Table of Cont

CW01468623

Tribute

This book is dedicated to the
memory of my dear mother
Doris. (Born 1927, died 1970)
At midnight, 26th June 1970
Mum became an Angel.
We became Orphans.

Throughout her life, she never once
complained about the tragic events she
endured. She smiled through adversity
but many times we heard her weeping
when she was alone. She loved us dearly
and made sacrifice for her four young
boys every day of her tragically short life.

Special thoughts go to my hero,
Grandad Cooper and the sweetest
grandmother any child could have
wished for. They are at peace in
Woodhouse Cemetery, Sheffield.
Mum being close by.

Her four sons, Orphans of an Angel
survived the ordeal, sadly mum didn't.
She made the ultimate sacrifice.

Preface

This book is the biography of my dear mother.
The true story is based on my memory of events at
the time, therefore some events have been created
to achieve the writing of the book. Though these
memories reflect those of a ten-year-old-boy, the
context has been written by me, now, as an adult to
allow the story to flow and be more understandable.

A quotation from Chapter 1 of the book epitomises
how perspectives change through time.

*'Most of these problems were shielded from us. I knew
nothing of deepening poverty, misery, and loneliness;
mum did, this was her life.'*

At the time in 1962, we were four young boys and like
every devoted, loving mother, she shielded us from the
anguish she suffered. She was an Angel in every sense.
Fifty years later, perspectives can change regarding
the events. Nothing could change the memory of how
mum struggled through destitution and chronic ill health.

British, USA & International Grammar

The book has been written and published in the UK using British grammar.

For USA and International readers, there will be some basic differences with
spelling certain words. The most common difference will be words ending
in "ise" such as "summarise" (UK) as opposed to "summarize" (USA).
Please bear this in mind when reading the book.

Chapter 1

She was hiding the truth. But mum's eyes said it all; pain, anguish, and tears permeated her delicate defeated face. Though her stomach problems were as yet undiagnosed, she knew there was something more sinister afoot. It was something she had not revealed to me, or my two brothers who waited at home. At this moment, in November 1962, I saw mum as I had seen her so many times before; bedraggled, forlorn and convulsed with excruciating agony.

The journey to Bradshaw's Grocery Store on Alexandra Road became a ritual. Though it was a two-mile walk to the opposite end of the village of Aughton, near Sheffield, it was a necessary evil. If the trek wasn't made, there would be no food on the table tonight for any of us. I 'sort of' enjoyed the arduous walk regardless of the weather as it gave me prime time with mum. Such time was a precious commodity, having two brothers, Alex aged twelve and Glenn aged five, and mum trying to juggle so many problems in her life. Most of these problems were shielded from us. I knew nothing of deepening poverty, misery, and loneliness; mum did, this was her life.

Now a debilitating stomach complaint surfaced. A health issue that could not be cured by tablets or medicine. Whatever the problem was, it wasn't going away. Mum wasn't scared of being admitted to the hospital; she was scared of not coming out. In her present condition, I couldn't imagine how she could walk the four miles, there and back, burdened with three heavy bags as dark, rainy skies hovered like an evil cloak. A biting northerly wind drove the icy rain in an almost horizontal direction. The raw driving rain hit her face like dry rice, but she could not cower away from its pulsating attack on cold skin.

I could tell from the tone of her voice, the journey was non-negotiable. Mum had a soft voice and an abundance of patience, but a tinge of the frustration of the raw deal of her life showed so many times. Her eyes begged to be in a distant world. Not because of raising three boys, single-handed; but because of the anguish, drudgery, and turmoil created by poverty. I got used to the challenge; the weekly two-mile trek along Alexandra Road' Rain, hail, and the wind was 'character building,' dad used to say.

"Are you a man or a mouse?" was the extent of his life-coaching skills.

Within minutes of arriving at the shop, another tortuous convulsion plagued her body.

"What's the matter, Mrs. Dalton? Are you alright?" Asked Mr. Bradshaw with empathy, his deep Yorkshire dialect resonated, laden with panic as he looked towards her with concern.

"Mum?…… Can you hear me? How can I help? Mum, can you speak to me?" I asked as my tears escaped. I knelt beside her, willing her to speak; to say something, at least.

Mum, Evelyn Dalton, thirty-six-years old, clutched her stomach, knotted like an over-tightened tourniquet. Her insides seemed crunched up and squeezed like a screwed-up newspaper. She writhed in agony as she curled up on the floor like a child. Her scream had a rawness to it, like an open wound, and echoed her pain, as though someone had stabbed her with a serrated knife.

"I must have fainted, Jeff. Woman's trouble, that's all," said mum in a strained, loud whisper. Her eyes squinted open to glimpse Mr. Bradshaw and me peering over her with concern.

"I'll be alright in a few minutes. Let me get my breath back," mum added with tearful eyes.

The pain restricted her ability to breathe and speak coherently.

"You're not okay mum. You need a doctor, urgently." I said, anxious that yet another sharp attack would grip her stomach.

"Here, sit on this chair, Mrs. Dalton," ushered Mr. Bradshaw.

"Let me phone a doctor or an ambulance."

Mr. Bradshaw was the kindly man who owned the Corner Shop. The weekly trek to his shop was mandatory. He became our saviour by offering *'tick'* to obtain groceries without paying until the following week. Fridays always became a critical day. There was no food in the house, not even a dry slice of bread for toast. There was nothing left in the pantry and no money left in her purse to buy anything. Mum was destitute; we were destitute, dad became indifferent. He was content as long as he had his 'beer and backy' money to play darts and drink beer at the weekend. In the Yorkshire coal-mining villages, this was known as 'tipping-up.'

Mum's housekeeping money paid the bills, the rent, and whatever remained was left went on food and clothes, if any. At least she could pay the bills before he spent the wages on booze, then wasted it against a wall. Dad, Eddie Dalton, thirty-six-years old, had been a coal miner since the war years of the 1940s. He struggled to get by on his poor pay. This had a massive knock-on effect for us all, especially mum. Today, he was on the afternoon shift which meant he didn't arrive home with his wages until after ten o'clock. By then the shops had closed. Three hungry boys needed to be fed and with no food or money, mum became destitute. Her meagre housekeeping money shrank below the poverty line over the past year. His wages remained the same, but bills climbed higher, more-so as we grew older. The only way mum could make ends meet and put food on the table was *'to rob Peter to pay Paul'* and the use of tick, to tide us over for two days.

Mum looked meek and mild in a biblical sense, vulnerable and child-like and weak from the endless burden of chores. These burdens became more arduous as mum's health deteriorated in the years following 1962. At random moments during every day, she seemed to be stabbed like a voodoo doll. The pain, so fierce and penetrating was as if her stomach had been ripped apart by a serrated knife. One minute she was fine and pain-free, within seconds, she was writhing in pain, incapable of anything but screams of agony.

As much as I wanted to, at the age of ten, I could offer mum no rescue. I could only give the love of a son and an extra pair of hands to carry two bags of the weekly grocery shop. Glenn, five, was at home, looked after by my older brother Alex, twelve.

"It's just a bit of woman's trouble, that's all," said mum, struggling to speak with convulsions.

'Woman's trouble' is the one phrase that prevented any inkling of male help. Determined to carry on, she stood up, gingerly, with the help of the back of a chair and a helping hand from Mr. Bradshaw. As mum sat on the wooden ladder-back chair, her skirt, sodden from the fierce rain, steamed gently near the electric fire in Mr. Bradshaw's shop. The musty smell of damp clothes was wafted by the convection of heat that intermingled with the smell of fresh bread and pastries.

"I know you mean well, Mr. Bradshaw, but I'm sure I'll be alright in ten minutes. I could do with some Milk of Magnesia if you have any on the shelf? It's the only medicine that seems to settle my stomach. Can you add it to my 'tick?'"

"It's not for me to say, Mrs. Dalton, but you really do need to see your GP. Those symptoms are way beyond heartburn or indigestion," said Mr. Bradshaw with a deep frown of worry.

Mum wasn't well. Aged thirty-six, she showed obvious signs of a hard life of poverty and hard work. A recent visit to the doctor suggested an ulcer. He prescribed Milk of Magnesia to supersede her use of hot-water bottles and taking Indian Brandee to soothe the pain. It never cured her grumbling pains, merely subdued them.

We had no car, no spare money for bus fares, no money for warm clothes for the winter, and not much money for food. The only clothes I had that fitted being the school uniform, paid for by a local authority school grant last September. I assumed most families lived like this. I realised in later life experts classified it as abject poverty and part of a socio-economic group of a Yorkshire working class. In 1961, I thought this was normal in a northern mining village.

"Your dad thinks he's Father Christmas when he hands over my housekeeping money," said mum. "He barely gives me enough to feed three blind mice, let alone three hungry boys."

There wasn't anything I could add to mum's jibe at dad. Her quip was rhetorical and true. For many, grocery shopping was an innocuous formality. For mum, it became tearful and daunting. Rows about money and housekeeping became a constant source of heated words between mum and dad after we had gone to bed in the evenings. We were three growing boys with an appetite. Clothes wore out much quicker as we grew. Trousers with holes in the backside and grazed shoes became the norm, worn out by kicking footballs and stones.

"I only work at the coal mine. I don't own it," said dad. "I sweat for a full shift in a slurry of coal dust and piss-water to earn my wages. There is no spare money. You have it all," continued dad, raising his voice a decibel with annoyance and frustration.

"We can't afford to live on the pittance you give me. I have to shop at Bradshaw's now. Getting food on tick is embarrassing and it's a long way to walk. All this is making me ill. I don't have time to be ill. There's no-one who can care for the boys if I go into hospital. They would go into a children's home. I will never let that happen," said mum with a tear and choked.

"Mr. Bradshaw's it is then. But I can't take you or pick you up; I'm at work. Alex and Jeff will need to help you carry the shopping bag back," said dad, indifferent to mum's difficulties.

Outgoings became a juggling act of *'robbing Peter to pay Paul.'* Using tick became essential in the fight for survival. Dad's poor wages meant incessant horrendous arguments festered daily. I heard mum cry herself to sleep, night after night. It became obvious poverty seemed to be a strain on their relationship. Mum had already visited her GP with an umbrella condition under the loose description of anxiety. He prescribed Milk of Magnesia and to have more rest.

Mum didn't have time to rest; she didn't have time to be ill and she didn't have spare money to pay for Milk of Magnesia.

Appointments with the doctor had become a complete waste of time against a backdrop of deteriorating health problems. There was no-one within the family willing to help care for three boys. By the end of 1961, burdened with destitution, mum found it more and more difficult to cope with raising three boys in a poverty trap. The consequence was a strained relationship and constant arguments with dad.

Mum continued to whimper between her tortuous outcries as she sat on the chair in the corner of Mr. Bradshaw's shop. As a ten-year-old, I didn't have a clue of how to help. Mum needed help, urgently that seemed to be life-threatening by its severity and suddenness. Reluctant to call an ambulance, mum didn't fear going into a hospital; she dreaded never coming out.

"You can't go on like this mum. You've had stomach pains for the past year. It's getting worse," I said with frustration.

"Magnesia seems to settle it," said mum, trivialising it all.

"It's more serious than an upset tummy Mrs. Dalton. Look how it made you collapse."

The fight to survive remained a constant challenge. Living on the breadline grew more difficult, week by week. Her housekeeping money lasted five days at a push. The final two days of the week required the need tick; some people knew it as 'the slate.' Desperate for food by six o'clock, mum had no option but to trudge from one end of the village to the other. With no transport, mum could only lift two bags of food. Alex and I took turns, week about, to help.

Mum squinted at her shopping list, with a screwed-up face, as she needed spectacles she couldn't afford to buy. A dewdrop fell from her nose, her fingers too cold and wet to prevent it from falling. A genuine tear escaped her face, caused by deep pain, and the embarrassment of asking for credit.

"Can I have it on tick? Pay you on Monday?" Said mum with a frown of hope. Her head partly bowed with embarrassment, and partly as emotional blackmail. Her runny eyes intermingled with hints of rain as the odd droplet trickled down her face.

"Of course you can, Mrs. Dalton. You're a good customer."
Thoughts of mum collapsing again, before we got home filled my head with realism and fear. Two heavy bags with string handles cut through her cold, callus palms. Though it seemed purgatory, she was too proud to accept defeat.

"You can't carry these bags, Mrs. Dalton. You're not well," said Mr. Bradshaw.

"I ain't got time 'not to be well.' We've got to eat," said mum.

"You can hardly walk two steps mum; let alone two miles. I can come back tomorrow on my bike," I said, hoping to quell mum's stubbornness.

"Let me take the shopping home for you, Mrs. Dalton. It's only five minutes in the van."

"Stop mythering will you? We'll be home in a jiffy," said mum, imitating a smile.

Mr. Bradshaw was a saviour for us. Without his service, we would starve until dad doled out his wages the following day. If there were six days in a week, we could manage. My heart was heavy for mum's plight. I wasn't crying, but I was tearful. At the age of ten, I was supposed to be a man. Men were not supposed to cry. My dad drummed that much into me every time I was on the losing side of fights with my older brother Alex. I could see the torture in her face that made me worry to the point of fearing for her life. By eleven in the evening, dad arrived back from work. Another heated discussion erupted about finances.

"We can't go on like this, Eddie. We are so short of money."

"I can't work any more hours down the coal mine. It's like hell on earth down there. I already work forty hours, and there is only one cage," said dad.

"There is no way we can cut down on food," said mum. "We are already on the poverty line. Anyway, where is our time? You take none of us anywhere, any more," continued mum.

"How the heck can we go anywhere?" Said dad. "Remember that rare thing called money? We ain't got any. What bit we have goes on food. There's only one thing to savour; that's the holiday to Great Yarmouth next summer. My holiday pay from the Coal Board covers that. At least it's a break from my wretched job and the boys can have a fantastic time."

Dad didn't realise how severe mum's health problems were. He accepted mum's classic response of it being a trivial concern.

Throughout the rest of the winter of 1961, mum's life followed the same path of toil and hard labour. The horrendous blizzards and freezing conditions made matters worse. Her pains recurred, some more acute and sharper than others. By the end of Spring, mum's poor health continued to dominate her horrendous life. She tried not to complain, but on occasions her pains became chronic. Mum persevered through her pains, trying not to make a fuss about it.

One of mum's long-standing issues came to the fore before our long-awaited holiday. Ever since mum and dad first got married fourteen years earlier, mum yearned for a baby girl. Since Glenn came onto the scene five years back, mum's lament grew stronger. At the third time of asking and hoping for a baby girl, it wasn't to be. *'Another one with a spout,'* mum joked.

"How on earth can we ever afford to have another baby, Evelyn? We can't afford to live now, let alone having baby number four," said dad, shocked by mum's brooding.

"You only ever think of the money, don't you? You never think about what I want," said mum.

"Another mouth to feed makes little sense. We've got three boys now. We have to be careful how we live. There is no spare money," said dad, raising his voice.

"You spend every bit of spare money on beer, darts and 'baccy.' You're at the Black Bull on Friday nights and the Holbrook Working Men's Club on Saturday nights. Where do we fit into your busy social life, Eddie Dalton? Oh, I forgot; I have to stay in and take care of the kids."

"I work all week down that bloody coal mine. I need a drink with my mates to clear my throat. Doesn't hurt to play darts, anyway. Does it?" Said dad becoming angrier.

"You know I always wanted a baby girl. My body clock is running out of time."

"We can't afford another baby and that's that," shouted dad and stomped upstairs to bed.

Mum felt dejected. Dad's rejection of wanting another child seemed common sense from his point of view. Another mouth to feed would plunge the family into dire straits. A colossal difference of opinion surfaced. Their relationship seemed weakened by it, as dad distanced himself from the matter. Her chronic stomach pains were spasmodic and were not going away and added to mum's stress levels. Dad didn't show empathy or kindness towards mum's plight. The holiday to Great Yarmouth crept closer. Mum hoped that if they all enjoyed a terrific family holiday, dad's lukewarm attitude towards another baby would improve. By the end of 1962, cataclysmic changes for the entire family and mum, in particular, would decimate us all. Life would never be the same again.

Chapter 2

Eagerly awaited, Great Yarmouth became the major event of our summer holidays. A visit to the Royal Aquarium Theatre was a rare treat, more-so since we had little spare cash. Lonnie Donegan topped the bill with Des O'Connor the compere. Donegan, a national treasure, reeled off his recording hits in the first fifteen minutes of his act. He was mum and dad's favourite singer. He also delivered witty punchlines in between his songs to provide superb entertainment. During his initial welcome, he asked the packed audience to settle and pay attention to a serious announcement. The theatre became silent in anticipation as he addressed the cavernous theatre with gravity and dignity.

"I have an important message from the management," said Donegan with a tone of serious concern in his voice and delivered with a dead-pan face. The audience listened with trepidation and hushed into respectful silence.

"There has been a ten-pound note found in the foyer tonight. If anyone has lost any money, please contact the manager at the end of the show. By the way, the manager is Mrs. Helen Hunt. The staff have informed me, anyone who wishes to claim the ten pounds tonight can go to Helen Hunt for it."

Raucous laughter and cheer reverberated through the audience. I asked dad if I could go to the manager's office and tell them I had lost the ten pounds. He initially agreed, but as I passed his seat, he clutched me onto his lap and explained the meaning of the joke. Naive gullibility, maybe, but disappointment on a massive scale. Dad made it up to me the following day as we stalked the never-ending line of gift shops en route to the beach. Occasionally, mum and dad stopped to look at one piece of cheap tack that was better than another piece of cheap tack.

"Dad. Can I have one of these badges?" I said with excitement.

I collected badges. Petrol stations gave them away with petrol. Robertson's designed a complete series of 'activity themed' enamel badges to encourage buying their jam and marmalade. Every shop we passed, I scoured the counter for badges. The latest trend appeared to be witty slogan badges, alongside the *'Kiss Me Quick'* cowboy hats, hit the gift shops.

'The Pistol Club' badge caught my eye.

A definite must-have, for my collection. It read:

'The Pistol Club, Drink All Night, Pistol Dawn.'

It was crude, but it tickled my boyish humour. Dad laughed whilst mum frowned. I won the day, much to mum's consternation. I bought it with my own money that I earned from my newspaper round. They drifted out of the shop, for me to pay my dues. At the counter, another badge caught my eye, but I didn't understand its innuendo. What the heck, mum, and dad had strolled outside the shop. I bought it and pinned them both to my chest before I left the shop. I strutted out as though the Queen had awarded me the Victoria Cross for bravery. Bravery to wear it, my chest stood proud, like doing the Lambeth Walk, with thumbs behind the lapels of my blazer. Mum, Dad, and my brothers sauntered along with the myriad of gift shops until I caught up with them. My newly acquired badges raised many eyebrows, boyfriends gave naughty nudges to girlfriends who blushed and giggled at the innuendo style badges. Mum and dad gazed into a shop window, then looked back along the promenade of shops where I strutted to catch up.

"Jeff, you can't wear those badges, they're vulgar," said mum.

"Eddie, tell him!"

They didn't know I wanted to buy the second badge, thinking one was enough for my collection. I learned in adolescence, the true meaning of the innuendo. It was a steep learning curve.

'The Muff Divers Club'
'All newcomers welcome.'

Dad let me wear them both. We had one trait in common, the same sense of humour. Mine innocent, dad's 'tongue in cheek.'

Great Yarmouth held so many vivid memories and became the happiest holidays we had spent together. Enriched with everything that was meaningful; sand, sea, sunshine, and happiness. Without a doubt, the Summer holiday of 1962 became a resounding success. As a family, we seemed to be as happy as we ever had been. It was the last time I saw mum laugh so heartily, with tears of laughter rather than tears of pain. Mum and dad appeared to be closer and laughed together. Appearances could have been deceptive. After two weeks of wall-to-wall sunshine, the holiday ended and the arduous journey back to Sheffield began. Only a day after the holiday, one simmering obsession resurfaced. It consumed mum's mind ever since she got married.

Unbeknown to my brothers and me, was mum's yearning for a baby girl. She still hoped that having a memorable holiday could persuade dad to see things her way. She yearned for a baby girl ever since she married dad thirteen years earlier. Since Glenn came onto the scene four years back, mum's lament and her obsession grew stronger. Part way through another heated discussion, mum grimaced as though someone had stabbed her with a hot dagger. Tears streamed down her cheeks as though being tortured. Dad was in a dilemma. He didn't know whether mum's pains were fake, as a twist of emotional blackmail, or whether her suffering was a genuine, ongoing issue.

"What's happening, Evelyn? What's the matter?" Yelled dad.
Mum couldn't speak; the pain was too fierce. Alex, Glenn, and I became worried, watching mum tortured with agony. Glenn being five, whimpered. Alex and I huddled mum, the only empathy and affection she could expect. I could sense a lukewarm atmosphere between them. This might have been a consequence of the arguments over the past hour, or a consequence of a serious difference of opinion. Whatever the reason, mum was suffering extreme pain. It seemed this was the early signs of dad's indifference towards us all.

My brothers and I loved mum with deep affection. She was echelons above the love and respect we held for dad. None of us felt the same about the relationship with him. I could sense that even though we had just returned from a memorable holiday, dad appeared to be more distant, as though his heart was elsewhere. It had seemed to rekindle a bond with dad. Their simmering arguments on our return swept that away.

"Evelyn, are you okay?" Snapped dad with apathy in his voice.

Dad wasn't a tactile person. He found it difficult to show compassion or even affection. A few minutes after the sudden attack contorted mum's face, the pain subsided to a dull ache.

"I'm okay, Eddie. Just a bit of woman's trouble. You know? It comes and goes. It's nothing serious" said mum, rubbing her sensitive stomach with a delicate touch.

"What was all that about Evelyn? Have you had anything like that before?" Asked dad.

"It flares up now and then, without warning. It could be a bit of indigestion. I take Milk of Magnesia for it; that helps."

Mum's stomach pains had plagued her for almost a year. They were irritable to begin with, a niggle of discomfort, but became gradually worse, becoming regular, intense and more painful. The pain came in spasms, subsided, then returned with a vengeance, even with strong painkillers. Cramps deteriorated into convulsions, over the next few months. Sharp stabbing pains worsened to screw her stomach into knots. She never divulged the true extent of her suffering, but fobbed us off.

Procrastination made matters worse. Mum refused to complain and became reluctant to contact her GP again. She preferred to persevere and conceal the severity of whatever the actual problem was. Mum recovered from her bout of extreme discomfort. Dad softened his stance and fudged the issue of enlarging the family numbers. He knew there were more important problems to worry about than adding another infant to the fold. Like trying to make ends meet as things stood.

"Let's see how things go for now. This year might be the last holiday we can afford for a while, my wages get worse.

"Now the holiday is over, I could get a part-time job when the kids are at school," said mum, trying to convince dad she was serious about another baby. She hoped by attempting to go to work, dad would agree to another baby. "Glenn starts school in September, so I'll have time on my hands to work a few days a week The extra cash will help to pay the bills."

Dad took mum at her word that the pain was not sinister. She knew there was something wrong. It seemed to be a medical problem tablets or medicine couldn't cure. Already stretched to the limit, he had little energy or stamina left to take on a cleaning job, even for a few hours each week. Spare time was unheard of in mum's wretched life. Her body was feeling the strain of caring for three growing boys, paying the bills, and living on the breadline.

"If we both got a part-time job, paying the bills would be easier. We need to get back on our feet before we can think about another baby," said dad, brushing aside mum's obsession.

Mum preferred to try for a baby straight away, but with reluctance accepted the need to go to work part-time. At the age of thirty-six, her biological clock was ticking away. She guessed she might only be able to have one more chance to have a baby girl, then she would be out of time. Within a week, mum took on an ideal part-time income. A cleaning job at a huge 1940's house in the nearby village of Ulley. Ideal, because the work schedule fitted in with child-care between nine and mid-day, and was within walking distance. She walked a mile to the job, every other morning after we went to school, another task on her already overburdened schedule.

Before the end of the month, dad got an evening job as a shellfish salesman and worked Friday and Saturday evenings from six until midnight. He travelled the pubs and clubs of Sheffield selling fresh seafood delicacies of cockles, crab-sticks and prawns from an oversized wicker basket. Mum and dad were both pulling in the same direction regarding finances, but the consequences would have far-reaching effects.

The year 1962 became a pivotal turning point in our lives as several issues came back on the agenda. Transport was his huge Royal Enfield motorbike, a hunk of 1950's brutalism covered in chrome, used to be an apt description. Coupled to the bike was a Combination sidecar with two seats, one front, one back, and a fold-back canvas sunroof. It gave us a four-seater as our means of transport in the late 1950's onwards. It became a popular mode of transport for working-class families who couldn't afford the luxury of a car.

Dad's part-time job seemed odd for a coal miner, selling seafood snacks from a motorbike and sidecar. He plied the pubs and clubs of South Yorkshire every weekend and it seemed to give him a buzz of being out socialising within his favourite venues. A few weeks into his job, dad asked if I wanted to go with him to 'help.' That felt important to me. The bribery of a packet of crisps and a bottle of fizzy Vimto seemed at incentive.

Cramped into the sidecar was like being in an Olympic toboggan, wedged in on either side. If that wasn't bad enough, flying down the cobbled, one-in-ten Whiston Hill was a bone-shaking experience. A steep gradient, with a ninety-degree corner at the bottom, was as frightening as a fairground ride out of control. By the time the hair-pin bend appeared, Whiston Hill had juddered my bones like operating a pneumatic drill. At long last, we came to a welcome stop in a car park behind a refrigerated lorry, near Rotherham Station. Salesmen queued with empty wicker baskets that needed filling with the evening's stock of seafood. I waited in the sidecar for dad to return with his basket full to the brim.

"Cor, dad. They wreak," I yelled in horror, with a screwed up nose.

The pungent seafood disgusted the senses, almost to the point of throwing up. The fully laden basket, thrust into my lap, beneath my nose, was not what I envisaged. Smells of vinegar, interlaced with seafood smells, wafted upwards and stung my eyes into tears. It seemed a nightmare. I hated seafood. Smell, taste, touch, and sight turned my stomach. Six hours of nursing this odorous concoction, laced with 'eau-de-vinegar,' half a metre from my nose became a stench too far. With no opening windows, it smelt like a sardine packers outing.

"You get used to that," came dad's philosophical reply, but offered scant consolation.

"Smelling of fish?"

Sat in the sidecar, the pungent smell of seafood overwhelmed me. I couldn't wait to get out and breathe fresh air rather than smelling of fish docks. Within ten minutes, we arrived at the next club. My clothes and hair wreaked. As dad grabbed the offensive smelling basket, I climbed out to take my first breath of fresh air. Unexpectedly, within seconds of stepping into the working men's club, my throat choked, congested with clouds of tobacco smoke. I held my breath long enough to walk into the hallway. Then sat at a table next to the entrance door that allowed my recovery.

"Cockles, crab-sticks!" Shouted dad, selling his seafood.

He seemed a popular character. Customers jostled past the bar and rummaged through his basket to find their favourite delicacy. Dad needed to deliver the seafood fast to keep it as fresh as possible. Sooner the better was my thoughts. The social clubs and working men's clubs were a coveted target with cavernous halls packed with scores of punters. Every table was full of pints of John Smith's beer and Britvic Orange. In a white coat and trilby, he looked every bit a cockle salesman. Good with people, an excellent talker, 'he can charm the birds off the trees,' said mum, so often, sometimes with a hint of concern. Salty crab-sticks, washed down with a few pints of beer, became a tradition. With bingo and a dubious off-key singer to follow as a finale, it was a popular Yorkshire night out.

"Dad, can I have some crisps now?"

"When we get to the next club, Jeff."

After a two-mile rush to Holbrook WMC, dad plied me with crisps and Vimto. As he worked his way closer to the exit, he squeezed past the bar with his enormous wicker basket. A blonde, attractive lady tapped his shoulder. He passed her a packet of crab-sticks with a smile and a wink, following her comments. Ash blond hair draped across her shoulders. A painted on, body-hugging, glitzy blue dress, contrasted with her hair, just like Monroe.

The following Saturday, I wanted to do the rounds again with dad. Though I had smelt of seafood and vinegar, feasting on crisps and fizzy drinks meant it was a hardship worth suffering.

"Can I come with you again on the shellfish run, dad?"

"Tell you what. Look after your mum tonight. I'll bring you some crisps and the Vimto."

"Suppose so. Make sure you get the Vimto, dad."

"Can we play dominoes, mum? I'm a star player at that."

"Sure. But you always beat me, don't you?"

"Better luck this time then, mum."

"I'll try."

Mum had an innocent, infectious smile. She generated warmth with how she looked at us. Her auburn hair, once so shiny and wavy a few years back, it now showed the signs of grey roots and frizzy dryness. Mum was now thirty-six. Her face wrinkled through her foundation cream. Her complexion had paled with time, hard work, and family chores. She smoked Park Drive, one of her few pleasures in life, she reiterated so often. They yellowed her teeth and gave her a regular morning smoker's cough.

"See you later," shouted dad, bound for Rotherham to begin his seafood sales.

"Bye. Be careful. It's cold out there," shouted mum.

"Sure. Don't worry. I'm always careful."

"Bye, dad."

As the coal fire crackled, I looked at mum as her hair silhouetted into a fiery red. Her sweet innocence, oblivious to anything other than pacifying my disappointment with dad. She saw it upset me.

Often I felt hurt because Alex was the first-born son, and I was the second. Not second best by favouritism, but he was two years stronger and wiser.

"Can I stay up for a while longer mum, to have my crisps?"

"Not tonight, sweetheart. It'll be late when your dad gets back home," said mum.

"But he promised to get me crisps and a Vimto, mum."

"I know he did."

"Please, mum…... Please."

I had to avoid the 'time-for-bed syndrome' at all costs. How to persuade mum to agree became a challenge of wits and emotional blackmail. A cute smile would never cut it to achieve much success with mum. She was far too wise. With dented pride, I managed a one-off measure of success. I tried my usual 'tilt my head to the side with doleful eyes' tactic and gazed longingly; it worked.

"Please, mum. Please mum. I'll make you a nice cuppa tea."

"Okay. You've twisted my arm. You can stay up until midnight. Dad should be back by then."

"Thanks mum. You're so good to me."

"Better give me an enormous hug as you beat me at yet again."

By midnight, I had dropped to sleep on the sofa in the lounge. Mum half-woke me to go to bed. She still suffered serious discomfort on most days, so lifting my weight wasn't an option. I shuffled to my feet, but still remembered…...

"Is dad back yet, mum?"

"Not yet, sweetheart. He won't be too long now."

"Can I just stay up longer to get my crisps?"

"It's late now, love. You can have your crisps in the morning."

I skulked upstairs as the last embers of the fire simmered and crackled, casting an orange glow to the walls. Sunday was a long lie in bed. At least I could look forward to my crisps. Dad continued his grand tour of pubs, and clubs on his shellfish circuit. He travelled alone, as I looked after mum and Glenn. By 10.30 pm, dad had arrived at the Holbrook Working Men's Club. As if by coincidence, he met up with the blonde lady he spoke with earlier on the evening before. Dad had met the flirtatious lady, known as Roxy when he first began his part-time job. They seemed at ease with each other as they chatted and joked. Banter seemed more than furtive.

"You made it then?" Yelled Roxy above the hum-drum of noise.

"Yep. Done my calls, dashed round and made this my last stop."

After a pint of 'Bitter,' dad and Roxy departed arm-in-arm. They walked for ten minutes to her house. She would go nowhere on dad's motorbike. With unintentional humour, she said it was beneath her standing, even though she had spent hours in the Holbrook WMC.

Chapter 3

Two hours passed by quicker than they realised. Beads of sweat filled the sheets. Steamy windows gave diffused lighting to the bedroom, fogged-up by fantasy and passion.

"You gotta be back tonight?" Asked Roxy.

"Ought to," said dad. "I could say that snow blocked the roads, making it impossible to get up Whiston Hill. Get home later than expected," dad continued, conjuring excuses for mum.

Dad had not arrived back from his part-time evening job. Mum became worried as the weather worsened. She feared dad could have had an accident on the treacherous roads leading to outlying districts. Dad always arrived back by midnight. Mum was at home with me, aged ten, and Glenn, aged five; Alex, aged twelve, had a sleepover with mum's parents, grandma and grandad Cooper. The dramatic turnaround in our lives began in the bleak, snowy winter of 1962. Roxy had sealed mum's fate, 'aided and abetted' by dad.

The clock chimed three, like a death knell. Blurry eyed, his back was as stiff as a long shift at the coal face. Dad extricated himself from her sheets, Roxy slept like a contented baby. He sneaked down the creaky stairs and dressed into his motorbike leathers for the fifteen-minute ride back home. He freewheeled down the hill, in neutral, so as not to wake the neighbours. Roxy had ignored social etiquette and gave them a rude and loud awakening, well BEFORE she fell asleep.

Snow sprinkled gently like pillow feathers and blanketed the ground, the first snow of the Winter of 1962. By three o'clock in the morning, the streets outside Roxy's house looked like a Christmas card setting. Roxy was sound asleep. Dad had awakened, racked by a guilty conscience. His motorbike was tucked away in the club car park, which meant he wouldn't wake any neighbours in the early hours. Dad left Roxy to sleep off the late-night drinks and sneaked downstairs. He donned his leathers and walked in the soft snow to his motorbike. Dad hoped the weather could be his 'saving grace,' his best alibi for being late home. Twenty minutes later, in atrocious weather conditions, dad arrived home. To avoid waking mum, he switched off the engine, and freewheeled downhill for the final hundred metres. He hoped she would be asleep. But woeful cries emanated from the lounge as dad turned the key of the front door, then placed his heavy, leather motorbike gear in the outhouse.

"And?…….." Shouted mum.

"Thought you were asleep, love."

"You mean you hoped I would be asleep. Where have you been until now? It's nearly four."

"My motorbike broke down love, on the way home. Must be the snowy weather and the bitter wind."

Mum's eyes were blood red with tears, her face blotched by anger and torment. She had laid in the chair sobbing and alone, daring not to believe the inevitable excuses that dad would conjure up. Gripped in knots, her stomach churned with anguish and pain, for two different reasons.

"Don't lie to me, you bas**rd." Hot tears pooled in her eyes, her throat became coarse.

"I swear. The bike broke down. Couldn't just leave it in the middle of nowhere. Could I?"

"Yes, you could? Couldn't you walk?"

"Not at three in the morning. No."

"The bike can't have broken down at three. I'm not a fool."

"Meaning?"

"Meaning, what were you doing between midnight and three? You are home by twelve. Always. You could have walked home in that time. Then I might have believed you."

Mum snivelled through a lull in explanations. She opened another box of Kleenex and dried her eyes and face. The wicker bin overflowed with wet tissues and weak excuses.

"Don't mean to be funny, but you don't smell," said mum.

"What?"

"Had you been at work, your clothes, your skin, and your hair would have wreaked of smelly fish. If you had been messing with your bike, you'd smell of petrol and oily rags."

Another stony silence filled the hallway as mum glared at dad. He couldn't muster any answers, let alone the right ones. He could only offer excuses. Mum's life began spiralling down a vortex. Her suspicions confirmed the female instinct of detecting whitewash.

"We need to do a hell of a lot more talking tomorrow," said mum.

"You can sleep with what's left of the night, on the settee," said mum. "Don't want you in my sight. Let alone in my bed. Did you bring the crisps and Vimto for Jeff?"

"Sugar! I forgot."

"You disappointed him, not taking him with you last night. It devastated him when you didn't come home by midnight. He'll be heartbroken when he wakes up and finds out you haven't brought them."

"I'm so sorry."

"Being sorry is not enough, is it? You've lost so much tonight. I hope she was worth it."

Mum struggled up the stairs dejected and slammed the doors behind her. Picture frames rattled on the wall. She needed to find out if dad's new flame was just a one-night stand or something more serious. Dawn was breaking with too many unanswered questions. Mum couldn't sleep. Her stomach churned with anger.

A few hours later, mum ambled downstairs into the lounge. Dad groaned his discomfort from the lumpy sofa as he struggled to lift his head from the shame and guilt of his night of passion.

"When did all this start?" Said mum with a raised voice.

"Look. It meant nothing," said dad, agitated.

"How long did you say? I didn't catch that."

"It was just a fling. That's all."

"How long?"

"Best part of three months, I guess," said dad.

"I don't want to hear about the best part of anything. You're having an affair, then coming home. And sharing my bed? That's disgusting," she said with anger, her voice getting louder.

"It wasn't like that."

"Proud of yourself?" Said mum.

"I am so, so sorry," said dad.

"Why lie to me? That's what hurts more."

"I didn't mean it to happen. Honest."

"You didn't mean it to happen?"

"That's right, love."

"You mean she forced you to stay the night? Then forced you to have sex? You must be desperate; forced into bed with a wench that offers everything on a plate? No questions asked? How often does that happen?"

"I've told you. It didn't happen like that."

"Look. She hasn't jumped into bed with you for your money. A cockle seller? She didn't go with you for your Ferrari, you've only got a motorbike and sidecar. She didn't jump on you because of sparkling wit and conversation, you're a cheapskate coal miner with a shovel."

"Come on, love. We can sort it."

"Oh, I forgot the obvious reason. It just happened, didn't it? What kind of excuse is that? How can you break the hearts of our boys? You know, Jeff's upstairs asleep now. You hurt him when you didn't take him with you. And why was that?"

"I had lots more deliveries last night."

"It happened 'cos you finished your round early and spent some time with an out-and-out floozy. Don't come near me. I don't want to catch anything."

"I had a few drinks. That's all," said dad.

"You had more than a few drinks. You're a liar."

"We can sort this out. I know we can," said dad.

"Jeff will be heartbroken. You couldn't even remember to get his bottle of Vimto and favourite crisps."

"We can sort this out. Whimpered dad with naïve optimism.

"WE? WE can sort it out?" Said mum, a decibel louder.

"I can make it up to you. We can get back to where we were, can't we? It's not too late."

"You've always smelt of oily rags from working on your stupid bike. Now, you smell of a tart.

"Where did I go wrong?" Said mum. "Oh, I forgot, I had three kids, a husband who plays darts every other night and provides not enough food to feed three blind mice."

"Let's talk about things. We need to give it another try."

"You still smell of cheap perfume. Women can smell cheap perfume. Another woman's cheap perfume smells unpleasant."

Mum was in a rage. Her blood boiled with anger. She tried hard to control her temper, but her emotions somersaulted between killing dad or loving him. Mum had loved dad passionately since her teenage years, her first love. There had been jealousy rather than suspicions at times, especially as dad enjoyed darts matches at the pubs and clubs. Though mum, now thirty-six, only looked fair for her age. Dad still had his looks; mum had us.

"So what's your wonderful master plan, Mr. Daydreamer? Does it live in your pants? 'Cos that's where your brain is. You know, over the years there have been opportunities for me to look elsewhere. To search for freedom. To find a way out of my mundane life of washing, ironing, and shopping. But you know what? I turned my head the other way. You know why? Because I love you and I love the boys."

"I am so sorry. I wish I could change it all."

"I used to believe every word you said, opposite to what my mother said about you."

"That's unfair," said dad.

"I saw the way other women looked at you with a coy smile. Every time, I wondered if she would be the one who broke your marriage vows. You looked at other skirts when we walked down the street. I often wondered if you had or hadn't been faithful. It was a game for you."

"I've always been faithful. You could never doubt that."

"Last night?" Asked mum.

"It meant nothing,"

"I'm sick of hearing you say *'It meant nothing.'* It did mean something or you wouldn't have done it. Would you?"

"Just believe me, please."

"So, if it meant nothing, is it open season to jump into bed with anyone that flirts?"

"I know what you're saying, but I am truly sorry."

"You know, in your case, some floozy comes along, turns your head with fluttering eyelashes and a wink, and you drop everything while she drops her knickers. How can you change that? Leopards can't change their spots. You can never change. Once a liar, always a liar."

"We can work all this out. It was nothing. It meant nothing."

"I thought today would be a special day for us," said mum in a quiet, defeated voice.

Mum paused for a few seconds. She contemplated sharing some important news, but hesitated.

"So if I went out for a fling tonight, and came back tomorrow," said mum, "that's okay, is it? It wouldn't mean anything, so that's okay. Is that a strong relationship? How would you feel if some virile stud made love to me all night? But that's alright because it meant nothing"

"I know what you're saying, but we have been good together over the years."

"I heard lots of stories and rumours about your affairs. It's a small coal-mining village, news travels like jungle drums. I turned a deaf ear because I loved you. Now I'm betrayed. You've taken the best years of my life and trashed all those happy memories. For what? A cheap tart who can't keep her knees together long enough to say no."

"I'm so deeply sorry. I can make it all good. Just give me a chance."

"Another chance? Another chance to betray me and our boys?"

"You wanted today to be a special day? It still can be," he said.

"Not now."

"What more can I say?"

"You just don't get it, do you? It's not what you say. It's what you've done. You can't undo what you've already done. When you spill milk, it's spilt. You can't put it back."

"Perhaps we've gone past the point of no return," said dad.

"Perhaps we have," said mum in a soft voice, dejected and hurt. Her voice quietened into a soft acquiescence of defeat. Mum never wanted it to be like this. She wanted it to be how it always had been. She loved dad. She needed him in her life, but her rage jettisoned hopes of reconciliation. Whether his fling was a genuine one-nighter, a moment of male weakness, or something more serious, mum struggled to balance trust and loyalty. She wanted to overcome her angst, but the opportunity seemed lost. Never a devout churchgoer, mum still had a high moral standing, but it had diluted through generations. Mum wrestled with dad's infidelity, the age-old dilemma of the acquiescence of his betrayal. In other words, a marriage of convenience.

Silence filled the room. They looked at each other. Dad with disguised guilt and faked remorse, mum with genuine bitterness and disbelief. A tear nestled in the corner of her eyes and dribbled to the corner of her lips. The bitter taste of defeat seemed to be so acidic and unpalatable. Her erstwhile news seemed pointless. Her enthusiasm became dampened by his inept whitewash. She revealed her surprise without natural excitement and exuberance.

"I'm pregnant...... How special is that? Baby number four?"

"Oh!....."

His disquiet painted a picture of indifference. The revelation was unexpected, so was the reaction. Mum felt he only considered his own importance, and how all these problems affected him. In reality, he created all these problems, in some way.

"Glad you're overwhelmed with excitement," said mum with sarcasm. "I'm going to my mum's. I need some space. Alex is there already. Jeff, Glenn `will catch a bus."

"What about us?" Asked dad.

"Is there an us? I need to think about everything. You will live to regret what you've done to me and our boys. One day ghosts will come back to haunt your conscience."

Dad went into shock mode; stunned into an abrupt silence. He couldn't conjure any explanations about why he had strayed. A mid-life crisis had never been on the agenda. He appeared to be sorry mum had found him out, rather than sorry it had happened. They had reached a major crossroads in life. Mum became shocked with anger. Life had dealt another savage layer of heartbreak. She struggled to cope with paying for the necessities of life; gas, electricity, food, and clothes. Three growing boys tested her patience daily. Alex and I were at loggerheads from daybreak until he went out to settle unfinished business.

Mum, now at thirty-six, had another baby on the way. She desperately yearned for a baby girl. It's what she had wanted for years. She desperately wanted dad in her life, but she couldn't come to terms with his unfaithfulness. Mum held the belief that a baby girl would help to create a special bond between dad and a baby daughter. To her, it would help cement their relationship, but her life had already become a struggle by the early 1960's. To care for four would create an extra challenge for her endurance and stamina amidst a backdrop of destitution and ill health.

Somehow, she kept it all together, but at the cost of her own health and emotions. The situation could go beyond breaking point if dad were to separate from mum. Her housekeeping money would become slashed to zero, income would be meagre, plunging the family into even deeper dire straits. Perversely, mum still loved dad passionately. For better, for worse. She needed to talk to her mum and dad, my grandma and grandad Cooper about the shambles of her life, maybe even the dying embers of her marriage. She didn't want to accept an irretrievable breakdown, but she couldn't see a way forward.

"Jeff, Glenn! Come on, you two. It's time to get up."
We charged down the stairs like elephants, skipping the odd step with a heavy thump.

"Hi, mum. Hi Dad. Did you get my crisps and the bottle of Vimto, dad?" I said with eagerness.

"I did son, but I left them at the club. Sorry. I'll get them later tonight. Alright?"

A tear loitered in my eyes. Dad disappointed me yet again. How could he forget?

"You can't even lie very well can you, Eddie?" Said mum with a croaky voice.

Her eyes rolled at his contempt, saddened by my malaise. More emotional than Alex, I inherited mum's softer traits. I took people's word at face value. A character trait within me that never receded. Up to this point, I always believed dad to be beyond reproach, honourable, a man of his word. He betrayed us all and mum. He destroyed trust within all of us. The vociferous argument subsided. Mum decided that she needed to visit grandma. She needed her love and emotional support. Above all, she needed a shoulder to cry on and a long chat to put matters into perspective.

"Let's get ready, boys. We're going to grandma and grandad's house. You know what that means," said mum. Her face became less blotchy from crying, but her eyes still sore and puffy.

"Cornish ice cream and trifle. Yeah!" I yelled. Bribery was so easy to nurture at my age.

"Only if there's no fighting with Alex when we get there.

"Okay. But he always starts it. You know that mum,"

"Don't worry. A little birdie tells me grandma Cooper has baked a gorgeous chocolate cake for us. Get washed and dressed. We'll catch the next bus. You can both eat toast on the way."

The ten-mile bus journey to grandma Coopers' meant mum, Glenn, and I needed to catch the first bus of Sunday at eleven o'clock; by lunchtime, we arrived at grandma's. There were issues mum didn't have answers for. Her mind became frazzled, racked with how to resolve them. She was not in a fit state to think straight. She hoped her own mother would give her the support she needed.

Chapter 4

Grandma and grandad Cooper were mum's natural parents. Mum also had two stepsisters, much older, by fifteen years, Ruth and Connie. Grandma and grandad recently moved to a pensioners council flat near Woodhouse, in Sheffield. Their old, stone-built house on Tilford Road was demolished as part of a modernisation program. Four small blocks of flats provided a massive lawned area at the back, created for resident's communal use. Alex and I had stay-overs every other weekend. The communal lawn became Wembley Stadium, witnessing fanatical football matches between us. Glenn was too young, other than to fetch the ball. He was happy to draw air-planes and paint in his magic painting books on his own, in the lounge.

Grandad Cooper was a precocious character. He encouraged my inventiveness. It gave me freedom away from Alex. I revered grandad; I listened with to his wonderful stories with awe, his philosophy on life and snippets of facts and immeasurable wisdom. I never gained this input from dad as he always worked or played his beloved darts. So often, mum said he was playing away. I didn't understand innuendo as a ten-year-old.

Grandad was sixty-six now and walked with a limp.

'*Shrapnel from the war, you know,*' he reiterated so often.

He was stocky and well built, but less than five feet tall. He reminded me of a good-humoured Toby Jug, not as an insult. I could never berate him. He was a gentle man. He instilled in me many traits I never gleaned from dad. He taught me how to complete a jigsaw puzzle and every birthday and Christmas, he bought me increasingly harder puzzles, going up to ten thousand pieces. For the first time in my life, I earned accolades for patience and calm. He had a beguiling sense of humour, a mixture of Yorkshire wit, and boyish escapades.

His stories and logic, so believable, bordered on irony. His infectious humour became contagious, as my character became enriched by his. A natural raconteur, his quips filled quieter moments.

"You know, when I was in the war, they fired bullets at me. But, the funny thing was, they always missed me 'cos I was less than five feet tall. The bullets went over my head."

I chuckled, but at the same time frowned with questioning truth. His jokes were light-hearted but with an innocence of childishness. Grandad was ten years old, the same as me.

"You know, when I was a lad at your age, I asked the building foreman why they called bungalows,...... bungalows? The foreman told me that after a few weeks, the bricklayers ran out of bricks, so they decided to 'bung' a low roof on it."

"Grandad. I don't know whether or not to believe you."

"God's honour, lad," grandad smiled and gave a wink.

His fascinating stories captivated my attention. They were semi-believable. He would physically tickle my ribs and plonk me on his knee with a huge squeeze of love and affection. Dad could never do this, but to grandad Cooper, it came naturally. Mum was a carbon copy of grandad in so many ways. Warm, caring, patient, humble and proud. Grandma Cooper doted on mum and us boys, as though we were her own loving children.

"Chocolate or Victoria Sponge?" Shouted grandma from the kitchen.

Alex and I decided by *'paper, scissors, stone.'* If Alex won, chocolate cake became dessert. If I won, Victoria sponge became dessert. Consideration was never an option for Glenn. He preferred ice cream anyway.

"We'll have Fruit Cake," shouted grandad to wind us up.

"Shut up, you silly old fool," said grandma, settling the issue.

"Less of the silly," shouted grandad, tittering to himself.

Grandma spoiled us rotten with cakes, buns, jelly and ice cream. Mum struggled to put these kinds of goodies on our table, but not for the want of trying. We didn't realise her many problems of destitution, poverty and chronic pain. Unbeknown to us, marriage problems began to surface between mum and dad. Heated discussions and tearful arguments unfolded when we were at school or in bed. Though grandma and grandad Cooper were pensioners, they still received a better income than mum and dad, probably as grandad used to be an insurance agent with pension awareness. It was nearer the truth that we were poor, rather than grandad being rich.

Grandad Cooper, a genuine hero in my eyes, was an icon of immense respect. We walked together to Richmond Park on countless Saturday and Sunday afternoons, and endless days in the summer months. As we strolled along, he reflected on so many aspects of life, my proper education. The true meaning of life eschewed from his lips, philosophical muses, perspective, endurance, and patience revealed as we ambled along. Eager for his wisdom and knowledge, his every word etched into my mind, meaningful and honest.

"Na' then lad. We have to stop for a while."
I thought he was out of breath. Perhaps thirst warranted our stop by the old drinking trough in the Market Square of the stone-built village of Woodhouse. We had walked a long way, through Richmond Park and up the steep hill to Handsworth, then beyond towards Woodhouse.

"Na' then, lad. See these black shiny cars coming towards us?"
A funeral cortege approached ahead of us. Glistening polished black limousines strolled nearer with courtesy and respect. Men sat with shiny top hats in each of the six Rolls Royces. The leading car alluded bystanders to lower their heads and remove hats and caps as a mark of respect.

"Yes. Has someone died grandad?"
"That's right lad. It's a funeral procession."
"Did you know him, grandad?"
"No lad, I didn't. But what you have to do is stop, take your cap off and bow your head. It's a mark of respect. To the person who's died, and to all his loved ones. A time to reflect, not just about that

person, but to reflect on life itself, loved ones, people who you care for, people no longer with us."

"Never knew any of that, grandad."

"We'll all get to that stage one day, you know. Even me lad."

"Don't say that, grandad. I don't want you to leave me, ever."

We stood motionless by the kerb edge and waited a few minutes in the afternoon sun, reflecting in silence. Grandad removed his flat cap for respect to reveal a shimmer of sweat on his bald head. The world had stopped for a while. Everyone I could see in the street motionless, heads bowed with respect as the hearse drew closer, then disappeared over the hill. Mourners grieved and cried. Many gave the Christian sign of the cross on their chest. Grandad re-placed his traditional Yorkshire flat cap and we continued our slow walk. From a naïve point of view, it made me realise grandad would pass away at some point. But at least if he lived to be a hundred, I would be many years wiser. Even these emotional, heart-rending moments became reflected upon by grandad. Every morsel of knowledge imparted to my attentive ears, absorbed as part of my education.

"Fear nothing in life, lad. Not even death. Death is part of life. A perspective of life. A statement of everything you've achieved. Remember that."

After two hours of walking uphill and down dale, we arrived back at grandma and grandad's house. He tired and gasped from his emphysema and struggled to walk up steep hills, always needing a rest at a roadside bench whenever one appeared. Level walks had become slower, football kick-abouts in the park non-existent. Exhaustion soon gripped his perennial, merry expression, contorted with age into a face of fatigue. He still mustered a quip of humour. His mind rumbled by thoughts of making others smile.

"You know, 'cos my legs are shorter, they're nearer to the ground. That means I don't have to walk as far as you," said grandad, chuckling to himself. At age ten, you're not sure whether that was true. I loved his boyish jokes. It was part of his fabric. I wished he was my dad.

"Grandad. Can I borrow your walking stick?"

"If you want to, lad," he said with concern and a wry smile. "Why on earth do you want my walking stick, soldier? You normally only go for a walk with me."

"Got a brilliant idea, grandad."

"What's that then, lad?" Grandad looked bemused and scratched his head.

"Golf, grandad."

Grandad beamed a smile of confusion with raised eyebrows.

"Golf?" He smiled. "Can't take you to Gleneagles. It's too far."

"Sure…... Golf."

"Well, I've got no golf balls or tennis balls. I know an old wartime ditty about not having any. I'll teach it you one day."

"Grandma. Can I borrow one of your balls of wool?"

"Why do you need my ball of wool?"

"Golf! I can use it as a golf ball and use grandad's walking stick to hit it."

"Alright then. Have a look in my knitting bag. There are plenty of old remnants in there you could roll up into a ball."

"If you're going to play golf outside, you'd better be very careful about Mr. Grumpy upstairs," said grandad. "He doesn't like little boys. He eats them for breakfast. He rants about everything, so don't upset him. Do you want him to eat you?"

"Trust me grandma, it's only a ball of wool."

"Grandma, can I have one of your leather gloves, please? Just one; like the golfers have."

"Go on then. But you hark my words! Do not upset Mr. Grumpy Pants." Said grandma with a meaningful tone.

Out I went onto the fairway, albeit the community lawn. A luscious green swathe of cut grass beckoned my first shot. Glove in hand, I glimpsed grandma and grandad twitch the net curtains back in the grandstand of their lounge. My thoughts trained on the BBC Sports commentator, as he began his eloquent commentary, in a quiet and deep captivating voice……..

"....And here we are, ladies and gentlemen. Jeff Dalton is now placing the ball down at the first tee. His famous wood driver now clasped firmly in his hands. He prepares himself for this lengthy drive into the distance."

Placing the ball of wool on the grass, I turned ninety degrees towards the distant brick wall. With unerring concentration, I held grandad's old wooden walking stick upside-down. After I wiggled my bum a bit, I stroked the driver backwards and forwards a few times. I had seen professionals do it on grandad's telly; I assumed for effect. Meticulous care needed, I summoned my technical skills, deep thought, and concentration.

'Raise the club above the head, eyes on the ball, another wiggle of the bum and...' Whack!

With surprise, the ball of wool flew a reasonable distance of thirty yards. I continued this across the wide lawn, up and down, backwards and forwards, to my heart's content. I often played alone. No older brother to create arguments. No-one to wrangle my trusty wooden club from me. Nobody to unwrap the ball of wool and tie me around a tree, like cowboys and Indians did. Nobody to fight against for once. Utopia.

'Next, I can try a little chip shot,' I mused.

A low brick wall bordered the raised lawn, itself being a metre above the normal pathway below. The wall finished a foot above the grass. An ideal chip shot, to get it over the wall and onto the pathway adjacent grandad's house. I raised the walking stick above my head, ready for the swing. Then I lowered it gently for practice and judgment and recoiled it back above my head. Woollen ball in place, thirty yards from the wall, I swung the upturned walking stick. A professional stroke of quality. My palms must have been clammy from earlier shots. The improvised golf club slid from my hands and missiled towards Mr. Grumpy's window, seemingly in slow motion. Fear gripped me. Images of impending doom created by an angry ogre flashed before me.

'Forgive me Mr. Grumpy, for I have sinned,' rang through my mind like the Lutine Bell, warning of imminent disaster.

'Noooo..! This can't be happening. Not now. Not Mr. Grumpy's windows. He eats little boys.'

The walking stick travelled like a guided missile. True and straight. Straight through Mr. Grumpy's window. It shattered with an ear-deafening, scintillating crash like a loudspeaker blared inside a library. Shards cascaded like the sparkles of a firework. Fragments of glass echoed between the flats as they hit the concrete paving slabs beneath the lounge. Each tinkle peppered the path in a surreal work of art. The walking stick disappeared through Mr. Grumpy's large picture-window like an Olympic javelin. I raced inside grandad's house and hid behind the sofa, terrified and trembling. The army closed in on me. I needed a place to hole up out of sight from 'Ivan the Terrible.'

"Na' then lad. Don't thee worry about it. Accidents happen. You stay there. I'll sort Mr. Grumpy out. It's about time I had a word with him," said grandad with reassurance.

A thunderous knock rattled the door. The metal letterbox flapped like a chatterbox.

"I want a word with that lad of yours! He's nothing but trouble," Mr. Grumpy shouted with menace in his voice. Retribution was high on his list of demands.

"Hang on a minute," said grandad in defiance. His barrel chest blocked the doorway.

"It's your lad. Your grandson, I should think? He's done it. He's smashed my bloody window. Where is he? You'll need to pay for that."

Mr. Grumpy, alias Mr. Hardcastle, a beefy six-foot, ex-army sergeant, hated noise, children and people in general. Every time we visited, grandad preached the same sermon. *'Don't be noisy! No running through the corridor! Don't even breathe in his direction."*

Now I had broken every rule in the British Army manual. Grandad's less than four-foot-ten-inch stature seemed inadequate, but his portly body filled the doorway as he stood like a Yorkshire bulldog. Mr. Hardcastle wasn't welcome. He could only remonstrate outside the front door, trying to peer past grandad. Although short, grandad still had the stance of a heavyweight boxer in a compact frame.

"Don't worry about that, Mr. Hardcastle. I'll pay for it. It's only a bloody window. Put your binoculars away now and calm yourself. I'll phone the council maintenance office on Monday. They'll sort it," said grandad, as a firm statement.

"And what am I supposed to do in the meantime? It's made my room draughty."

"Try closing your mouth. That's where most of the draught comes from," quipped grandad.

"Well, I'm not happy. I can tell you that much," said the angry Mr. Hardcastle, frothing at the mouth.

"Nothing new there then. You've never been happy since you moved in," said grandad.

"Balderdash. You'd better get it sorted, that's all," he said.

The only way I could prevent a loud giggle was to cover my own mouth with my hands. Mr. Hardcastle marched away, disgruntled by verbal defeat and snappy wit. Grandad had an answer for everything; his mind was so alert. He had a way of putting people down but in tandem with raising a smile for anyone within earshot. I feared a venomous battle as if two cobras weighed each other up before a strike. Grandad stood his ground and defused the argument. He spoiled Mr. Hardcastle's desire for a slanging match, who 'about-faced' and gruntled as he stomped back to his own house. Mr. Hardcastle wanted a full-on verbal war of words, most of them unpleasant. He got little chance as grandad closed the door in his face, mid-sentence.

A draught swept through the corridor of the four flats, thanks to me improving the ventilation. I expected both grandma and grandad to be furious. Grandad looked at me and laughed. His face beamed with wry approval. He stretched his arms out and lifted me onto his knee. Then he sat in his rocking chair and cuddled me for a few minutes. His warmth radiated through me like a soothing heat lamp, to dispel my worries.

"There you go. No need to worry, was there? He's gone now."

"Why are you laughing, grandad?"

"Mr 'Grumpy' has been bothering me for some time. Now we've both brought him down a peg or two. Best get your hands washed. We'll have some cakes, eh? Well done, lad."

"Thanks grandad."

It felt incongruous to commit a cardinal sin, then pat me on the back for it. Dad always scolded me if I upset the neighbours. I'm sure grandad could see himself in me. In later years, this proved to be true as a total stranger vividly described and confirmed his manifestation. She reassured me not to worry and that grandad was indeed my Guardian Angel.

"So you won at the golf" A hole in one, eh? Well done, lad!"

Chapter 5

Grandad tried to impart as much of his knowledge into my mind. He knew I had an eagerness to explore new avenues of information. His set of Encyclopedia Britannica, a fountain of knowledge in its' day, engrossed my mind as I absorbed a colossal amount of information. Pride of place for the dozen leather-bound volumes was above the Grundig radiogram, below the retro-style wall mirror. Grandma polished them every day as the distinctive smell of leather oozed around the room. They kept each volume and page in pristine condition, as new as the day they left the printing press. Grandad showed me a myriad of skills; he knew I had enormous patience from completing ten-thousand piece jigsaws. He showed me how to make plastic Airfix models with meticulous care. Then showed me how to paint them using tiny tins of Humbrol paint. As grandad was now in his sixties, he suggested I understand ancestry and how to do a family tree. He showed me how to get information from birth and marriage certificates, using his own as an example.

"Tell you what, lad. Let's see if you can put our family tree together," said grandad in his soft Yorkshire dialect.

"Have you got some drawing paper grandad?" I asked with enthusiasm.

Drawing paper was the end of unused wallpaper. I realised I could draw a family tree, stretching back a thousand years. Two metres of wallpaper could accommodate hundreds of names and dates. The only limit was how much information I could investigate and collect.

"Here you are. Pencil, paper, ruler. Let's get started."

Grandad sat beside me as I began the diagram of a family tree. He brought me a small rubber so I could draw perfect squares around the edge to create small boxes to add names, and to rub out my mistakes. He showed me how to measure distances between each box. It looked professional for a ten-year-old. I was so proud that grandad spent so much time and patience with me.

"Na' then lad. That's the bottom section done....... Alex.... Jeff..... Glenn. You now need to put their dates of birth inside the boxes if you know them," said grandad.

"I need to ask mum about their birth dates. I only know mine."

"Why not ask your mum if you can stay for the week? It's half term; we can go for our walks. Then you can go to the library across the road for one of those books you need."

"That's a brilliant idea, grandad. I need to get as much information as I can to get organised. I'm sure my mum will let me stay for a few days. Gets me away from Alex as well. I think mum is upside down at the moment. When she goes back home later, she might feel as though she needs a break from me and Alex. Alex is always out of the house, messing about with his friends. That way, there's only Glenn to look after, and he's no trouble," I said.

As mum returned home, I had every expectation she would patch things up with dad. She was always the peacemaker, the pacifier whenever arguments arose. By far, the events of the weekend had been more vociferous than any in the past. Dad's attitude now bordered on indifference most of the time, coupled with relentless silent moods. Learning from past quarrels and tiffs, mum became submissive and did whatever facilitated an improvement in relations. She needed to keep the peace; a status quo of how life was a week ago. She pussyfooted around him and pampered him as best she could. She could only pamper to his moods from an emotional point of view. I expected that whatever had flared up between mum and dad, they would gloss the situation over within weeks. Dad would continue his selfish life as though nothing had happened. Mum would continue her struggle against poverty and slave at home with deteriorating health. Grandad always preferred me to find the information for myself instead of him giving the answers to make it easy. A few days away from Alex was always high on my agenda.

This gave mum some breathing space after the upheaval with dad, one less person to feed and take care of. Mum thought that was an excellent idea and agreed for me to stay with my hero. As Monday morning arrived, I skipped across the road to the library, eager to continue learning about ancestry. I was a member of Sheffield Libraries as I called in every other week when visiting my grandparents. The library was quiet; nobody about except the female librarian. I searched the aisles of all the books, but couldn't even find the subject.

"Can I help you?" Asked the polite female librarian, tiptoeing along the aisle to where I stood, placing returned books back onto the shelves.

"Hope so. I'm looking for a book about Gynaecology."

She looked at me with a deep frown and surprise but asked again for me to confirm my search.

"Are you certain that's the book you need?" Asked the lady.

"Yep. I'm sure. I'm just trying to find out where I came from."

"Well, if you're sure. Follow me this way. I'm sure we have something that covers that topic. It's unusual for anyone coming in to find books about that. Are you certain?"

"Yes. I'm certain."

"Here you are. I do hope you find the right book for yourself," she said with a diplomatic retreat.

After a few minutes, I found half a dozen books on the subject. I opened the first book I came to but dropped it in shock. They didn't seem to be the right books I wanted. The librarian looked across towards me, but I disappeared before she said a word. I was so embarrassed, for her and me. I ran straight home to grandad's house as fast as I could.

"Who's chasing you, lad? I'll sort 'em out whoever they are."

"It's not that grandad. I went into the library, but the lady showed me the wrong books."

"They must have some. They have books on everything, lad," said grandad, disappointed on my behalf.

"I told her the books I needed, as you told me."

"That's right. A book about Genealogy. The study of ancestry and how to draw a family tree."

"Genealogy......? I got it, wrong grandad. I asked for a book on Gynaecology. She showed me some weird books I didn't understand." Grandad sniggered and kept a bemused smile.

"Don't worry, lad. Let me have my cup of tea. We'll go to the library. I'll explain and apologise. I'm sure she'll understand."

"Thanks, grandad."

Grandad and I returned from the library with the correct book about Genealogy. When mum arrived the following week, to take me home on the number 21 bus, everybody had a rib-tickling laugh about my mistake. Embarrassed, I thought I had asked for a book about ancestry. Grandad thrived on this kind of humour, even though the faux pas was unintentional. Empathetic as ever, he smothered me with a reassuring hug. He didn't want me to feel as though the joke was on me, rather to laugh about the situation.

"Come here, you. Let me give you a 'whiskers,'" said grandad as he gave me a gentle bear-hug of empathy. His neatly trimmed white whiskers, the scourge of many kids, produced a guaranteed giggle as he rubbed his chin across my stomach.

Mum and grandma had talked for two hours about mum's quagmire of escalating problems. They both cried and hugged each other at sensitive moments. Grandma seemed able to come up with the right answers. With mum's state of mind, she knew she could trust her mother to be able to offer her support, whether it be physical, emotional, or financial.

"So what's the matter, love?" Asked grandma.

"Where do I begin? There are so many problems. I just can't cope with life," said mum, her voice began a faint quiver.

"I knew something had upset you when you. What is it, love?"

"It's one problem on top of another. Money, or lack of it, is the root of many of our problems," said mum.

"They say money is the root of all evil, love," said grandma as she hugged mum.

"That's only if you've got money. We haven't got enough money to buy food or clothes for the boys," said mum. A tear formed in the corner of her eye.

"Eddie works down the coal mine all week, but his wages are as poor as a shop assistant. And he risks his life for a pittance. He doesn't take time off work and he still doesn't bring enough money home to feed us and pay the bills. I have to walk to Bradshaw's, four miles there and back, in all weather to get some food for the weekend on tick. Can't do it any more, mum,"

"Your dad and I, don't have a lot of money on our pension, but we can give you a hand."

"I appreciate that mum, but that's unfair to you. We don't want cash handouts. Eddy and I have just got part-time jobs to make ends meet. The extra wages do help a lot, but it means I am working myself into the ground. Looking after the boys, the household chores, and the shopping are killing me. The boys help with carrying the groceries with me, but Jeff is only ten and Alex is only twelve. It's purgatory on a cold wet evening," said mum, her throat choked with emotion.

"What about Eddie? Can he do any overtime?" Said grandma.

"He works in a team, mum. The cage goes down the mine shaft once at the start of the shift, then brings the men back to the top at the end. Overtime is not available at the coal face. He's just started a part-time job selling seafood snacks at the pubs on weekends. The extra money is handy, but none of us see him anymore. Whatever spare time he gets, he plays darts with his mates," said mum. Defeated by a cascade of uncontrolled tears.

Mum burst into tears as she revealed how much of a struggle life had become. Grandma put her arms around her and gave a motherly squeeze. Grandma saw the pain and anguish in her mum's eyes. Tearful pools glazed over her emerald green eyes. They cried for help; they cried *rescue me from these depths of torturous existence.*

Only grandma and grandad could hear and see her plight. Mum was near to a nervous breakdown, and had to fight against that sombre place, fearful of losing us to fostering.

"Come on. There's no need to lose hope, love. How about if I come across during the school week and take care of the boys? I can go shopping and help with other chores around the house. That will make your life a lot easier, more so as you go to work three mornings a week," said grandma.

"Could you do that mum? The boys can be hard work, especially after school."

"We can share cooking the meals and the shopping. It will cut your workload in half.

"It would be an enormous help for me, mum. Every bit of help is a bonus at the moment."

"And what about your stomach problems? Is that getting any better?" Asked grandma.

"I keep taking the medicine, mum, but there's no improvement. The doctor reckons it's all down to stress and anxiety. He said I should eat proper meals, but up to now, I haven't had the time or even the money to look after myself properly. Maybe the problem will improve with you helping me out, mum"

"Well, I hope you'll be able to cope better with me coming over. Maybe in a few weeks, we might notice an improvement in how you feel. Everything alright, with you and Eddie now that you all had two weeks away together?" Said grandma.

Grandma hit a raw nerve. Mum burst into a deluge of heartbreaking tears of pent-up emotion. She blubbered for a while as she had to reveal problems about their relationship. Her blood pressure seemed to create a blotched face seemed. As she cried, her heart gave way to the enormity of her grief. She sobbed into her trembling hands as her tears trickled between her fingers. Her breathing degenerated into palpitations. She cried until her eyes were sore. Within her soul, she felt empty and lifeless, drained of spirit.

With dad's revelations, she felt as though there was nothing left and no reason to go on living.

"Eddie is having an affair, mum. I don't know how to handle it." My mum gave an emotional outburst. She couldn't hold back her pent-up distress any longer. Trickles of emotion spilled down her face. Her outpouring of anguish became loud and out of control, her tears escaped onto her blouse before grandma got the tissues.

"How do you know he's cheating?" Said grandma.

"He didn't come home last night until nearly four in the morning. I caught him sneaking in. He hoped I was asleep, but I waited up for him. At first, I worried because heavy snow had fallen. I waited and waited and got myself in a tizzy. I was so worried about him, I was beside myself. It distressed me. Then I feared the worst," said mum.

"It gets you like that, love. You can't help but worry when it gets so late, and he's still not home. Anything could have happened on the roads. So he crept through the door; and….?"

"Straight away, I could smell perfume on him," said mum. "His face, his hair, his clothes. He gave a load of weak excuses, but I knew he was lying. A row broke out and then a slanging match. I went to bed and left him downstairs at about five this morning. I don't know how I can forgive him, but for the sake of my boys I might have to," continued mum.

"Think carefully about all this, sweetheart. Don't throw the towel in until you've had a considered the consequences. It's not just you that's affected. Think of those three lovely boys. Let's have a serious talk about it all. I'll make us both a lovely cuppa. Then you can calm down for a while," said grandma.

"That's not half of it, mum. You said to think about my three boys. It could be four now."

The surprise stunned grandma into a jaw-dropping silence. For once, she was lost for words. In an instance, grandma recognised the dilemma her daughter faced. A moment when grandma could say nothing until she knew how my mum felt.

"Oh, Evelyn. My sweet angel. Are you sure? How far on are you? Does Eddie know?"

"The doctor confirmed it on Friday, just gone. The baby is twelve weeks. I was so excited on Friday, but I couldn't tell Eddie; he was just on his way out. I couldn't wait for him to come home after his evening job. When he didn't come home on time, I became distraught and tearful. He crept in at four, we had a big row, then I told him."

"So how did he react? What did he say?"

"His exact word was… 'Oh'…. Followed by total silence. That sort of summed it all up," said mum, weeping into her tissue.

"Do you want to have the baby?" Asked grandma defensively "I always dreamed of having a baby girl, mum. This time, it could be. What do I do if we split up? Do I have the baby?"

Mum decided she needed to go ahead for her own peace of mind, and hoped to God, this time the baby of her dreams would become a reality. In the 1960's, there was no way of predicting the baby's sex. At the fourth time of asking, it had to be a girl. There was an obvious strain on mum and dad's relationship, noticeable by the constant arguments each time he returned from work. Finances had improved, but only to the point of being able to afford to live. There was still no surplus cash, it being consumed by the usual household bills, rent, and food. Dad's assessment of the situation proved accurate. With mum, now seven months pregnant, ending her part-time job was imminent. She relied to a great extent on her own mother, grandma Cooper. Household chores, cooking, and shopping, as well as helping to care for three growing boys was strenuous. For a seventy-six-year-old woman, this was a monumental task. Mum had no other options; it was fortunate grandma volunteered to help. As a knock-on effect, this left grandad Cooper on his own for five days of the week. His health had suffered markedly over the past year.

"Look, Evelyn, our finances are becoming a problem yet again," said dad, exasperated at never quite getting on top of household budgeting.

"Things have been better since we got extra money from the part-time jobs," said mum.

"You're packing in work next week. We're back to square one yet again. I have had enough of trying to make ends meet."

"What is that supposed to mean?" Said mum, taken aback.

"We can't keep going like this, can we? This is not what life should be. Burdened by debt, collectors knocking on the door. No money to buy anything and another baby on the way."

Dad grabbed his coat and stormed out mid-sentence. Mum burst into tears as he slammed the door without saying another word. Grandma comforted her as she wept on her shoulder. Once again, finances plunged the family into severe difficulties. Dad had no enthusiasm for another child. There appeared to be cracks in the relationship. Dad returned a few hours later, smelling of beer. The usual cold treatment kicked in; the atmosphere became as icy as the air outside. Words needed to be spoken, but none were said. Neither mum nor dad saw fit to speak about the existing turmoil. Arguments continued every time they were both at home. Their relationship was in a downward spiral, getting deeper into an unknown abyss. Mum was excited and hopeful of a new dawn as the special date drew nearer. She needed the support of a loving husband, now more than ever. Such hope was becoming no more than a pipe-dream.

Chapter 6

With irony, dad had become more distant as Easter 1962 approached. Mum's efforts and toil continued unabated, though she was heavily pregnant. There was a mountain of household chores to carry out. At least, grandma Cooper shouldered most of the burden, least favourite was the Friday night epic journey to Bradshaw's Corner Shop, now with grandma bearing the load. The arduous weekly two-mile trudge continued, this time with grandma and myself. In grandma's autumn years, her health and strength deteriorated markedly. Her natural body language showed tiredness, a jaded face, perpetual smile showed a grimace.

"Na' then young man," exclaimed the burly Mr. Bradshaw. "Where's your mum today, then?"

"She's not at all very well Mr. Bradshaw," I said, exhausted and windswept from the lengthy walk.

"And who's this fine lady?"

"It's my grandma."

A tear escaped and rolled down her cheek as the stiff wind had brushed her eyes. The bitter winter had not given up its icy grip. She shivered and rubbed her hands to rekindle a semblance of circulation, then looked at her wet shopping list.

"Hello, love. So how is your daughter?" Said Mr. Bradshaw.

"She's coping. The baby is due next month. Fingers crossed for a girl," said grandma.

"Has she got the top side of those stomach cramps yet?" Said Mr. Bradshaw.

"The pains come and go. Who knows what it might be? She's got the baby to worry about on top of that as well. The big downside for us is she's started drinking cabbage water. The entire house smells of boiling cabbage. There's no escape from it. She says it helps," said grandma.

Grandma knew there was something more serious about mum's health. Her stomach pains had caused agony for too long. They were getting worse, more painful, and more often. Mum knew the pregnancy wasn't causing extra problems as the GP advised her to continue with Magnesia.

"I'll help you pack those bags, love," said Mr. Bradshaw.

"That's most kind of you. You're a gentleman," said grandma.

Grandma lifted the two heavy bags in her wrinkled, callous hands. Her knuckles whitened with weight as I grabbed the other two with trepidation.

"Four bags this week, Mr. Bradshaw, but I might be back."

"We're always here, son. Give my regards to your mum."

We laboured along the trek to our house, like sherpa Tenzing climbing Everest. Alexandra Road seemed never-ending, only a perpetual horizon, no matter how far you walked. Grandma's back arched and ached with the heaviness of years of hard work but never complained. Glenn, now five, had started primary school. Mum had to walk a mile each way on the 'school run.' At the age of thirty-six, nurturing a baby would create more strain. I didn't realise it then, my battles with Alex added another layer of anxiety to an overburdened mum. Her face aged beyond her years. Her complexion had turned from sallow to a milky paleness. Her hair, greying away from auburn, seemed as brittle as a Brillo pad, ironic for a woman of her age.

Moments full of fun, laughter and adventure had all but disappeared from our lives. The magic seemed to have disappeared from mum's life years ago. A satin veneer had replaced the gloss. Though mum struggled from a physical, emotional, and financial point of view, her stepsisters, aunty Ruth, and aunty Connie kept their distance. Only grandma Cooper stepped in to help. Mum was her own true daughter, aunty Ruth, and aunty Connie were not.

They were always a distance apart, not just a physical distance, but also emotional. Ironically, by a cruel twist of fate, aunty Ruth would create a cataclysmic effect on us all. Her well-meant support turned out to be ill-judged, heartbreaking, and life-changing.

Grandma Cooper helped for most of 1962. School holidays, normally a gigantic task for mum, became a Herculean task for grandma. Just after Easter, baby number four arrived, 'spout and all.' Mum's dream wasn't to be. It overjoyed mum to welcome baby David into the world. Dad seemed distant and underwhelmed. He didn't see a newborn baby, he saw debts spiralling out of control. We saw his affections drifting away from us and mum. The icy cold Spring had not thawed, more-so in our family. A few weeks went by into the Summer months, dad was hardly ever seen at home. He was either at work, playing darts, or doing his part-time job. Mum went back to do her part-time cleaning job as soon as she could. After an arduous three-hour stint, mum walked up the mile-long country lane, leading out of the village of Ulley, where she worked. She stopped to catch her breath at the top. It was just after mid-day. Grandma was with us during that summer.

Uncle Jack and aunty Ruth dropped in to see grandad, making sure he was alright on his own. He was agile enough to look after himself for a few weeks, but now at seventy-six, his emphysema caused him to be short of breath. His walks were now becoming less frequent. He often said his old war wound was playing up. Ironic that the War Department had never enlisted him in the army, but I accepted that fact long ago. Grandad sat in his favourite armchair by the gas fire as aunty Ruth made him a cup of tea. He seemed happy enough, then in an instant, he dropped his tea on the floor, clutching his chest.

"Dad, what's the matter?" Said aunty Ruth, in shock.
Aunty Ruth put her arms around him, but he was fighting for breath. His face turned ashen and gaunt within an instance as aunty Ruth burst into tears. Seconds later his head fell back into his pillow, his face and eyes became transfixed. His shoulders had slumped back into the armchair.

There was no response; he was lifeless.

"I'll run to the phone box and call an ambulance. Be back in fifteen minutes," said uncle Jack.

"There's no need to rush Jack. It's too late. Dad's gone."

Uncle Jack returned, breathless. He leaned over to aunty Ruth and huddled her with warm affection.

"The ambulance is on the way," said uncle Jack. "They'll be here as soon as they can."

The ambulance arrived within fifteen minutes, but it was too late. There was nothing the crew could do. Resuscitation was futile. His face was already gaunt and grey. His entire body seemed unresponsive. Uncle Jack and aunty Ruth feared the worst. They were right. The two ambulance crew gave an empathetic look of sadness and held aunty Ruth's arm for a few moments.

"There was nothing we could do for your father. He slipped away in an instance. At least he didn't suffer. The important thing is that you were by his side." said the medic. "Just so there's no distress for you, we'll move Mr. Cooper into the bedroom. We can cover him with a bed-sheet to make the situation more dignified," continued the medic.

Moving grandad was a thoughtful act of kindness. At least he was at peace as aunty Ruth and uncle Jack awaited the doctor. Meanwhile, Aunty Ruth hyperventilated as shock overwhelmed her nervous system. Though she was the eldest of three sisters and had always organised everyone around her, she could also be irrational sometimes. That moment had arrived like a thunderbolt.

"Sorry we couldn't save Mr. Cooper," said the ambulanceman on his way out. "We'll get in touch with a locum doctor. He will need to examine Mr. Cooper," he continued.

"It's too late for a doctor now?" Said aunty Ruth, abruptly.

"A doctor has to attend a bereavement, love," said uncle Jack with reverence and empathy.

Aunty Ruth became hysterical and confused. Anguish clouded her actions as she bit her nails in desperation. She twisted her necklace like worry beads and began mumbling incoherent noises like monastic chants. She rocked back and forth, childlike, as though on a rocking chair. Shock had jarred her mental state, as psychiatric issues resurfaced from years ago. Uncle Jack was worried the tragedy might trip her back into an obscure dark world. The treatment worked years ago, but now another trauma questioned her mind. Irrational words spewed out like ticker tape.

"The ambulanceman has already pronounced my dad had passed. So why call a doctor?" Said aunty Ruth. confused,

"It's what has to be done under the circumstances," said uncle Jack, trying to calm her.

"This is ludicrous, Jack. We have to stay in the house for God knows how long? A doctor is of no use now, is he?" Said aunty Ruth with pangs of frustration.

"You're the eldest sister, Ruth. You're the one who will have to let everybody know about your dad. I know you're devastated. But especially your mother and sisters need to know."

Aunty Ruth sat motionless. Her mind buzzed incessantly. She rested for a few minutes until she recovered from the shock. Too much was happening too quickly. She sat back and stared at the old lampshade, a kaleidoscope of colours, like her mind. Already, the musty smell of the absence of furniture polish drifted as uncle Jack opened the top windows.

"I know you're right. I can't get my head around any of it at the moment," said aunty Ruth, her body exhausted.

"Perhaps you want a few quiet moments with your dad, to say some kind words and reflections? I'll make you a nice cuppa tea. Some paracetamol might help calm you a bit."

"You're right, Jack. I'm just being stupid," said aunty Ruth, regaining some composure as the tablets and strong tea settled her nerves.

"You've had a terrible shock, love. All this only happened less than an hour ago. At least you were with him. He wasn't alone. His eldest daughter was by his side. None of that's stupid. Shock, devastation, and hurt are natural reactions," said uncle Jack with his soft voice.

"Sit down for a minute and get your breath back.

"I know you're right. My head's spinning. But I feel a little better now. I think I will have a few minutes with dad. Just to let him know I'm here, with him."

"That's right, A few quiet words before the doctor comes."

"Alright, Jack. Just be with me for a while. I feel sick," said aunty Ruth.

"I'm not going anywhere, love. Just sit yourself down. We've got to wait for the doctor, anyway. He could be another hour yet. Someone has to stay here for the doctor to arrive."

Aunty Ruth walked into the bedroom with trepidation and turned back the sheet to reveal her dad's face, as he slipped into eternity. She looked around at the many mementos and photographs of loved ones. She stroked a small photograph of her with her dad from the bedside cabinet. Memories of playing with grandchildren at Scarborough before they grew up. The room had a chilly air, as though vapour would emanate from her breath. She held his hand and stroked his forehead. A shaft of sunlight peeped through the curtain onto their wedding day picture that looked across to him. In between tears, she wrestled with words of compassion and humour, traits of his character.

"I've always been here for you, dad. You know that. You were always here for all of us; me, Connie and Evelyn. You'll always be in my heart and everybody's heart. You will look down on us, helping to sort out our problems. You'll be a guardian angel for mum, your girls and all the grandchildren. Your work will be cut out up there, you know. You'll be working harder up there than you ever did down here," she said with grandad's wit.

Aunty Ruth continued with reminiscences of glad times until delicate taps at the door broke her sombre reflections. She gave a sad smile before she left the bedroom with a bowed head.

"Morning doctor. I'm Jack, Mr. Cooper's son-in-law. Please come in."

A short while later, the doctor had completed his examination. Administrative forms completed and empathy proffered, the doctor signed the Death Certificate and left within minutes.

"It seems strange to leave dad alone in the house. It doesn't seem right," said aunty Ruth, her voice choked with sadness.

"I know. But your mum and sister need to be told."

"I can't think straight. There's so much to do. I don't think I can cope with all the grief," said Aunty Ruth.

"I know. But think about how your mum will feel. She's just lost her husband of forty years. It will devastate her. Then there are your sisters. They're all going to be shocked."

"How do I tell mum that dad has gone?" Said aunty Ruth.

"I think it's time to go now, love. There's nothing more we can do here. Maybe a bit of fresh air might pick up a bit?"

Aunty Ruth appeared to be in a trance. Most of uncle Jack's comments drifted over her head.

"I just feel so lethargic and useless. Everything seems beyond me. I can't help but think of dad and how mum will feel. How will the grand-kids feel?"

With grandad passing, everybody must have grieved in their own way; some inconsolable, some stunned into numbed silence. Many couldn't let their emotions spill out for a long while. Then emotions would spill out for no apparent reason. Sometimes, in the blink of an eye, a random thought or image flashed through the brain, releasing pent up grief and sorrow. Floods of tears could erupt in a supermarket, or at work, or at a bus-stop.

"I know you're right. Maybe it's time for us to tell mum and sis.' I'm not looking forward to this, Jack. Not at all," said aunty Ruth with a sad face frown and heavy eyes.

Twenty minutes later, uncle Jack and aunty Ruth arrived at our house. Grandma was about to prepare lunchtime snacks for us all. Mum had just arrived back from work. She was about to enjoy her first sit down of the day with a cup of tea.

"Right then. I need to get you lot fed," said grandma. "It's just like feeding the five thousand."

"Yay!" We all shouted, except David, who by cried for a feed.

"Beans on toast? Or potted meat sandwiches?"

"Chips, grandma," I yelled back, tongue in cheek.

She glared at me with exasperation and consternation. A raised eyebrow and a curled lip showed indignation of my quip.

"Alright Jeff, you can have chips. What about you, Alex?"

"Tomatoes on toast," he said, just to be awkward.

An unexpected rap on the door surprised us all. The door flew open. Curtains blew in the cross-wind of a draught. Glenn's birthday cards tumbled to the floor like tenpins.

"It's only me," yelled a female voice, crying as she spoke, with a strong Yorkshire accent.

Before we could muster any greeting, aunty Ruth burst through the door. Her face was ashen, contrasted by reddened eyes from crying. She paused, as though she was thinking of what to say, and how to say it.

"Evelyn. Mum. I've got some terrible news," said aunty Ruth.

"What's the matter? What's happened?" Said mum, sitting.

She struggled to hold back her tears and stumbled to the sofa, barely able to breathe. Her voice whimpered with panic as she stuttered to say a word. Her hands smothered her face as shock gripped her emotions.

"It's dad…. It's dad…He's….He's dead," said aunty Ruth.

"No…No…… He can't be…... Not dad……," mum screamed.

Mum collapsed back on to the sofa, stunned by shock. Ruth stretched across to mum and put her arms around her. They both hugged with affection and consoled each other. I had never seen this spontaneity before. I clutched mum as I had done so many times before when she cried. She cuddled me and hugged me with so much warmth. Grandad's passing was unexpected. She knew my grief was as great as hers. Devastation, despair and disbelief shocked us into numbness. Grandma Cooper, in the kitchen, oblivious to the commotion until she heard screams, barged through the door. She looked around at heads bowed with devastation.

"What on earth's happened.... Ruth?.... Evelyn?....." yelled grandma, visibly shocked.

"I can't believe it. Dad's had a heart attack," said aunty Ruth, sniffling, wiping away teardrops.

Fear splintered grandma's heart. Her arm stretched out to hold the doorway to steady herself from fainting. Her fingers shook with the devastating news.

"Mum. He's gone. It was instant. A massive heart attack. Gone. Jack and I called to see how he was this morning, with you being here. He was fine one second, supping his mug of tea, then he seemed to just collapse, gripping his chest."

"Oh, no!.. Screamed grandma. "I can't believe it, not my Joe."

God took grandad's life without warning. Life seemed unfair. Aunty Ruth explained what had happened, after a short while of sobbing. Handkerchief boxes quickly emptied. "We dropped in to see him only an hour ago. He was bright and cheerful; then gone."

Chapter 7

Plucking up courage, grandma stood, wobbled on her feet, and grabbed the back of the chair to prevent herself from falling. Her eyes radiated fear and shock and stared without blinking. Her head seemed anaesthetised and motionless, set with rigor mortis, as her brain wrestled with reality, or she was in the middle of a ghastly nightmare. Seconds later, her eyes snapped into rapid blinks, waking up from her trance. She snapped into life, irrational blurb spewed from her dry mouth. She was alone, grandad was alone. Grandad transcended into a dark unknown world beyond ours; grandma into a dark corner of her own mind. In a quiet moment, she stopped and gazed with a blank expression, tears of memories seeping down her cheeks through her foundation cream.

"I need to see him. I need to speak to him," she said. Her voice quivered with anxiety.

"No mum. It's not good for you to go to the flat now. Somebody needs to be with you. You can't be alone tonight. The place will be cold and lonely," said mum.

Uncle Jack seemed to be the only person to be rational in a time of crisis. A veteran of the war and countless tragedies below ground at the coal face, he saw panic and hysteria at first hand. He saw comrades disappear before his eyes, lost in a flash. Scores of friends wandered, dazed with shock, with incoherent voices, bewildered by instant trauma.

"Let me take your mum, Evelyn and the two boys, this afternoon, while it's still light. Ruth could stay to look after Glenn and the baby."

"You're right. Glenn is too young to go. He's only five. Seeing his grandad would be a big shock. You happy with that, Ruth?"

"I guess so. I said a few words to dad a while ago. You all need to go over to the flat. He's alone over there. I'll be fine looking after David and Glenn for a while."

"If you're all there together, you can support each other."

"That's the best idea, Jack," said aunty Ruth nursing David.

"You need your loved ones around you; us. Close all the curtains and open the top windows. Pay your respects to your dad. I can bring you all back later, to Evelyn's house. Perhaps have a cup of tea, a ham sandwich or something."

"That's so good of you, Jack. I appreciate that," said grandma. "Can I come back to stay with you tonight, Evelyn?"

"Of course you can. We can then keep each other company, have a cuppa, calm our nerves."

Uncle Jack's car ambled along the country road as if it were a funeral limousine. In a surreal twist, this would be the exact journey we would take for real, maybe a week later. We dawdled up the steep hill from the village of Aughton and on to Woodhouse. We passed the old railway station where I sat with grandad, watching the trains hurtle past. The occasional dribble wiped from her nose, grandma sniffled in unison with mum. She wrapped her arms around her, and hugged her as they both whimpered, along the ten-mile journey to grandma's flat.

Grandma, always dressed in her long black winter coat and black velvet hat, sat motionless thinking of grandad. Like many locals, she only possessed one warm winter coat, and that was it. Mum grabbed her solitary dark blue winter coat, Alex and I grabbed our dark green school blazers. The morose atmosphere, only enlightened by the contrast of green rolling hills, grandad had walked with me many times. As fields of green rolled by, so did the tears of pain and anguish that trickled at random down mum and grandma's cheeks in unison. Words seemed inappropriate, thoughts and memories triggered a cascade of hot, salty teardrops, dribbling down into the corner of their lips. Alex and I were likewise hurting, but mum and grandma's pain seemed greater. The ratchet of the handbrake signalled our journey's end, outside grandma's house. Everyone sat in the car for a few minutes, contemplating the chilly room where grandad lay. Net curtains twitched with furtive glances as the car doors opened, then thumped shut. Neighbours strained to see what was happening. Disturbed by cars arriving, ambulance, doctor and now bereaved members of the family, ensured immediate neighbours were aware grandad had passed.

I sensed an eeriness, a ghostly presence of spirits that enveloped the hallway. Grandma and mum seemed reticent to continue. They both took deep breaths to summon inner strength and bravery to walk the few steps to the front door. They supported each other, arm in arm, with the help of Alex and I, holding their arms on either side. The gloom of the hallway enticed an anxious glimpse into the bedroom. The door, open by a fraction, but ajar enough to see grandad, at peace, awaiting his ascension to a higher life. I could only squint through the narrowness, a fleeting glimpse, enough to see my fallen hero. Stomach cramps of fear coincided with the musty smell of death, even with windows opened. Blackout curtains plunged all the rooms into sullen darkness, except for a shard of light, guiding our path into the room where grandad lay; an impromptu chapel of rest.

"Are you seeing grandad now, Jeff? I'll come with you. There is nothing to worry about."

"If you would mum," I said, a quiver in my voice.

Until now, I had shed no tears, even though I sat next to my hero, grandad Cooper. I felt guilty and dishonourable to him as I had not out-poured my emotion. Of all the people in my life. It seemed callous of me. Perhaps he was by my side, in spirit, making me strong. Perhaps I had grown up, matured by tragedy. People around me said it makes you grow up quicker. I didn't want to grow up. I wanted to be seven, the same as grandad. I had to reconcile the fact grandad taught me to be brave, and there was nothing to fear when someone passed. It didn't scare me. Even though I was alone. I was with my hero.

"You alright son?" Asked mum.

"I think so. I just want to talk to grandad."

I reached out and touched his cheek with the back of my hand. His body had a supernatural coldness. A coldness I had never experienced before. I held his hand again with an icy chill. I had only ever felt warmth from grandad; his touch, his voice, his warm personality, his warmth of love. As I whispered to him, he seemed to grip my hand. He seemed to acknowledge my presence, a reassurance everything would be alright. I could not help but reiterate Psalm 23.

> *'Though I walk through the valley of the shadow of death, I fear no evil, for thou art with me.'*

This strange and surreal experience held a resonance within me for the rest of my days. I felt the spirit of grandad within me, as though he had drifted into my body. Years later, a total stranger, unknown to me or the family, described grandad's presence to a 'T', his features and his name. She said he was my Guardian Angel and for me never to be afraid. From that day onwards, I walked taller, head high, without fear from anyone.

Grandma sauntered along the gloom of the unlit corridor to the bedroom. Her head bowed, heavy with grief. Her hazel eyes, leaden as a storm cloud and sunken with tears, building into pools, semi restrained by her eyelashes. Two cards, hand delivered by near neighbours, lay on the floor beneath the letterbox. Well-meaning sympathies and condolences gave a kindness of thought.

The bedroom door gave a mousy squeak as she stepped with trepidation across the worn out rug. She climbed on to her usual side of the bed, cuddled him and held his hands in a warm clasp. Her head nestled below his chin across his barrel chest.

"You said you would never leave me love, but you have, you waited until I was out of the house. Well, I'm with you now just like I've always been, by your side, forever, my love. We spent lots of wonderful years together, didn't we? With our children and grandchildren. All those lovely days at the seaside, you making everybody laugh and giggle. Playing stupid tricks on the grand-kids. We'll all remember you forever. We'll all miss you.

I miss you, my love. I'll always cherish your memory."

They laid side by side, eyes closed, gazing to the ceiling. Grandma thought of the many happy memories they had shared.

"As we sat together in the long grass, we shared a daisy, pulled off its petals one by one, and took turns with trepidation to say,

'She loves me, she loves me not.'

Later that afternoon you proved it. Evelyn is the living proof of that memorable day," said grandma.

A serene quietness engulfed her kaleidoscope of images playing with mum and the grandchildren in the billowing fields of wheat.

"We made daisy chains on warm afternoons. Held buttercups under each other's chin to see if we liked butter. Pennymoon flowers stood tall and swayed in the warm breeze. Grand-kids made posies and gave them to me so I could marry you again."

Grandma became choked by her memories. A shy tear hesitated to ruin her powder foundation but escaped down her cheek. She reached for their wedding photograph and held it to her chest.

"I just want to say thank you for loving me. Thank you for being with me and thank you for saving me. Without you, I would have been nothing. Thank you for giving me the most wonderful, beautiful daughter in the world. In more ways than one, Evelyn and I would not be here now. We would not have survived. For that, I owe you my eternal love. Always did, always will. You will be with me all the days of my life, and thereafter. In my heart, in my soul, in my dreams. You said we would go to different places. No, we're not, I will follow you wherever you go. I promise I won't let my tears mar the smiles you have given me. Thank you for giving me a wonderful life. Thank you for loving me."

Grandma kissed him on his lips and cheek and gave him a loving hug. She looked back from the door and blew another kiss of warm affection as another tear escaped and trickled effortlessly.

"Bye love. Until we meet again."

Grandma retreated from the bedroom, deep in thought, wiped her face, and cleared her throat.

"Anyone fancy a lovely cuppa?" Said uncle Jack.

"I could do with one. He was a kind man." Grandma lamented.

"No grandma. He WAS the best," I added with pride.

"You're right, lad. He was the best. The best to us all......."

Grandma burst into tears. A gush of emotion spilt into a deluge, her body shook into tremors of grief.

"Perhaps we ought to say a meaningful prayer for grandad," said mum, struggling to speak through her own flood of tears.

Grandma agreed and retrieved her bible as we all held each other's hands in a circle. Not one to be religious, but it seemed right to me.

"That would be good. Just a brief prayer to say thank you for the wonderful life he gave us all and how he enriched everybody's world," said mum, stuttering for composure.

"Just a little message for you dad. We just want you to know we're all here. We all learned from you not to be afraid. You taught us to be brave. We miss you terribly already, dad."

Mum cut short her message with another surge of pent up emotion, then continued.......

"You know, dad said so many times.....

'Cos I'm paying for the funeral, you're all going to bloody well enjoy it. I'm not paying for people to be miserable at my party."

"I know it might be too early to talk about it, but any thoughts about the funeral arrangements, Gracie?" Said Jack to grandma, as the sombre mood lifted somewhat.

"Can you take care of that for me, Jack? Maybe go into the Co -op Funeral place tomorrow?" Said grandma, glancing at Jack, her voice croaky and fragile with constant outpourings.

"Of course we'll do that, love. Not a problem at all," said Jack.

"Joe wanted to be at rest alongside his mother and father, next to the family grave, sharing the same position in Woodhouse Cemetery. Just a normal low key funeral, but with red carnations. We had red carnations when we got married. So did Evelyn when she married."

"That's alright, Gracie. Leave the arrangements to me. In a few days, you might be strong enough to think about the church service, the prayers, the hymns?"

"I'd like that. But now I need time to think," said grandma.

Dad, being down the coal-mine since five in the morning, knew nothing of the tragedy that unfolded that July morning. He had showered the top layer of coal grime and sweat from his body at the colliery pithead showers. An extra bath at home was always necessary to get rid of the deeper gunge from his pores. Whether clean and fresh or rank and fusty, the dour smell lingered on skin and clothes like a disused poultice. He walked across the black, sludgy quagmire of the yard. Thick oily clag and coal dust stuck to the boots akin to a heavy clay sludge. It stuck like syrup to a blanket; almost the weight of deep-sea diver's boots. Into the car park, onto his motorbike, he revved up the steep hill and home on to the White City miner's estate.

He arrived to find an empty house, as deserted as the 'Marie Celeste' and as tranquil as a mountain pond. Normally, we were all at home during the school holidays, plus grandma Cooper, who now helped. They had left no messages or notes on the table or on the sideboard. Everyone had left everything as it was as if it was an apparition, and jumped into uncle Jack's car. Only aunty Ruth stayed behind to look after David and Glenn, but they were out for an afternoon walk, to get David to sleep.

As with many coal miners, calling at the pub on the way home became a time-honoured tradition, 'to quench the northern thirst.' A tried and tested formula to rid throats and lungs of a lethal concoction of coal dust, black mist and methane. Many miners used Black

Pigtail, a chewing tobacco to masticate the black goo of saliva and choking dust. Scores of coal miners walked home through the village, and 'grebbed up' black treacle spit into the road or hedgerows. The disgusting noise of a guttural *'oicht'* followed by a cough, a greb and then a spit, a common occurrence, and many a time, a disgusting sight. Positioned for convenience and hygiene, spittoons hid behind the entrance doors to pubs. Miners jettisoned the black phlegm out of sight of ladies, akin to some form of etiquette and diplomacy.

Dad changed into a navy blue blazer and fawn cavalry twill trousers once he had finished his morning shift. He splashed on his *'Old Spice'* after-shave lotion across his face and a smidgeon behind his ears as ladies do. Back on with his heavy bike leathers, resembling a quick costume change in between pantomime scenes, and out again, racing his motorbike down the street. Fifteen minutes later, he arrived at Roxy's house.

"Fancy a drink, love? I'm as parched as sandals on a hot beach."

"I'm game if you are," she said with unmistakable innuendo.

"Come on then. Grab your coat. I'll treat you to a Martini."

"Not like you to be around these parts during the day. Only see you at the weekends."

"Everybody's out for the day. Must have gone to Millhouses Park, swimming at the lido or something, I suppose."

"Still glad you came though. I always am."

"Another drink and then back to yours?"

"You can't get me into bed with just a Martini and lemonade."

"You wanna bet?"

"Come on, then."

By late afternoon, amorous affections created aching bones and groans.

"Got an ailing back love?" Asked Roxy with a sardonic smile.

"Well, I have been down at the coal face all morning."

"So heaving coal out is the problem, is it? Perhaps you're not used to a good workout."

"Complaining?" Asked dad, tongue in cheek.

"I've got nothing to complain about, big boy. You're just what the doctor ordered."

"Well, that's alright then. I'd better be on my way now, love, the kids will be home."

"That's not romantic. Is it? *gotta go 'cos the kids will be home.*

"You know what I mean?" Said dad.

"You'd better make it up to me at the weekend?"

The unmistakable beat of dad's Royal Enfield motorbike arrived back home. The house still quiet, apart from a few kids who played and squealed in the backstreet. Kick-the-can echoed between the houses. Mum asked if aunty Ruth had seen dad at all. She had been out and walked to the far end of the village with Glenn and baby David in the pram. Once home, mum cradled David to sleep again in the corner before he returned.

"Where the hell have you been while now?" Shouted mum.

"You been crying?" Asked dad. A rhetorical question.

"An understatement…. Yes, I have," said mum, hands-on hip.

"And your mum? She looks upset."

"You're full of understatements today."

"Where the heck have you been? Well?"

Dad looked across to us, with a weak smile. Mum glared at him, turned back to us, and said:

"Uncle Jack has given you boys some pocket money to get some sweets. Aren't you lucky?"

"That's right," said uncle Jack.

Dad didn't say a word. There was never any money for sweets.

"Shall we jump in the car and go to Bradshaw's, Evelyn?"

"Sure. Let's go," said mum, stirring dad's jealous feelings.

The car pulled away as Jack sensed a row brewing in the air.

"It's been hell down the pit today. Can't a man have a pint?"

"You ain't been to the pub. I know it."

"I can't go to the pub with my mates, without you moaning."

"You never go to the pub in the middle of the week. You have to be out of bed by four in the morning. You wouldn't get to the cage on time. No cage, no work."

Mum pressed for the truth. Feeble excuses didn't cut it. His steely eyes drifted away from her stinging bloodshot eyes, bulged with fury and frustration. Her chest heaved with elongated, deep sighs of exasperation.

"Just went to the Black Bull. Had a few pints. A few games of snooker. That's all. What harm is there with that?" Said dad, as his defence. The soft tone of his voice seemed insincere.

"You need to lie well to be convincing. I'm not your naïve little teenager any more. I can't trust an instinctive liar again."

"What are you on about, woman?"

"Well? Where have you been until now?" Screamed mum, her anger at boiling point.

Mum glared at him with disdain. She gave him short shrift for his contempt and inept excuses. The room quietened with unease but contrasted with her simmering cauldron of anger. He stared out the window. The unkempt garden, once his pride and passion, now showed his indifference and neglect, resembling his attitude.

The back door from the garden burst open. Uncle Jack charged in, concerned by the noise.

"You alright Evelyn?" Asked uncle Jack.

He had heard arguments as he walked down the path. Once inside the house, he strutted forward and brushed past dad with aggression. He hoped for a response in retaliation, verbal or otherwise. They were not good together in the same room; the atmosphere became electric, as the argument continued. Grandma and aunty Ruth took us into the garden. They sat and chatted on the garden seat about what had happened at home with grandad. Aunty Ruth rocked David in the pram as he lay asleep contented. The garden was large enough for three of us to play kick-about football.

Chapter 8

"What are YOU doing here, Mr. Goody-Two-Shoes?" Shouted dad, goading uncle Jack.

They both faced each other, eyeball to eyeball. Dad stuck out his chest for bravado. The atmosphere transformed as though pit bull terriers wanted to square up to each other. They fought hammer and tongs in younger days; both were abrasive with each other. In years gone by, dad became more than suspicious about uncle Jack's closeness to mum. He preferred to avoid any contact with his brother-in-law, uncle Jack.

Bad blood existed between them ever since mum became pregnant, carrying Glenn. As the years passed by, an uncanny resemblance became evident. Glenn was the only one of us to have butter blonde hair and blue eyes the same as uncle Jack. Alex, me, and baby David inherited mousey coloured hair like dad's. Whispers on the grapevine of a clandestine affair remained, but were unproven, but plain for all to see. The impasse between them flared up occasionally at close quarters. It would take a blind man not to see why.

"You've got enemies, Eddie," said Jack. And I'm one of them."

"Just go away. You're not wanted here," yelled dad, pushing Jack backward a step. His eyes narrowed with anger and breathed heavier with each deep breath.

"You got that wrong, mate. Go away. YOU don't belong here," shouted Jack, his face tightened with anger; fist clenched and recoiled for a punch on dad's jaw.

"Please don't start all this again. Not today, of all days. "Please," said mum summoning inner strength to deflect more upheaval.

"What do you mean, not today?" Said dad, wary of the remark and the gathering of mum's family. The last gathering happened at Glenn's christening, five years back.

"Not told him yet, Evelyn?" Shouted Jack, glaring at dad.

"Why is everybody here? What's going on?" Asked dad, marooned and ostracised. Everyone glanced towards Evelyn for a reaction. To see if she was strong enough to utter the words that bottled up deep inside her. She hesitated, then took a deep breath, and looked at sad faces.

"Dad's died," said mum, standing next to aunty Ruth.

The lounge, full of family, created an 'ad hoc' minute of silence. They all glanced at each other, expecting someone to offer words of comfort. Everyone seemed afraid of saying the wrong words or patronising instead of empathising. Mum broke down, drained of energy. Aunty Ruth stood up and caressed her shoulder as an older sister would.

"I'm so sorry sweetheart," said dad with diplomatic respect, but with little compassion.

"Save the sweetheart comments for that tart you've been with," said mum in a sharp tone.

At a low ebb, recent marital problems became mum's focal point. To make matters worse, dad found himself in the direct line of fire. Mum's family trapped him on all sides of the small lounge. To air dirty linen in public might be juicy gossip for neighbours, but that showed at first hand the plight that mum suffered. Dad, having spent the afternoon in absolute joy, contrasted by irony with mum, who spent the afternoon in the depths of depression. A full-on domestic argument suggested when guests and family should leave. Dad was in the wrong place at the wrong time. Dad was in someone else's bed, instead of in mourning.

"What? That old chestnut again?"

"Don't lie, Eddie. Her smell is on your clothes. Ash Blonde hairs are on your blazer?"

Uncle Jack lurched forward towards dad, grabbing his throat with both hands as um screamed with fear of another bust-up.

"You're not fit to be a father, Eddie," shouted uncle Jack.

They pushed and shoved a while. A chair hurtled across the table, breaking a chair leg. Jack raised his colliery swagger stick to bludgeon dad to the ground. Aunty Ruth and the door frame thwarted the strike.

"Don't Jack! Don't do it. He's not worth the effort," shouted aunty Ruth, terrified of another full-scale physical battle.

"He's a dead man. He could have died long ago when I should have left him for dead."

Uncle Jack dropped his swagger stick. A relic of coal mines in the last century used to keep miners in order. Now he used it as a walking stick in his early retirement. The swagger stick was a beast of a weapon. Shaped like a baseball bat. It could hurt, it could kill. It almost did, years ago.

"Pack that in you two. Grow up and move on," begged mum.

Dad stared, *'rescue me,'* at mum across the room. Sympathy was not forthcoming, but his eyes looked hurt, his body dejected. His respect in tatters, fragmented by deceit, laid bare before mum's side of the family.

"You've not offered any condolences to anyone. Everyone here has lost an enormous part of their lives. Mum, my sister Ruth, the boys. What about me? Who cares about me?" Said mum.

Dad stepped across to comfort her, but too late. Mum snubbed his embarrassing, ill-timed gesture.

"I am so sorry to you all. I was unaware of anything about this. I left for work on the morning shift......" said dad.

"Don't lie. Eddie. Just go away. This is no place here for you today," said mum, furious by his presence.

They appeared to have arrived at the point of no return. The reality of grandad's passing and a marital feud saddened mum's mood. She needed quality time to grieve with her mother.

"Just go," continued mum.

Mum's mind was exploding with stress. She couldn't worry about marital problems. If anyone needed a break, mum needed one now. But she still carried the burden of being destitute, and the weight of looking after four boys, and all the while, still racked by stomach pains. She could do without more worry in her life.

"What about my boys?" Said dad, realising his exodus was imminent.

"They don't recognise you are any more. You saw them half-an-hour ago, but never spoke to any of them. When did you last say you loved them? What's the colour of their eyes?"

"I need to say goodbye to them."

"They're outside if you want to speak to them."

"If you don't go now. I promise, I will kill you with my bare hands," said Jack, with aggression and impatience. He strutted towards dad and ushered him out of the door.

"Jack. Cool things a bit. Eddie's going okay. Leave the situation at that," said mum.

"I need my bike gear. It's in the outhouse."

"Get your leathers and go and don't come back. Ever," said Jack emphasising his greater annoyance.

"Back off, Jack. You've said your piece," said mum, who had experienced enough traumas for one day.

As we played in the back garden, strangely dad came out. Rowdy behaviour meant being chastised. Unusually, a tear pooled in his eye like everyone else in the house that day. A sombre event, consumed by the enormous tragedy of grandad's passing. I never saw dad shed a tear for anybody. Unbeknown to anyone, dad was leaving our lives at that moment, forever.

Dad gathered us around, as aunty Ruth and grandma stepped back into the house to be with mum, all still grieving the loss of a hero, my grandad. For many months, closeness to dad never existed. He lived at home with us, but rare leisure time seemed to be elsewhere. We seldom saw him. The happy Sunday picnics at Millhouses Park seemed to have ended. Consigned to history, there were memories of the occasional family day trip to Whitby or Scarborough. If dad didn't want us any more, why should we care about him? I assumed dad's passion for darts consumed most of his leisure time. Mum lost out to a younger, vibrant charlatan, able to offer more than the deep love she could offer. The wink of an eye, curvaceous looks and the promises of a good-time-girl commanded elicit attention. Aunty Ruth and grandma brushed passed dad, with David in the pram. Dad beckoned so as not to wake David.

> "Listen guys. Your mum and I have chatted about things and we've both decided things would be better if I moved out to live somewhere else. I want you all to know I still love you very much. I always will."

Alex, Glenn and I listened to his tearful comments, but they seemed to be crocodile tears. His comments seemed shallow. Empty promises seemed to be like the others he made over the past year. From his days in the Territorial Army, mum always commented on his role as a Gunner. As mum admitted so often, I call him *'Gunner Dalton.'* He forever promised he was *'gunna do this'* or *'gunna do that,'* but never did. Now, dad appeared to have cut the last few strands of their relationship. He lost respect from mum and from us. We no longer saw him in the same light. Dad wasn't part of our lives any more. He abandoned us a year ago.

> "Hey. Give your dad a hug," he said as the first of random tears dribbled down his cheeks.
>
> "Don't you love us any more dad?" Said Glenn.
>
> "Of course I do," said dad. His voice quivered with emotion.
>
> "So why are you leaving us and mum?"
>
> "Your mum and I need some time apart, that's all," said dad, giving Glenn a hug. "I'll still see you all when I can."

It seemed humorous saying: *'when I can.'* In retrospect, that meant if he could be bothered to make the effort. Meaningful words were not said, even on this tragic day when honest words were important. Perhaps that's how it was. There WERE NO honest words. The words *'I love you'* were a distant memory. A time to reinforce loyalty and devotion. Though mum and dad were splitting up, and dad leaving, we might still team-up with dad. It may have been possible that they got back together again.

Even though dad had betrayed her love and trust, mum still loved him. Dad gestured to Alex and me for a hug, but we couldn't be that close any more. Those moments seemed false. Not having any contact and closeness for over a year, then expecting a hug seemed surreal. Dad still forced a reluctant hug from us. I felt angry and hurt. I felt sorry for mum. She suffered the most. Mum and dad had been together for twenty years. We seemed to be a content family, albeit living a humble life with barely enough money to survive.

During the past year, dad changed. Caring appeared troublesome, even a chore. He didn't seem to try any more. Perhaps in hindsight, dad struggling to support mum and three growing boys was not what he envisaged. As David was born, 1962 became a major turning point in our family fortunes. Bringing up four boys, an extra mouth to feed, seemed to be a commitment too far for dad. Mum somehow brought us up single-handed. Dad, always at work, mum did everything else. There was no wonder she often said: *'Next time, I'm coming back as a man.'*

For years, mum craved for a baby girl. At the fourth time of trying, it wasn't meant to be. It wasn't until many years later; we found out that mum did indeed have a baby girl. Her first baby, stillborn. Dad spent less time at home with us. It was heartbreaking to hear mum cry at night. She must have known dad was slipping away. Even though she guessed he was having an affair, she hoped and prayed it was only a fling, a moment of weakness in troublesome times. She wanted to forgive his indiscretion, but couldn't see a way forward yet. Many times over the past year, she tried her best to weep in the privacy of her lonely bedroom, with lonely thoughts *of 'why'.* For a moment, he seemed emotional. I didn't want to admit or show it hurt me. I didn't want to shed a tear. I was a man now. But I still cried. I don't know why; after all, I hated dad for his treatment of mum and us.

I couldn't help but think of grandad. He was my genuine hero. Always was, always would be. This was grandad's day. I poured my heart out at grandad's bedside earlier in the day. I found it easy to say the important things to grandad. I found it easy to love him. He taught me to be brave. He was by my side for eternity. Grandad deserved oceans of tears, my dad deserved none. In my heart, I would cry for grandad every day I thought of him. Tears for dad's parting of the ways were non-existent. Grandad had departed through natural causes, without choice. Dad departed by choice. As a twelve-year-old, I felt that emotion, but I was stubborn and proud enough not to show it. Dad was abandoning what had been a contented family, maybe forever. Life could never be the same.

Ten days later, black gleaming hearses parked outside our house. A stark contrast to the pure white colliery houses of the White City. In a Yorkshire mining community, many things were black and white, rich and poor, existence and subsistence, life and death. A sedate ten-mile drive brought the Rolls Royces past the stone-built houses of Woodhouse, through Market Square. It paused a few seconds in front of the seventeenth century Cross Daggers pub. Grandma cried; memories of her and grandad, as vivid as yesterday, filled her thoughts.

Mourners stood statuesque up Tilford Road, their first house. Many more lined the streets leading to St James Church. It was no surprise grandad commanded so much respect. Tearful noises through the nave reverberated as grandad's coffin progressed sedately down the aisle. The aisle they walked along forty years earlier, to marry his beloved bride. Red carnations adorned vases in the church. Two wreaths lay on top of the coffin, '*DAD*' and '*GRANDAD*' comprised red and white carnations. My eyes glazed over for the entire ceremony. I was aware grandad was with me. Singing hymns and saying prayers choked me.

My eyes blurred. Words were intelligible. Hymn books and prayer sheets shivered in my fingers, sermons drifted over my head like passing clouds, eulogies became interesting as I could listen to anecdotes about him. My eulogy was within my own thoughts, inside my head, inside my heart. They were real times, real stories from a real hero, grandad. I listened to the hymn, *'All things bright and beautiful,'* a simplistic tune, but that broke my heart. I wanted my grandad. I wanted him to hold my hand. He stood by me when I recited Psalm 23 subconsciously.

'Yea, though I walk through the valley of the shadow of death, I fear no evil, for thou art with me.'

Chapter 9

Massive voids permeated mum's life. Grandad had always been her guiding star from being a baby girl. His wisdom guided her in the right direction. His love created warmth and stability in her rocky life. Though she despised dad's deceit and adultery, she still loved him with all her heart. Mum still cried at night and hoped she could resolve the separation. Mum felt there had to be a break to come to terms with grandad's demise and dad's indiscretion. She prayed he would come back every night and believed she could forgive him for his indiscretion. If he wanted a reconciliation, he needed to be more caring and attentive to mum. Dad neglected us all for ages and abandoned us only since grandad had passed. Mum hoped they could get back together sooner than opposed to later. A powerful measure of her love and devotion.

Months later, a loud knock on the door just before five o'clock in the afternoon caused surprise. Alex, Glenn, and I sat in the lounge reading comics or doing homework. The sudden noise awoke Baby David. Mum, with the help of grandma, was preparing food in the kitchen. Grandma still stayed at our house and allowed mum to work part-time, as dad provided less and less financial support. He left mum to cope as best she could manage. As mum answered the door, she became worried by the portly figure stood in the doorway. A stern-looking dark-suited official with a frowned face looked concerned by the latest news.

"Mrs. Dalton? I need to speak to you for a few moments. I'm Mr. Francis. Deputy Manager at the colliery."

"What is it? What's happened?" Mum shook with fear. A suited man from the Coal Board meant trouble.

"Can I come in, love? I have some terrible news," he said.

Mum's heart sank to a new depth. Even though mum and dad had separated, her love was undying. As they had been apart for six months, she yearned for dad to come back. Alex, Glenn, and I took the opposite view. He had abandoned us. We couldn't understand why mum viewed dad differently. She still held an overwhelming love for him. We didn't. I was twelve, Alex was fourteen; we didn't understand the depth of her love for a man who had betrayed us all. Too young to understand the complexities of relationships; being male, we had developed male instincts seeing things, black and white. Dad was a chancer, he took a chance with his affair, and mum found out. Dad had lost his chance from our point of view. Mum was the evergreen, eternal romantic.

The colliery Deputy Manager's knock on the door could only mean one thing. A tragic accident involving the man she loved. Tears streamed without effort down her face. He had delivered news of sorrow countless times before in the village; always the bearer of terrible news. A hazard of the job, he was unaware dad no longer lived with us; the only reason he called was to bring horrendous news of dad. As luck would have it, grandma was still staying at our house and could help share the burden of any more bad news. We still lived in a Coal Board house, hence his visit.

"Mrs. Dalton, I have to tell you some awful news."

"No. Please. Please don't tell me…..... No…….."

Mum fainted and fell on to the sofa. Grandma rushed to her side and tried to comfort her. Alex and I put our arms around her. Glenn rocked the pram to keep baby David calm but stood in the corner, unsure what was happening.

"Any smelling salts in the house?" Asked Mr. Francis with due concern. He saw these catastrophes several times.

"Yes. I've got some in my football bag. I take it to football practice, just in case it's needed."

"Okay lad."

She came around within an instance as the strong smelling-salts were working. Dazed and lethargic, she was oblivious to the last few minutes.

"Are you alright Mrs. Dalton? You took a really nasty turn for the worst there. You must have fainted."

"Sure,…..I think so. I must have passed out. What's happened down at the coal mine? What's happened to Eddie.? Please, for God's Sake, don't tell me……....."

"Try to calm down Mrs………."

"I gotta be at the pithead. I have to see…….."

Panic-stricken, mum burbled and mumbled words of incoherence. Fear gripped her as tragic scenarios flashed through her mind.

"I'll call a doctor. Your mum needs sedatives to calm her nerves," said Mr. Francis.

Another round of smelling salts brought mum back to life. Mr. Francis clasped her hand as her head drooped with despondency.

"You alright Mrs. Dalton? Perhaps a nice cuppa tea?"

"I'm alright now. Thank you. A cuppa tea would be welcome."

Grandma, always helpful, did the honours and made a cup of tea. It allowed mum to calm her nerves, even though her mind pounded with terrible thoughts of dad's survival.

"There. You're getting a bit of colour back to your cheeks now," said Mr. Francis.

Mum breathed out an enormous sigh of emptiness. Her mind was resigned to the impending news of a tragedy. *'Beware the Grim Reaper'* hung heavy in the room. The black cloak of uncertainty wreaked chaos amongst every mining village when mining disasters struck. The Reaper's presence gave sleepless nights of vigil to scores of potential widows. Loved ones, trapped, perished or 'unaccounted for' in a tomb hundreds of feet below ground, created thoughts of impending sorrow.

"As I was about to say, Mrs. Dalton, I have to tell you some unpleasant news."

Mum's veins trembled. The first shock-wave had subsided, but Mr. Francis contemplated the enormity of the after-shock, much greater than the first. He revealed a tsunami of dire news and tragedy. Mum became stunned into disbelief, numbness swamped her body like anaesthetic.

"It's not the best of news, love. I can only tell this straight."

"What on earth's happened? What's happened to Eddie?"

"There's been a roof collapse down the mine; an explosion, caused by a build-up of methane, maybe firedamp. From what we can understand, the timbers creaked and finally gave way. There's one fatality according to the rescue teams. Nine men are still missing."

"And the body. Is it….?"

"No, it's not your husband, love. But many miners are still missing," said Mr Francis in a solemn tone. "There could be more fatalities. There will definitely be injuries."

"Rescue teams are on site, working as fast as possible to… "

"Retrieve……..?"

"Please don't jump to any conclusions, Mrs Dalton. There's a decent chance the rest will be safe; perhaps in a small pocket of air. We simply don't know yet."

"Or methane," said mum with an air of despondency. "You said a build-up of methane caused the explosion…. So there is every chance he is…..." continued mum.

She baulked at the possibility of losing the man she loved. Mum looked dejected. Her face became tormented with bedraggled hair. Reddened eyes submitted to the sting of relentless tears; her mind devoid of hope and spirit, drowned in a sea of torment.

"Why is life like this? Why is life so cruel?" Said mum.

"There's still hope. There is an excellent team working round the clock. We'll soon have those brave men out," said a worried Mr. Francis, trying to raise her optimism.

"Alive?………."

"There is a good chance….."

"Of what?...... the Coal Board could avoid payment of little or no compensation?"

A silence settled the angst and outpouring of grief. Alex and I could only sit and comfort mum. We had never experienced any of the tragedies of coal mining disasters.

"You know what's really hard?" Said mum with curt sincerity. "That bloody coal mine has taken the lives of one hundred brave men, from this village, in the past twenty years. Brave, decent lads in their prime. Older men looking forward to hanging up their boots in retirement. I know mothers and wives who still grieve, mourn and weep at the graveside. They still talk to their teenage sons, with names etched on a gravestone, faces still real but cast into a distant memory. Men have lost their lives; snatched from their loved ones. Tell me, for what? For bloody profit. That's what."

Contempt showed through as latent anger. Mum hated dad working down the coal mine. Over the years, there had been near misses, minor roof falls and the occasional methane gas leak. His body showed signs of scars and abrasions of toil and hard work.

"I know it hurts.........."

"No, you bloody don't. Not sitting on your arse in your cosy little office. No-one knows what hurt and pain are. Ask any widows in this village. The bereaved can describe what pain and heartache is. Many still look at old photographs and mementos. They are the proper heroes. The ones who suffer pain for the rest of their lives are the ones left behind to grieve. The dead don't suffer pain anymore."

"I do understand it's a horrendous time for you, but we are doing the best we........"

"He's dead. Dad's dead. He's not coming back." Alex shouted out with pent up emotion. He ran off upstairs to his bedroom and slammed the door behind in anger.

"Let him be, Jeff. Let him get it out of his system," said mum.

Mum hugged me with a deep, loving caress and wrapped her arms around me; my head snuggled into her beating chest. Her heart rate must have been off the scale.

"I have to be at the pithead. See how things are going. I will come back as soon as I know anything," said Mr. Francis with a deepening grimace. Mr. Francis seemed as morose as mum had seemed dejected.

"Best to stay here, love. Everything is chaotic down at the colliery. People milling about and ambulances screaming back and forward with injured men. An absolute nightmare."

"It's a nightmare here. Waiting and crying. Three boys sobbing and a baby screaming for food," said mum with total honesty.

"That's what I'm saying. Your boys need looking after at home, not at the colliery gates on a freezing, rainy day in February."

"I suppose you're right," said mum, reluctant to agree.

The living room clock seemed to get louder with each passing minute as mum, Alex and I looked in desperation. We had no telephone at home. Out of fifty houses on the White City estate, only one family had a telephone. The nearest public telephone box placed half a mile away. Every day, a constant stream of worried women queued to phone the Coal Board offices at the colliery for news. Each potential widow trudged home yet again, void of news and void of hope. Many travelled to the colliery offices to gain first-hand information of loved ones, not yet recovered or not yet returned like soldiers from the Somme,…...

'Missing, Lost in Action.'

A rapid knock at the door, two hours later, jolted us all from a time-watching hypnosis.

"I have some excellent news and some grim news, Mrs. Dalton. The rescue teams have found your husband," said Mr. Francis. Mum stumbled with fear and grave worry. Grandma hugged her to prevent her from falling.

"Is he…...?"

Mum wept more than she could breathe. Intakes of air stuttered into palpitations.

"Mrs. Dalton….. your husband is alive. That's about as much as I know at the moment. An ambulance has taken casualties to Northern General Hospital in Sheffield, love."

Mum screamed as adrenaline raced through her body like an electrical charge. Her heart pulsated with exhilaration. She jumped up and down like a child and grabbed me and Alex for hugs. Elation streamed from her eyes within an instant. But the euphoria was short-lived. Her sub-conscience begged more details about the injuries. Though her initial anxiety had eased, there were more questions than answers.

"How is he? Is he injured? Will he survive?" Mum fired her questions in a frenzy. A multitude of thoughts of severe traumas and disabilities clouded her initial excitement.

"I can't tell you much more than that, love. As we speak, he's in the ambulance, at speed to the hospital. Is there any way at all I can help?" Asked Mr. Francis.

Mr. Francis feared the worst. He knew because of the number of fractures incurred and the acute loss of blood. Dad may lose his life, maybe that night, or in the next few agonising days. The odds were not in dad's favour. Wives read prayers late into the night. Candles of hope adorned many window sills throughout the village. The vicar led a vigil at the pithead. A crowd of hopeful wives gathered and huddled together in the bitter wintry night.

"Can anyone from the Coal Board take me to see my husband at the hospital? It's an hour on the bus; I can't afford a taxi."

"Without a doubt, I can take you in the car, love. Get yourself ready. We can be there in half an hour."

"Thanks so much, Mr. Francis. I am sorry about what I said."

"I know, love. Forget all about that. It's a massive shock, isn't it? Get yourself sorted and we'll be away. My job's done at the colliery for today. The Coal Board Rescue team will continue searching through the night until they have found every man."

Grave anxieties arose about dad. Mum was distraught. She was apprehensive, but she hoped and feared for his chances. She understood from experience, many miners lost their lives to disasters down the coal mine. Mum sent prayers, hoping dad wouldn't become one of them. Some of mum's friends were widows. Only coal-mining villages experienced this phenomenon. Every person in the village knew of friends or relatives who had either perished below ground, in the quagmire and heat of the underground coal mine. Or there were many who were disabled or had amputations or walked with a limp. Soldiers returning from the wars experienced similar misfortunes, except that the enemy of the coal-miner was methane, firedamp, or emphysema.

Mr. Francis dropped mum outside the primary entrance to Northern General Hospital. The car journey avoided an arduous expedition, by bus, from the village. Mum's health became an increasing concern. But she was adamant of being at dad's bedside. Dad's injuries could be life-changing at best, or life-threatening at worst. Hope was all that mum had. She needed to be with dad, by his side, the minute he regained his consciousness. Mum still loved dad; she needed him to know they had a future together.

Chapter 10

With trepidation, mum climbed the stairs of the old Victorian hospital. Mum, almost at the first floor, wheezed for breath and stopped at each level. The unmistakable aroma of antiseptic filled the corridors and the nostrils. Tall ceilings echoed the occasional clatter of stainless steel pans and equipment like a crescendo of cymbals at a concert. As mum asked about dad, the Sister directed her to speak with Mr. Daniels, the consultant.

"Mr. Daniels. I have Mrs. Dalton with me," said the Ward Sister. "She has just arrived to see her husband, Edward Dalton. You wanted to meet her?"

"Thank you, Sister. Mrs. Dalton, please take a seat. I'm Mr. Daniels," said the consultant in a grave voice, his head bowed as he read some notes through *'pince-nez'* specs. His outlandish dickie-bow, a telltale sign of a senior consultant.

"Mr. Dalton has received several serious injuries from the mining accident and also, many of his injuries could be life-threatening. There are internal injuries, but at this stage, to what extent is unknown. He was unconscious on arrival."

Mum cowered forward with grief and concern at the severity of the consultant's comments.

"Is he?.... Is he going to die?" Asked mum in a tearful voice.

"At the moment, your husband is under heavy sedation; we have administered morphine to ease any pain. I've decided to keep him in an induced coma for twenty-four hours…."

"Is he going to pull through this nightmare?" Asked mum, her voice dry and coarse.

"We will do our best, but……………"

"But what?"

"Look, Mrs. Dalton. It's too soon yet………"

"Please don't say that. Please say he will be alright," mum said, barely able to speak.

"Mrs. Dalton, you have to realise………"

Mum broke down and slumped over the desk, head in hands. She knew those words meant something sinister. Life-changing injuries, a common occurrence at any coal mine, came with the dangers of the job. Coal mining villages saw men with arms and legs amputated, men hobbled about with prosthetics, scars and deformities. These were the 'medals of action,' a reminder of their sufferance. A daily reminder of a lucky escape from fatal injuries. The local cemetery, speckled with war heroes and dead miners, young and old, friends and comrades. Mum's head rested on her forearm, splayed in front of her, buried within her elbows and arms. Cries echoed down the corridor; shock plunged her body into paralysis. Her mind rattled with spasmodic snippets of news like a human pinball machine. Comments bombarded her mind:

'You must realise…' 'It's too soon yet….' Euphemisms for *you won't like what you'll hear'* or *'you won't like what you'll see.'*

"Sister. Come to my office, please," summoned Mr. Daniels via his intercom. Sister Alison stepped in to find mum, body drooped and limp, across the desk. Mr. Daniels, waved his finger in mum's direction, gesturing help from a nurse.

"There, there, Mrs. Dalton," ushered the Sister, who offered tissues and hugged her shoulders for reassurance. "Let me get you some tea."

Sister Alison returned with a teapot and three cups, then she put her arm across mum's shoulder. The outpouring of grief reduced to a whimper as Mr. Daniels continued with his initial findings.

"Mrs. Dalton. Your husband is in the best place possible as we can monitor his condition day and night. By tomorrow, we hope to have a full prognosis of his injuries and treatment. We'll keep him sedated to keep him stable. We've controlled his breathing with oxygen. His airways are clear from any foreign matter, but we think his lungs contain substantial amounts of coal dust. Hot gases have scorched the Bronchial tubes. We have stemmed the external bleeding, but indications are there may be internal bleeding. He's weak, but we're confident he'll improve, given time and intensive care."

Mr. Daniels stood to attention, his chair shuddered backwards with haste, ending the meeting with mum. He brushed past as though an alarm had sounded; his desk-side manner seemed poor.

"Rude, isn't he?" Said mum, taken aback by his swift exit.

"Most consultants are like that, Mrs. Dalton. They don't mean to be abrupt; they're busy. To be honest, we're expecting a lot of miners to arrive from the colliery. We don't have space for multiple disaster cases, but we seem to cope, somehow."

"Suppose you're right. There are many miners trapped."

"Anyone at home with you, Mrs. Dalton?" Asked the Sister.

"My mum is staying with me, she's been helping for a few months, with me not being well. With four boys to feed at home, it's difficult to live on pennies."

"Your husband should be stable enough to have more x-rays tomorrow. He'll still need heavy sedation to keep him comfortable. We may need to keep in a coma for a few days.

"I'll still come in every day. He's my husband. I need him."

Mum walked towards Room 4 with tears in her eyes and feared for what she might see. As mum opened the door, she burst into uncontrollable weeping and stepped closer to dad's bed. A heart monitor bleeped in unison with the blood pressure monitor that peaked and troughed like a mosaic. The breathing machine hissed like a mad professor's lab, inflating and deflating the round rubber bladder with a flexible pipe attached to his breathing mask.

"Eddie? Can you hear me?" Asked mum in a soft voice, as goosebumps chilled her arms.

Dad, swathed in bandages from head to toe, looked frightening, like a scary monster film, by Boris Karloff. Only the holes for his eyes and mouth visible through his dressings. The one clue to his identity showed by his name on a card above his head:

'Edward Dalton. Nil By Mouth.'

"Eddie. It's me. Evelyn," she said, her voice quivered.

Dad lay motionless, a neck support guided his head in a straight position, staring at the ceiling. Both arms, in plaster casts, prevented any movement in any direction. Reams of bandages clutched his body like an Egyptian mummy and disguised any of the horrors of the accident. After forty-five minutes of emotional outpouring at dad's bedside, the warning bell rang to signify the end of visiting hours. It was now eight o'clock in the evening; mum was reluctant to leave. She continued staring across towards dad, but he remained lifeless. Only the monitors that were bleeping showed any visible signs of life. Dad was in a critical state, kept alive by machines.

"You must leave now, Mrs. Dalton, visiting time is over," said the nurse. "Your husband is as comfortable as he can be at the moment. Not in pain; sedated, he'll sleep for quite a while."

"Anyway love, I'd better go now 'cos it's eight o'clock. It's getting late to catch the bus home," said mum, tearful and stressed to the limit.

Dad never moved. A medical cage prevented bed sheets from irritating his fractured legs, while morphine injections numbed the pain of countless injuries. Mum left the ward weeping, unaware whether dad would survive his horrendous injuries throughout the night. The following day, mum arrived at the hospital. An arduous journey, catching two buses and a fifteen-minute walk across the city centre to catch the next bus or tram to the Northern General. The final three flights of steps left mum breathless and strained her problems further.

"How is he today, Sister?" Said mum, raising a hopeful smile.

"Mr. Dalton is stable. His numbers have improved today. He had more x-rays this morning, but he's still in a critical condition. He's sedated to keep him pain-free, but you can see him for a few minutes; Mr. Daniels is doing his rounds soon."

"Could I speak with Mr. Daniels when he's finished?"

"Maybe tomorrow."

"Tomorrow?"

Sister Alison paused for thought and deliberated on speaking out of turn. Doctors and consultants could get tetchy if nurses ignored protocol. In their mind, nurses existed for a doctor's convenience, for the menial tasks of emptying bedpans and other undignified bodily chores.

"Mmm… well. I shouldn't tell you at this stage, but there's an important meeting later today with all the consultants. Your husband's injuries are high on the agenda. They'll discuss a prognosis from the x-rays and decide their next action."

"Not looking good is it, Sister?"

"You need to be brave, Mrs. Dalton, for your husband and for your children's sake."

"Is that gobbledegook for a disfigured body, a disfigured face, plastic surgery….?"

"Surgeons are excellent nowadays; they perform wonders."

"Yeah, but not miracles. So are you saying his face WILL need plastic surgery?" Said mum.

"Not for me to say. Doctors are gods, nurses are nurses."

"They can't make a blind man see; they can't make a legless man walk, can they?" Said mum with frustration.

"Maybe prayers can be a way forward for you."

"I don't believe in all that religious stuff, Sister. I lost my dad only six months ago, to a heart attack; the Lord didn't save him, did he?"

"It's not for me to guide you, Mrs. Dalton. I'm just the Sister. We have a chaplain if you would like him to counsel you and pray with you. He visits every patient in the hospital."

"To read the last rites before…..."

"It's not like that, Mrs. Dalton. The chaplain is there to help, to comfort and support you. They can help to give a fresh perspective on life; to reflect on love, faith, and hope."

"I understand what you're saying, but with four growing boys, a crippled husband and little money. Can the church fix that?"

Mr. Daniels arrived and spared mum a few minutes as he led her into a compact interview room.

"I can't imagine how tough life is for you, Mrs Dalton. But my job is to help your husband recover, with all the professional care we can give. He has severe disabilities, perhaps for life, and unable …..."

"Unable to see? Unable to see our baby grow up? Unable to play with his children. Unable to have a normal life?"

Mum slumped back into an easy chair in the office. Layer upon layer of problems drained her strength, physical, financial and emotional. Her heart and mind agonised to breaking point. Her stomach, gripped and convulsed with panic and an undiagnosed medical condition.

"Don't jump to conclusions. Take it day by day; you need to be everybody's unsung hero."

"You're right. But I'm not a hero, I'm a mother."

"To your boys, you'll always be a hero."

"I can only do what I can," said mum.

"We are having an important meeting tomorrow morning. I can tell you much more about your husband after the meeting."

Sister Alison clasped mum's hand as the consultant left, and looked deep into her bloodshot, green eyes. She could see pain and anguish, fear and despondency and needed more than human strength. She needed the love of her husband, the love that once shined bright and radiated in her heart. Mum walked with despondency to Room 4. Dad still with little signs of recovery. The Sister empathised, but Mr. Daniels was more pragmatic. His words gave mum fear rather than hope.

Mum made the strength-sapping journey back home once again. There were no signs of any noticeable improvements with dad. Mum's life had worsened, she could barely live on the poverty line. With dad deserting the family, what meagre support from dad over the past six months diminished to nothing. Mum was destitute. Now that dad's injuries seemed critical, his recovery seemed a long way off, perhaps months.

Trying to bring up four boys on social security handouts became nigh on impossible. Dad abandoning us threw mum into a life of purgatory. With anguish, trauma and distress in her life, mum still harboured undiagnosed abdominal problems, at times, convulsing her with excruciating agony. By chance, Grandma Cooper could give still support and care for us. But now, in her seventies, for how much longer remained a question. Without grandma, mum could not cope. Mum was at the point where she couldn't sink any lower. She was already at the lowest depths of her endurance. Little did she know, this was only the start of her nightmare.

Consultants met the following morning to assess dad's injuries.

"Gentlemen. Good morning. Thank you for taking time-out from your busy departments. We have now received the first casualties from the mining disaster at Holbrooke Colliery," said Mr. Daniels, senior consultant from Orthopaedics.

"Those poor souls trapped down the mine. Horrendous injuries……..." said the senior consultant from Neurology.

"This morning, we need to assess Mr. Edward Dalton, who is in the Critical Care Unit. At the moment, we have sedated him, and his numbers are improving all the while. His x-rays are here on the screen. We can see he has three broken ribs, a broken right, and left arm, a fractured pelvis, and a broken femur. We believe he has intestinal trauma and trachea-bronchial injuries. His airways have been severely burnt. He has 25% burns to his face, legs and back. Can we all work together gentlemen to co-ordinate a 'modus operandi' between departments? It would be an understatement to say this particular case is most critical. The workload will be immense, but I pride my team on doing an outstanding job here."

The meeting continued for an hour, discussing technical issues and prioritising surgical demands. Mr. Daniels, as lead consultant, stipulated his requirements. Each department had specialist teams focusing on their own specific areas, but within their diaries, Mr. Daniels took precedence.

"Any other matters, gentlemen?........No?..... Very good. Let's go to it. I will approve the removal of dressings wherever possible to speed up the healing of scar tissue and other lacerations. Mr. Dalton will be with us for quite a few weeks, maybe months. From what I've seen on the x-rays, his life will never be the same."

The meeting adjourned just before lunchtime, as mum arrived at the hospital. Mum hoped for improvements, at least to raise her spirits from a devastating low ebb. Dad was now in traction as cables and pulleys raised his legs at a forty-five-degree angle for pelvic bones to set in the correct position. Cables and pulleys festooned above the bed, plaster casts covered his broken arms, bandages covered the rest of his body. Dad's body seemed more like a construction site. Mum managed to speak with Mr. Daniels before visiting dad.

"Mr. Daniels? Mrs. Dalton has been waiting to see you if that's possible?" Said Sister Alison.

"Of course; send her through to my office in ten minutes. Two coffees, please, Sister."

"Mrs. Dalton. I'll take you through to see Mr. Daniels shortly."

Chapter 11

"Mrs. Dalton. Thank you for waiting. Let me tell you the excellent news first. Mr. Dalton has a splendid chance of pulling through. He is still in a critical state but improving daily. His airways are less sore and his breathing is normal. We found his lungs contained substantial amounts of coal dust, but that's normal for a coal miner. His lungs will become stronger over the next few weeks. He is still suffering from caustic burns, because of inhalation of hot toxic fumes. There are external burns and lacerations that will heal. There is no requirement for plastic surgery, but there will be scars to his back and legs. His pulse has stabilised, but his blood pressure is a little high because of all the traumas. He will be weak for some time. Recovery will be slow. Please be patient, Mrs. Dalton."

Mum sat back in a daze of disbelief and tried to absorb and comprehend the doctor's prognosis. Mr Daniels assessed dad's results. Mum frowned at most of the big words, but also at the frightful injuries. Mum pondered the challenge as she sipped Cappuccino with closed eyes.

"And that's the good news? What's the bad news," said mum.

"Mr Dalton's major organs are satisfactory, but contusions exist. They're contaminated by the explosion. The broken bones and fractures can take a long time to heal. We will operate on his three broken ribs tomorrow, which will allow him to breathe easier. We will operate on the fractured pelvis in a few days, along with the broken femur, if he is fit enough. There is an enormous amount of surgery needed. He's lucky to be alive; we have to build on that."

"What about any disabilities?" Will he be able to walk again?"

"This is where the biggest problem could be. Mr Dalton will walk again. However, there could be a pronounced limp caused by multiple fractures. When a thousand tons of rock and coal collapses on top of you, there will be substantial side effects. There are minor fractures to the vertebrae and spine that will limit his ability to bend. He won't be able to run or kick a ball. The roof fall has crushed the left leg, so that will dramatically reduce the strength. In all honesty. He won't be able to do a manual job. His days of digging coal are over."

Mr Daniels paused to sip his black coffee. He peered over his specs to monitor mum's reaction; she appeared subdued.

"This afternoon, nurses will remove some dressings where possible. At least you'll be able to see your husband and speak to him. There are several procedures to perform so we will sedate Mr Dalton much of the time. His hearing abilities are suspect at the moment because of the explosion, so you may have to repeat yourself, maybe speak a little louder. Make sure you face him when speaking, it will help him to understand what you say."

The extensive list of treatments required for dad shocked mum. This was no sticky plaster solution, it was a virtual rebuild of broken bones and repaired tissue.

"This evening, you will be able to see him, but he could be asleep. Can I suggest you come without your children for a week? Sometimes the sight of severe injuries can frighten children. Mr Dalton will be drowsy and he may not be able to cope with loud noises. There may be flashbacks to the explosion. Must go now Mrs Dalton, Good day."

Mum gazed towards the setting sun over the seven hills of Sheffield, and beyond to the Derbyshire Peaks. It seemed like only yesterday, that the entire family picnicked alongside Ladybower reservoir and explored the caves at Castleton.

'*Finally made it. Now three flights of stairs for the climb to Ward 8.*'

Mum said to herself.

After each flight of steps, a fifteen second breather became necessary by leaning across the metal railings. Mum wheezed to a stop and gazed up to the summit. On the next floor, swing doors slammed open, hitting the wall that echoed down the corridor, only to 'whoosh' and slam closed again. Mum half climbed the last flight when the fire doors swung open with gusto. She didn't pay much attention as they slammed open and closed every few seconds all day. A lady scurried along the corridor towards mum and brushed past her like a rugby player. Nurses stood aside for their own safety.

"Hey. Watch where you're going," shouted mum, her handbag catapulted broadside as the woman barged past her.

Visitors clung to each other for their own safety. In dismay, they tutted their annoyance. Mum grabbed a handrail to steady herself from falling. The lady was in a hurry; she wasn't stopping for anyone, as though passers-by were invisible. Her long white winter coat flapped open in the wake of the rush, to show a bright red mini-skirt that just covered her dignity. Red leather boots echoed the patter of footsteps on the tiled floor.

"Sod off!" Yelled the mysterious woman.

"Bitch!" Said mum with venom.

The rude lady stopped five metres beyond, half turned and glared daggers at mum. Her eyes locked onto mum's like radar, narrowed with fury. The pause, only seconds long, was enough to glimpse a snapshot of each other. Within an instance and with no further unpleasant exchanges, the woman hurtled down the stairs, as mum continued to Ward 8. She thought it deserved a complaint if the woman was a member of her staff.

"Excuse me, Sister. Who caused all the commotion in the corridor?" Asked mum.

"She's just been visiting your husband in Room 4. I thought you would have recognised her, as she said she was Mr. Dalton's sister," said Sister.

"My husband doesn't have a sister."

Before Sister Alison had finished speaking, mum had gone. The woman had brushed past only minutes before. The stand-off in the corridor created a fleeting image of a stranger, like a Polaroid snapshot; captured in the blink of an eye. Mum had a strong suspicion who she was, and did not want her anywhere near the hospital, let alone next to dad's bed. She wasn't a relative and had no right to visit dad in hospital. If it was her, she would end up at the Women's Hospital herself, Intensive Care Unit.

Mum tried to catch her before she disappeared. If it was dad's 'other woman,' mum needed to confront her and speak her mind to get things off her chest. She hurtled down the stairs as fast as her middle-aged body could take her. She clutched the metal railings in the stairwell to act as a brake. Out of breath, mum paused outside the hospital.

The mysterious woman had disappeared amongst passers-by. She glimpsed her dodging between traffic to catch a bus bound for the city-centre. It had just pulled away en route to town. Impossible to cross as cars, buses and trams whizzed by in both directions. This barred any attempts to catch the bus, except to wait at the zebra crossing with a dozen other hospital visitors. A white-coated lady with red boots had just boarded the bus, visible on the rear platform of the boarding step. Her blonde hair radiated like an atomic beacon. Even from a distance she looked like Monroe, the blonde bombshell. It was too late, she had gone. It hurt mum. She was furious that the other woman was visiting dad.

Inside the hospital, mum climbed the staircase yet again. At the age of thirty-six, she looked haggard. Her weary legs, weakened from the chase, needed a sit-down. She had been on her feet all day from seven o'clock. Even though grandma Cooper was at home and toiled hard to help mum, the task was monumental. A typical day involved getting the kids ready for school, then walking to her job as a cleaner, then back home to help care for baby David. Wash the clothes, put them on the line, iron, a quick slice of toast, then pick Glenn up from primary school. Food was next on the agenda as we came from school. The stress continued with the lengthy journey to hospital, but first, the bus into Sheffield, then the next one to the hospital. On arrival, climb three flights of stairs, then visit dad with a brave face and an hour later, back home again on the eight o'clock bus. Overall, mum endured a fourteen-hour workload, with no time for herself and little time to be with us.

Now the tragedy of dad being involved in the mining accident added another layer of anxiety. Even if he survived the horrific injuries, disabilities seemed inevitable. Grandma's health and strength deteriorated in a brief space of time. Our fragile mother looked after four boys in abject poverty. If that wasn't horrendous enough, it became impossible for a seventy-two-year-old as her years of toil showed in her face.

Though dad had been unfaithful, mum worked hard to keep the man she loved. She needed him in her life, and she needed to discover more about the mystery woman, her adversary, and who she was dealing with, as painful as that might be.

"I'm so sorry, Mrs Dalton. I didn't realise that woman was not your husband's sister," said Sister Alison.

"It's not your fault," said mum, her mind swamped with suspicion.

Mum had hoped the affair was over, even though dad had left the family home. His departure had been acrimonious at a horrendous time for mum with grandad passing. Without warning, she doubled up in excruciating pain, holding her stomach like a stab wound. Mum stumbled to the chair, weeping, her eyes transfixed to the floor in paralysis.

"Nurse! Hurry, I need a hand," shouted the Sister.

"What's the matter? Where is the pain?" She asked.

"Really, I'm okay. Period pains, that's all. It became worse when I chased that mysterious woman," said mum. A tear of pain drifted down her cheek.

"Better call a doctor," said Sister Alison, alerted that it could be something more sinister.

"No, honestly. I'll be alright in a few minutes."

"All women have these problems, don't they?"

"Sure, but you don't look at all well. Nurse, get Mrs Dalton some water."

"If a doctor gave you an examination, I'd be a lot happier. There has to be a reason you are suffering such pain."

"No. Please Sister. I haven't got time to be ill."

"Just rest for a few minutes. Let me take your blood pressure."

"Don't worry, I'll be alright in a few minutes."

Unconvinced, Sister Alison knew something was wrong, but mum rejected any medical help, adamant she needed to persevere with her problems. She feared being admitted to hospital, but more important, she feared the truth. Unable to look after her boys tantamount to placing them in a children's home. Mum crouched by the wall, holding the door frame for support, and winced as she tried to stand. Sister Alison asked her to sit in the office for a few minutes to regain her strength.

"Nurse, can you get Mrs Dalton a cup of tea, please? Can I have one, please?" said Sister.

"Thank you. It must be all the stress and worry," said mum.

Mum recovered somewhat as her pains subsided. The cup of tea and rest was a welcome respite, but she was distraught about the unwelcome visitor. Mum convinced herself the suspicious woman was 'the other woman.' She had no proof of ID, they had never met and there was no address given.

"Sister. I need to speak to her face to face."

"You say she's not a relative. So who is she?"

"Don't know yet. Saw her in the corridor. But she's not a relative. Never seen her before today."

"She arrives just for the afternoon visits."

"That's a coincidence. I can't visit in the afternoon but she can," said mum. "My kids come home from school, baby to feed, go to work. I can only visit in the evenings," said mum.

"If an unwelcome visitor comes onto my Ward, I need to know who it is for security reasons. I've got an idea," said the Sister.

"How do you mean?"

"How about if you come onto the Ward half an hour before visiting tomorrow afternoon?"

"My mum could look after the kids for a short while. I could come in just the once."

"You could sit in the staff room next door and wait. Maybe have a cup of tea? Security Officers can ask who she is."

"It would help me to sort this out," said mum.

"Not at all. She hoodwinked me; it annoys when people try it on with me. Senior staff could reprimand me, allowing a total stranger to visit a patient without permission; breach of regulations. We both benefit."

"Thank you, Sister"

The following day, Sister Alison set the scene for the plan of action. Mum had organised things at home with grandma. As planned, mum arrived on Ward 8, half an hour before normal visiting times. She had pent up outrage and resentment and needed to confront her adversary, no matter what the outcome.

"Hello, Mrs. Dalton. Are you alright?" Said Sister Alison as mum arrived as arranged.

"I am nervous about what might happen."

"Don't worry. I've organised everything. Just come with me."

Sister Alison escorted mum to the staff room, beyond her desk.

"I'll get a nurse to make you a cup of tea. Could do with one myself, to be honest. No-one can use this room this afternoon, only me. I'll be back in ten minutes and explain the plan to you. There are no windows in this room, so it makes our task easier."

Sister's desk, midway between the swing door and the ICU Room allowed quick access to all rooms on the ward. Cabinets restricted observation towards Room 4, but Sister Alison could see comings and goings through the main swing doors. A square window in the doors allowed a vantage point without the need to enter. Sister Alison had a view down the corridor to the staircase from her desk. The plan now became a waiting game. Sister Alison buzzed her intercom to Main Reception.

'Hello. Sister Alison here, Ward 8. Send me two Security Officers to the staff room, Ward 8."

"Is this an urgent security incident, Sister?"

"This isn't an incident at this point. But it could be. I need backup, just in case."

"Very well, Sister. Someone will be there ASAP."

"Can you ask they wear white coats, not their normal security uniforms. They must be discreet. I need them in five minutes."

"Understood, Sister."

Two security staff arrived within minutes, met by the Sister as they entered Ward 8. They all sat down and waited events.

"Security?" Said the Sister.

"Yes Sister. You asked us to see you?"

"Just follow me. I'll explain the plan."

Mum stood with a jolt as the door opened abruptly. Her nerves jangled, her heart raced.

"Mrs. Dalton. These are the two security officers. They will be here with you, just in case we need them. That lady might not come today. She may guess we have revealed her identity."

"Thank you, Sister….. for organising this today."

"Not a problem, patient safety is our principal concern. That lady may not be who you think she is and might want to harm Mr. Dalton. This is in everybody's interest."

"Never thought of it that way, Sister. I was only thinking from my point of view."

Sister Alison turned to leave and looked back over her shoulder.

"Oh. By the way, there is an intercom here. I've pressed Room Four to listen. We have the intercom so we can monitor all patients, but please don't press any other buttons, as I can hear what's going on from my desk. I'll wear my earpiece so no-one else is aware."

Mum smiled, reassured they would not compromise her own safety. They all sat down to await any developments. Mum's fingers shook as visitors arrived. Amidst the scurrying of staff, the high pitched clomping of ladies' shoes echoed up the stairs.

Uncle Jack stayed in the lounge with mum as the argument became more heated. Uncle Jack had always admired mum. He treated her with fondness ever since she was born. He was twenty years older and protected her as a baby sister. As they grew older, uncle Jack took on the mantle of her guardian, especially as she married dad, a known rebel in the village. Uncle Jack was forever suspicious of dad because of his womanising before he married mum. Dad and uncle Jack worked at the same colliery. Rumours always abounded in the miner's canteen. Most of it linked to dad. Uncle Jack was keen to stand up for mum in the latest round of arguments, but mum didn't need upset on a sad day.

Chapter 12

Fire-doors creaked open, then whooshed closed as a recoil. The echo along the corridor grew louder and closer, then stopped at the swing doors. A blonde-haired woman peered through the small square window and furtively scanned the ward to make sure it seemed safe to enter. Sister Alison looked from the corner of her eye, without moving her head, and faked checking medical notes. Other visitors hadn't arrived, only nurses staff flitted about doing routine chores, checking monitors, recording numbers.

The woman pushed the doors open gently to evade notice and sauntered towards Room 4. She was on a mission. Sister Alison sat at her desk looking down and reading patient notes, pretending to be busy and unconcerned. Mum and two security officers waited for the right moment to confront the lady. As the blonde woman passed Sister's desk, she buzzed to alert the staff room.

"The woman is here!" Sister Alison whispered at the intercom.

Mum became agitated as she had set her mind on a belligerent confrontation. She now stood only feet away from the woman who destroyed her marriage, her family and her life. Mum was in no mood for an adult discussion; only a mood to inflict her own physical pain. She needed to fight for herself and us.

The woman peeped through the Venetian blinds of Room 4. Dad lay motionless, his bandaged leg in a traction hoist. Head bandages, now removed, showed his cuts and bruises. A dressing covered his forehead. Safety regulations demanded the wearing of a hard helmet which protected him from even more catastrophic injuries. Dad's eyes blinked back to life, but were half-closed by shots of morphine. Sunbeams presented his first sight of daylight since the blackness of the explosion. He shook with fear each time doors creaked, stainless steel pans clattered or alarms echoed. The mysterious woman opened the door with trepidation. Dad was alone. She reckoned it was safe enough to enter the room, but the intercom listened-in discreetly.

"Can you hear me darlin'? It's Roxy." Dad's head turned towards Roxy's voice, but couldn't speak or smile.

"Been worried about you, darlin'. But I'm here now."
A passing nurse poked her head through the creaky door. Dad gave a spasm of distress, his brain tormented by images of creaking pit props that signalled an instantaneous roof collapse. Roxy turned in shock, surprised by the unexpected intrusion. The woman feared another confrontation at any moment, as tension raised each time the door opened. Her unauthorised presence had been a serious concern for Sister Alison.

"Everything alright?" Said a nurse, carrying out her routines.

"Fine. Thank you," said Roxy, continuing her pretence.

Mum listened in from the staffroom. She stood, 'spitting feathers' with rage, her fingers tapped the desk with frustration like a drum roll. Her breathing became deeper as blood pressure increased. She lurched forward with venomous anger and hate, then attempted to open the door.

The two Security Officers restrained her from leaving the staffroom to attack Roxy; her arms flailed randomly against each one. To hear the woman's voice incensed mum beyond endurance. At that moment, Sister Alison stepped into the staff room. She could hear the disturbance through her ear-piece. Obscured windows hid the room. She hoped the woman had not rumbled her plan.

"Just calm down for a minute, Mrs. Dalton. Let's listen to the intercom for a short while longer. At least now, we have four witnesses to what's going on. We need to be certain who she is, and listening to her chat should prove her identity. We need to get our timing right to get evidence. If we follow Security into Room 4, we can confront her."
Sister Alison sat next to mum and gave her a hug to settle her down; she was like a coiled spring, ready to explode. Mum trembled with

annoyance and contempt as Roxy stole her identity. Mum had so far only seen Roxy with fleeting glimpses in the corridor. Roxy had shown her face. Mum bayed for blood. The intercom continued to relay the conversation from across the corridor.

"Put your black jackets on lads. I think sh*t is about to hit the fan. Mrs. Dalton's protection is paramount. No-one knows who we're dealing with here," said Sister Alison.

"I know you can't hear me very well, darlin' but I'll keep coming every day until you're on your feet. I think your wife might know who I am. The bitch. I just want you to know I'm here for you. I do love you…..."

"Okay, guys. That's it, Security. Let's have a chat with her."

At that point, mum could not bear to hear those words being spoken to her husband, by a woman who she despised, but had never met. She wasn't in a mood to talk. Mum beat the Security Officers to the door, pushed them aside and ran into Room 4. No-one would hold her back this time. Mum ran out of the door, across the corridor, and into dad's room and surprised the Security Officers. Bewildered, Roxy just about turned her shoulders before mum grabbed her bouffant hair and wrenched her backwards to the floor. Mum pulled her hair. Then a rapid-fire torrent of fists reigned in on Roxy before she could draw breath.

Eventually, Roxy turned to face mum and began fighting back; but mum had the ascendency. They scratched at each other with fury and with fingernails. Punches landed from both of them, some into the face, some into the kidneys. The two Security Officers prised them apart, having received some unwelcome punches themselves. Medical equipment became in danger of being thrown to the floor. The safety of dad became critical as monitors rattled to the wall, his breathing equipment in danger of being ripped apart.

Mum shoved Roxy against the wall, cracking a wall mirror.

"You're an evil bitch," mum screamed in tears.

"Look in the mirror, darlin.' What do you see? What does Eddie see?"

"You're a devious, scheming cow," said mum.

"Eddie sees a worn-out witch. You've gone past your prime, love. Do yourself a favour, let go of what you can't have."

"You're heartless. One day, you'll live to regret what you've done to my family."

"Is that a threat?"

"You'll rot in hell," said mum.

Mum felt a sharp pain in her stomach, brought on by anxiety, and made worse by fighting.

"Alright, ladies. Let's sort this out. Shall we?" Said Sister Alison, dashing into Room 4 with another nurse.

"Bitch!" Exclaimed Roxy, her blonde coiffeured hair destroyed like a haystack."

"Hey. Come on now. We're in a hospital; patients need quiet and rest. They are seriously ill."

"You'd better save a bed for her as well," said mum. "The bottle blonde tart."

"Officers. Escort these ladies to the Conference Room, please. It's more private down there. At least the walls are soundproof. I'll be with you in a few moments," said the Sister.

The walk to the Conference Room calmed rattled nerves. A respite in between hostilities. Mum glared at her rival, looked her up and down with disdain, revulsion and full of hatred.

'*Fight for what you want,*' echoed through mum's mind.

Roxy epitomised most things mum could no longer aspire to. Roxy was twelve years younger, so had age on her side. She nurtured her gorgeous looks, her satin-smooth skin, her manicured long fingernails and above all, her ash-blonde stack of hair. She personified movie stars in '*Harpers Bazaar*' magazine, her character personified by '*Cosmopolitan Magazin*e,' her athleticism personified in '*The Perfumed Garden.*' Mum had four kids and little else.

"Home-wrecker. You lousy whore," shouted mum.

"If things panned out at home, he wouldn't search elsewhere, would he?" Shouted Roxy.

"Looks like a tart, walks like a tart, speaks like a tart. What is it?……. You."

"You can't keep a fella' Evelyn. Accept the fact. No point you wasting your time here or anywhere else, is there?"

"Eddie is still MY husband," yelled mum.

"Possession is nine-tenths of the law, darlin.' He sleeps in MY bed."

"You're possessed. Possessed by the devil," said mum, hurt by Roxy's painful gibes.

"Eddie needs to make up for lost time, I guess."

Mum was losing the war of words, she was losing a love tug of war. She was losing the will to live as she collapsed in agony, brought on by stress. She convulsed with excruciating pain, and clutched her stomach in tears, then struggled to stand up as her stomach clawed for relief.

"No need to look for a sympathy vote darlin'? Eddie has no sympathy for you."

"You don't know that," said mum, whimpering with a sense of verbal and physical defeat.

"I do know, love. Where does Eddie go home at night? It's not to you any more, is it?" Said Roxy, with spiteful sarcasm.

"Eddie doesn't love you; he never will. You'll find that out one miserable day in your life." said mum. Tears glazed her eyes.

The fierce argument subsided. As Roxy saw mum for the first time, it made her realise she had nothing to fear from someone fifteen years older. Roxy became conciliatory. She understood mum needed to visit dad with their boys. She had spent so much time with dad and knew his intentions were to be with her, when he recovered from his injuries and left hospital.

"Rather than argue, I don't mind you visiting Eddie at night, I'll visit him during the day," said Roxy, taking the lead in the conversation.

"Depends on the Sister. You're not a relative. You'll not even get in if I say so," said mum.

"Wrong darlin.' In another week, Eddie will be able to talk. If Eddie needs to see me every day, that will happen. Trust me."

The meeting ended in a mudslinging fight between mum and Roxy. They exchanged insults and home truths with aggression. Roxy knew *'possession is nine-tenths of the law'* and she possessed him, mind, body and soul. She learned from an early age, how to keep her man from straying away. Mum took the old-fashioned idea of marriage vows.

"Alright then. I'm no marriage counsellor or vicar but I can see it working," said Sister Alison, having listened to the slanging match. "Roxy is right, Mr. Dalton can choose who can visit him; family, friends or otherwise. If the patient cannot decide because he may be too ill or in a coma, hospital staff make that judgement on his behalf in the fairest way possible. In Mr. Dalton's case, he cannot speak to anyone for at least another seven days. I have to make this judgement based on what I see," Sister Alison continued her logical summation.

"That can't be right. I thought only family and next of kin could visit?" Said mum, tearful.

"Shut up and listen, darlin!" Said Roxy with a surly grin.

"I assume that you, Mrs. Dalton, is his lawful wife, and you have children?"

"That's right, Sister."

Mum thought the guidelines would favour her. She expected Sister Alison to bar Roxy from visiting the hospital. It would have been a moral victory, at least.

"I assume that you Roxy…..?"

"Roxy Maltravers."

"I assume that you are his partner Ms. Maltravers and Mr. Dalton lives with you? Then it's obvious to me that Ms. Maltravers should continue daytime visiting. You, Mrs. Dalton, should visit in the evenings, with your boys and other members of the family.

If either of you disagrees with my decision, you would first have to address your complaint to Senior Management at the hospital or seek legal advice. The hospital may deny visits to patients if there are any safety concerns. Can I add Ms. Maltravers, you have caused the hospital and Mrs. Dalton tremendous upset because of your secretive actions."

"I am sorry Sister, but based on what you've just said, I couldn't have visited Eddie for weeks. Even worse, if Eddie had passed away, I wouldn't have seen him at all."

"I've got to get back to Ward 8. I have a busy ward. I hope this arrangement is the end of this matter. Security will escort both ladies out. Goodbye."

Mum felt betrayed by the hospital's visiting system. It became obvious dad had betrayed her. She still vowed to fight for his love and affection. A week later, dad had gained enough consciousness to permit seeing his boys. Mum visited with Alex one evening, then me on the next to avoid tit-for-tat skirmishes. Sometimes she was strong enough to take five-year-old Glenn, but never able to manage baby David.

The evening visit to the hospital became a monumental task, a one-hour journey by bus and a hectic walk across the city to catch the next. Mum's stomach cramps became debilitating and more frequent. Grandma Cooper stayed at home to care for us, a struggle for her, weakened by arthritis, age, and bereavement.

The argument resolved any awkward situations about visiting times. At home, the situation continued as precarious as ever with grandma trying to cope as best as she could. Antagonism between mum and Roxy continued while dad recovered in hospital. Mum needed decisions about his loyalties, beyond when he left the hospital. Mum's visits to and from the hospital continued to be burdensome by bus, but had no choices.

After two months of steady recovery, dad was getting nearer to being discharged. He could walk, but with a limp; bending was likewise difficult. On his final evening at the hospital, mum trudged on her usual evening bus journey. There had been no talk of a reconciliation. Mum's determination to win back his love on the final evening at the hospital could be her last opportunity.

"Hello, Eddie. You alright?" Said mum, out of breath and glad of her first sit down of the day.

"Yeah. Not bad, under the circumstances. Painkillers are doing their job," almost indifferent to mum's visit.

"Eddie, we need to talk," said mum.

"About what? There's nothing to talk about. It's over between us," said dad in a curt tone.

"Why is that tramp so special? We've met. She is what she is."

"Don't say that. We are good. The boys will meet her one day."

"There is no us. Jack threatened to kill me. Remember? You didn't say a word."

"My dad had just died. Remember? My head buzzed like there was no tomorrow," said mum.

Mum looked around the room. A photograph, upturned on the nearby cabinet, showed evidence of Roxy's presence. Mum refused to look.

"I suppose SHE is in that photo?"

"Roxy and I with her little boy, Jamie," said dad, but was fearful of a jealousy row.

"Her little boy? Or yours?" Asked mum in a frosty tone.

"Hers, of course."

"Her boy? You left us to be with her and HER little boy?" Said mum. A tear escaped her eye.

"I didn't leave. You and your chaperone pushed me out, remember?"

"He's just my sister's husband. Don't exaggerate," said mum.

"It always seemed more than that."

"Only in YOUR head."

"I needed your support," said Eddie in a sharp tone.

Mum didn't like where the conversation was going. Dad seemed to make negative vibes towards mum with his indifferent attitude.

"I need you, Eddie. The boys need you. I love you more than anything. You know I do."

A tear welled in the corner of her eyes as she looked with deep concern into his. Dad couldn't hold any eye contact and closed his eyes with indifference and shook his head with contempt.

"Let's talk this through, Eddie. We can continue to have a happy future together, all of us, I know we can. There have been some tough times, but we always came shining through," said mum, reaching for a handkerchief to dry her eyes.

"It won't work, Evelyn. Not anymore."

"Why don't we give it another try?"

"I'm a crippled man. I can't work down the coal mine ever again. Do you know what that means?" Said dad, unwilling to listen to mum's pleas.

"You can get a job somewhere else. You know you could do much better than working in a coal mine. Let's face it, you nearly lost your life in that pit. Let's just give our marriage another try."

"I can't do manual work anymore; I can't lift anything heavy; I struggle to walk."

"The Coal Board will give you a job in the office. I can go to work. It's not a problem. We can get through this, Eddie."

"I can't work in an office with some mamby-pamby clerks pushing pens all day. It's not me."

Mum was a pacifist just like grandad, but at this moment, bitterness prevailed. "We're a fantastic team, Eddie. Don't destroy what we had together. Please, Eddie. Don't destroy us. We can fix things, believe me. Please," said mum as her tears trickled.

"As you said. That's what we had. It's all changed now. Life can never be the same."

Mum burst into tears. She didn't want to hear those words. Nothing she said could persuade dad to feel any different. After nine months apart from mum, he knew his future happiness lay elsewhere.

"Please, Eddie. Don't give up on us. I love you. We all love you. Doesn't that mean anything?"

Dad turned away. He didn't want to listen. Mum covered her eyes with her hands and sobbed. She had worked with tireless passion to save her marriage and had sacrificed so much to care and provide for all of us. Mum sacrificed her own health to add a paltry bit of extra cash to prevent us from starving. She worked until she dropped. She pacified dad in so many ways to prove she loved him and would do anything for him without question. She was one of life's true, unselfish givers. Now, more than ever, she not only loved dad throughout all these difficult agonising times, she begged him with heartbreaking tears to come back to her.

Even though his affair had lasted close to a year, she still wanted him back. She cared for dad and needed him back in her life. As dad had closed his eyes with indifference, mum felt dejected and hurt by his callus snub. She retrieved some photographs from her handbag. They all showed fun times with us all, either on holiday or at Millhouses Park; memories of us when we were younger, even ones of us as babies.

"I've brought you some photographs for you to see Eddie," said mum in a soft voice. Dad sat up in bed but said nothing as mum passed him a few photos.

"Do you see this photograph of us at Great Yarmouth? The best holiday we ever had. How they've changed in ten years," said mum, dad smiled. "Do you remember this one when David was born last year? He was so tiny that you held him in the palm of your hand," she continued. Her tears streamed down through her make-up, mascara ran down her face, blotched by emotions.

Dad continued to gaze at the photographs that evoked happy memories of us all together as a family. His eyes became glazed as he lay silent. Dad seemed to have decided about his future. He didn't seem to care about ours. We were his past. Mum reached out to hold his hand, but without a response. This provoked more painful tears. Mum pleaded with dad not to leave us. She tried hard to show how much she loved him. With her head drooped in bitter sorrow, stinging tears rained down her cheeks. Her eyes blurred by teardrops. She was heartbroken.

"I love you, Eddie. Always did, always will," said mum.

Chapter 13

The following afternoon, dad left hospital with severe disabilities after three months of bone reconstruction. Disabilities meant he could no longer work down the coal mine, depriving him of an income. What meagre maintenance payments he made to mum before the accident came to an end the instant he left.

As he walked down the long corridors of the hospital, it felt as though it was his release date from prison. The world outside looked surreal, the air smelled fresher; the noise seemed louder and more chaotic, people walked about quicker, trams clattered up and down Exchange Street. Dad had major decisions to make. The mining accident brought those decisions a step closer.

Three months of recovery gave him time to reflect on where his loyalties lie. Unable to work down the coal mine had made him jobless. Jobless and penniless meant that we would become homeless. We would lose the Coal Board house, provided only for miners. Without the stability of a home, starved of income and being in a fatherless relationship, Social Services Child Welfare would now become involved. Mum would lose us to a children's care home. She vowed that no matter what, losing us to a children's home would never happen.

Outside, mum waited with us in the hospital grounds. Her heart was full of yearning and hope that when dad emerged, her love and devotion would win him back. She borrowed a pretty dress, handbag and high-heels from her stepsister, aunty Ruth. She borrowed her most expensive perfume, hoping to convince him she could make the extra effort. Mum had not bought for herself in ages. We were all excited to see dad walk for the first time since his accident, albeit with a walking stick.

Mum tried her best to keep us under control. Dad appeared as the entrance doors swung open and squinted into the afternoon sun. We all walked towards him. Mum shed tears as she smiled with happiness. Alex and I were reticent. Glenn, five years younger, ran across to him and hugged him with obvious elation. He grabbed dad's legs in a huge squeeze and caused him to wobble because of his injuries. Dad couldn't lift him for the same reasons. We took a casual stroll in the hospital grounds to allow dad to adjust to the outside world. To him, that had changed forever.

Dad peered over mum's shoulder. The unmistakable figure of a blonde-haired woman appeared through the entrance gates that led into the spacious grounds. She sat on the nearest park bench, legs crossed, and exchanged glances with dad. Another awkward confrontation loomed between mum and Roxy. Mum glanced in the same direction, hurt by her adversary's presence. Dad's attention focused beyond mum as she looked into his eyes, needing him to recognise her deep love.

"That speaks volumes doesn't it Eddie?" Said mum, dejected by the awkward situation.

"It's the end of the line, Evelyn. My future is now with Roxy." Dad walked away from us with mum in tears, Glenn screaming for his dad. Dad had seemed to want to be with us all, but within minutes, he walked the other way. Glenn clutched dad's hand and tried to pull him back from leaving, then slipped backwards onto the lawn. He sobbed and kicked his legs in frustration, anger, and heartbreaking disappointment. Mum struggled to lift Glenn from the ground, then cradled him in her arms and hugged him with deep affection. He squealed as dad and Roxy disappeared through the tall iron gates of the park.

Mum stood still for a while, numbed with shock. She couldn't believe dad could just walk away, leaving us all without even a goodbye. Glenn was heartbroken. He was inconsolable and sobbed with hurt. Mum squeezed him with her deep love, then held him close, wrapping her arms around him. Mum had to sit down. She suffered her own anguish of dad leaving her. Tears, in constant streams, trickled down her cheeks. People walked by and stared at mum's grief, all of us abandoned in the middle of the hospital grounds. After a few minutes of outpouring, she wiped her tears. Across from where she sat holding Glenn, red carnations reminded her of happier times. They blew gently in the soft breeze and seemed to wave goodbye. The bitter sting of seeing dad walk away with someone else was like a knife cutting through her broken heart. The saying, '*The first cut is the deepest,*' rang true. Now all that remained were memories.

Alex and I showed no emotion; we were teenagers. Dad had abandoned us all the year before. As much as we knew, dad didn't want us anymore. He didn't care about us. He was unconcerned about mum's plight. Mum's life had plunged to new depths. Her misery had deepened to a new lower level of heartache. Mum now had to gain inner strength. We all huddled next to her on the park bench. Somehow, she had to rise above her own bitter disappointment.

Amid her own deep distress, she needed to catch the next bus away from the hospital. Taking three boys, a baby and a pushchair on a bus packed with passengers was a monumental task. With annoyance and frustration, passengers tutted when David cried, and insensitive even when mum broke down. Racked by grief and distress, adding her own colossal health problems virtually brought her to her knees. She knew she had to soldier on. There was no-one else to help her. She needed some emotional support. At that moment, she needed the love of someone who cared. There was only one person who understood her anguish; her own mum. grandma Coop She needed to be with her but was an hours' bus ride away.

"Come on, sweetheart. Let's visit grandma Cooper. I'm sure she's got some ice cream and cake for us all. You know she loves to give you a big squeeze," said mum, tearful herself.

The following three months crawled by for mum. Life at home, living on the breadline, grew more difficult, week by week. Food on the table, no matter whether it was '*bread and jam*' or '*bread and dripping,* ' 'sometimes only achieved by obtaining food '*on tick*' from Mr. Bradshaw's shop. The fight to survive remained a constant challenge of how to '*rob Peter to pay Paul.* '

A sharp rap at the door alerted everybody in the house. It sometimes signalled an important visitor. Maybe an irate creditor, hopeful of a few shekels of payment. The louder the knock, the higher the debt. Sometimes it was the rent man, the gas man, the milkman, or the TV rental man. It became an exciting challenge as mum said in a loud whisper, '*hide behind the sofa,* ' or in the pantry or under the stairs. In reality, it was the creditors demanding last week's instalment that mum couldn't pay the week before, or the week before that. I didn't know at the time how the crippling debts mounted week by week. The need to buy food from Bradshaw's Corner Shop grew increasingly important.

"Come on, Mrs. Dalton. Open the door! I know you're in there," shouted Mr. Reynolds, the TV rental collector.
We had only been renting the TV for a few months, then mum struggled to afford it. Even though the normal method of payment was to put coins into the slot meter, it was still a luxury. A few sniggers of defiance came from Alex and me, followed by '*Schhhh'*.....from mum until he became tired of waiting. How to rob '*Peter to pay Paul'* became endemic in the village. Mum peeped through the narrowest of gaps in the curtains, only to see Mr. Reynolds, the TV man, hands-on-hips, huffing frustration and despair. Mr. Reynolds' Morris van parked outside someone's house seemed ominous. It hinted that they may take away their television because of arrears. TV's were too expensive to buy in the 1960s.

The first television I ever watched was at grandad Cooper's on sleepovers. A 'Bush' TV with a 12" screen, surrounded by mahogany and weighed half a ton. A rollback wooden sliding door to blend in with furniture looked snazzy and avant-garde at the time. The novelty of being able to slide the rollback door, back and forth, like the doors of an aircraft hangar, became an irritating pastime when anyone wanted to watch TV. Television rentals became a national institution, only affordable to rent. To rent a television, a working male living at the address was necessary. Dad had left the house, but his name was still on the Coal Board rent book. That fact would have devastating consequences later.

Alex practised forging dad's signature and became an art form. He could now sign many rental agreements, provided they left the paperwork at the house for signing, then handed over a few days later. Alex wangled a way to get free television programs and virtually pay no television rental to the company. His ingenuity astounded me so many times, but the ploy worked for a while. The television had a slot meter fitted on the back. Alex's ingenious trick used one of dad's darts. He showed me the dodgy technique with enthusiasm.

"Get the dart and poke it into the slot where the coin goes. Then turn the key with care and precision. Hey-presto! There you are. As easy as picking a lock. How simple is that?" Said Alex, proud to show his technical skills. Free television every day. What a bargain," he said.

Alex never thought of consequences. If the needle broke inside the coin slot, we were in trouble. If there was no money in the coin box, it would become really difficult to explain. A month later, the unmistakable three thumps on the door meant Mr. Reynolds had arrived. It appeared to be safe enough to open the door. He only needed to empty the coin box. No payments to make. If the box contained more than the normal rent, they would give a refund. Mum knew nothing about Alex's devious master plan. Each day, he turned the key with the dart in place and gave us six hours of free viewing. So the television never switched itself off in the middle of a program. A pile of five coins sat on top of the coin box, ready for the dash to get the TV back on again. If Alex wasn't around, especially in the middle of a *'Lonnie Donegan Special,'* it would be a disaster.

"That's strange. There are minus ten hours of viewing this month. I need to take the TV back, Mrs. Dalton. It seems to have a faulty coin box mechanism," said Mr. Reynolds, as he scratched his head in disbelief.

"What on earth.....?" Said mum with genuine shock.

"Seen nothing like it, Mrs. Dalton."

"New-fangled gadgets. I don't understand them," said mum.

The metering system worked well, a means to an end.. Metered gas and electric supplies became the norm in the coal mining village. Coin-operated meters created a disproportionate demand for a pile of shillings. Every day, mum sent me or Alex to neighbours for a 'shilling for the meter,' in case it switched off.

"Ask Mrs. Turner if she's got a 'gas bob' to spare."

Rang through my ears every day in search of a kind neighbour who became a saviour, just before 'Coronation Street' was due.

The television contract required a £3 monthly payment. The company preferred slot meters as a cast-iron certainty of receiving payments, so customers didn't fall into rental arrears. Every month, the collector expected £5 worth of coins, then reimbursed a £2 overpayment, a welcome bonus. With only 20p in the coin box instead of £5, raised an eyebrow of disbelief. A faulty television could be the answer. When he asked if there was a problem with it, mum, with innocence, said there weren't any decent programs to watch on TV. He checked to make sure the mechanism was working as it should, by inserting a coin of his own. It worked, so the TV worked fine. He still took it away for checking, in case there was a hidden fault.

A replacement TV arrived a few days later, but Alex still continued with his TV skills. Three months passed before the scam became obvious. The counter at the back of the slot meter monitored TV usage for the month. On average, we had received over 100 hours of viewing, but precious few coins to count. There was no daytime television in 1962, apart from the odd children's programs at lunchtime. Strangely, even *'Muffin the Mule'* made mum give a wry smile. A beefy accomplice arrived with Mr. Reynolds to retrieve the heavy TV set.

"Are you replacing it with one that isn't faulty?" Asked Alex with a cheeky grin.

Mr. Reynolds glared a *'no comment.'* They bustled the television into the back of his van, with exasperation and annoyance. Alex could only smirk as he looked at me. Mr. Reynolds then revved his van in temper and stopped at his next pickup, fifty metres down the road. Another neighbour unable to pay the TV rental would be about to receive an aggressive thump at the door.

Settlement day had arrived. As a general rule, Mondays became settlement day. The day creditors knocked on doors in the misguided hope and belief of getting paid their dues. An opening joke at the local Working Men's Club became,

'Come on, settle up,' rather than *'Come on, settle down.'*

We bought most goods in the village on *'tick'*, 'buy now - pay later' the only means of getting through, day by day, week by week. Whether it be food, clothes or expensive items, credit became an essential way of life. The long trek to Joseph Peck's Department store in Rotherham was a Mecca for most things anyone needed, an Aladdin's Cave of goodies.

Every few months the journey to Peck's became essential. At Christmas, the trip to Rotherham became awe-inspiring. The latest toys adorned an entire floor, like Macey's store in New York. Joseph Peck became Father Christmas. Mum bought clothes for us all, with no need for 'hand-me-downs.'

Thursday was Family Allowance day. Friday was 'tip-up' day. Husbands tipped up the housekeeping money before they had time to get tanked up with beer on Friday and Saturday nights. Many wives waited at the pit gates to grab the week's wages before husbands spent it in the Black Bull on the way home. Mondays presented the best chance of bills being paid.

Rapid thuds on the door sounded like the dreaded bailiff.

"Hide, quick. Behind the sofa. Don't move and don't make a sound, anybody."

We scuttled away into our favourite little cubby holes, like mice hiding from the big bad cat. Another few bangs on the door alerted nosey neighbours. One-eyed faces peeped from behind twitchy curtains. Neighbours revelled in the intrigue and juicy gossip of another non-payment.

"Now come on, Mrs. Dalton. You know why I'm here," yelled Mr. Turnbull through the letterbox. He was the intimidating Coal Board Rent Collector, collecting last week's arrears.

"Alright. I'm coming. Don't break the door down," shouted mum from under the stairs.

"Alex, Jeff, Glenn. Go up to your bedrooms out of the way. Turnbull isn't a pleasant man," said mum, fearing there could be an argument.

Worse than the bailiff, Mr. Turnbull stood outside, looking unconvinced at the closed curtains to hide any secretive movements. Waiting for the door to open, his toes tapped in frustration. He was a gargantuan man. He was a bully through to the core. He filled the doorway when it opened.

"Sorry. Can't pay you until next week. Husband's off work."

"That's why I'm here. I need to see your husband," he said.

"Remember the explosion? Damned nearly killed him. Have you no respect, Mr. Turnbull?"

"A word with your husband, Mrs. Dalton?"

"Sorry. He can't see anybody. He's not well."

Mum needed to bluff dad's whereabouts. The longer it took for the Coal Board to realise dad no longer lived at home, the longer mum could hang on to our house. Even though it was cheap to rent, as it was a coal miner's house, mum still couldn't afford to pay the dues. The choice was a stark contrast between paying for food or paying the rent. Mr. Turnbull suspected dad no longer lived with us, but of over-riding importance to him was the fact dad no longer worked at the colliery. Therefore, a Coal Board house was not an entitlement. Mum's plight was about to become critical. If mum became homeless, it would condemn us to a children's home for an indefinite time.

"Still in bed?"

"He's asleep. Painkillers knock him out."

"Open the door, Mrs. Dalton!"

Mr. Turnbull knew scores of reasons for miners not going to work. He knew scores of reasons why tenants didn't pay the rent on time. Mum opened the door and peered beyond him to see if curtains twitched. She noticed a few neighbours across the road, hands-on-hips, tutting and cocking-a-snoot in the air in mum's direction. Many gossiped over the garden wall and glanced across in-between sarcasm. The ubiquitous scarf, tied above the forehead, hid their need to brush their hair. A 'pinnie' (pinafore), a full wrap-around sleeveless cotton house-coat, tied around the waist, meant they were doing their housework that day. It proved to their husbands they had been busy all day, while he was at work down the coal mine. Folk were hard. Nobody crossed their paths. They knew who knocked on doors in the daytime to collect their dues. They knew who knocked on doors at night when husbands were at work. They knew everybody's business and revelled in tongue splitting gossip.

"I told you….. he's not well," said mum.

"I'll be the judge of that, love. I'll come in and wish him well."

Mr. Turnbull breezed past mum with well-practiced arrogance, rudeness and indifference. His aggressive nature intimidated to the point of being nasty. Few people in the village dared to miss a single payment of rent.

"Hey. You can't come in here uninvited."

"Oh yes I can," said Mr. Turnbull.

"This is my house. Get out before I call the police," said mum.

"This is Coal Board property."

"It's still my house."

"Mrs. Dalton, you only borrow the house. It's only your house if you pay the rent; you ain't paid the rent."

"My husband's not here. He's at the hospital."

"First you said he's in bed. Then you say he's in hospital. Where is he? Do you know?"

Mr. Turnbull was impertinent enough to barge his way in to check if dad was hiding from paying the rent. He sent shivers down mum's spine. Wherever he called, he demanded payment. Mum was now in a precarious situation with no-one to turn to. Her life spiralled downwards in free fall.

"Mr. Dalton. No need to hide now, if you're upstairs," shouted Mr Turnbull from the bottom of the stairs. It was obvious the house was empty apart from mum.

"Didn't think so. I reckon he's out working on another job, moonlighting. It's against Coal Board regulations and the Terms and Conditions of your tenancy."

"There's nothing I can do," said mum. She didn't have a penny in her purse. Bureaucracy now confronted her. She was about to lose our home. The anchor that kept us all together.

"You've had at least a week to catch up with your rent arrears. Now you need to pay, today."

"One day. Someone will sort you out. Mark my words."

"Your husband should have gone back to work last month. They offered him an office job because of his injuries, but he told us to shove it. He's not done a day's work in months."

"I can't make him go to work," said mum, feeling the pressure and beginning to shed tears.

"As far as it bothers us, he no longer works for the Coal Board. The rent is in arrears."

"I don't have any cash to pay the rent. I don't have any money to feed the kids."

"I'm not a social worker. I collect rent. It was due a week ago. You need to pay. Now."

"I don't know where I can get the rent money today. I need more time. Please, Mr. Turnbull."

"If you can't keep up the rent, leave. Children or no children."

"Please, Mr. Turnbull. It's been difficult since my husband was in the pit accident. Please allow me time to come up with the money; please. I'll borrow it from my sister."

"Rules are rules. I don't make them. You broke the first rule; you didn't pay your rent."

Mum broke down in tears. Mr. Turnbull needed the rent, there and then. He wasn't about to compromise. His aim was self-centred. He wasn't running a charity shop. Alex and I stood by mum's side. We could only offer moral support. This giant of a beast looked threatening to us all. I was barely thirteen, Alex almost fifteen; we could do nothing except give mum moral support. Sometimes, Alex would become involved against overwhelming odds, but not now.

"Cry all you want. It doesn't alter what you have to do."

"You're a heartless person. Do you realise it's a struggle?"

"Read your Tenancy Agreement. Abide by conditions, or else."

"Are you threatening me?" Asked mum, sensing his heavy-handed approach.

"Just advice. You have only one choice. I won't say it again."

"Please, Mr. Turnbull. Please help me. It can't do any harm."

"You don't leave me any choice, Mrs. Dalton. Tomorrow, I'll hand-deliver a Notice to Quit for a serious breach of Tenancy Conditions. Mr. Edward Dalton no longer works at the colliery.

He no longer lives here and his rent is one month overdue."

Sure enough, Mr. Turnbull delivered the Notice to Quit the following day. He brandished the Notice above his head, as Neville Chamberlain had brandished his famous declaration in 1938. He gloated at his power as though his piece of paper became a gauntlet, thrown down to others who had not paid their rent on time. A punishment by embarrassment, as nosey neighbours enjoyed juicy gossip and wallowed in other's misfortunes.

"There you are, love, as promised. Signed, sealed and delivered. I like to keep my promises."

"I don't know how you can sleep at night, Mr. Turnbull?"

"Extremely well, as a matter of fact. My conscience is clear. I do my job; I do it well."

"Turfing out a mother and four children onto the streets. Proud of that, are you?"

"Your husband doesn't work at the colliery any more. You're not entitled to have a Coal Board house. End of story."

Dad had disappeared from our lives. He abdicated all of his responsibilities. Mum said he lived with 'the other woman' from Rotherham called Roxy. I had caught a fleeting glance of her a year earlier when dad took me on his part-time job. It had been my turn to go with dad that evening, Alex's turn had been the week before. I didn't know it then, but this woman would become a catalyst for our destruction and devastation.

Already the walls of security crumbled around us. Mum was destitute. We lived as paupers below the government's subsistence level. But we didn't realise the true meaning of poverty. We didn't know any different. This was our life; for mum, a living hell. We were victims of circumstances; dad's. He could have prevented this turmoil. Instead, he created it and walked away. A gossiper or 'do-gooder' had alerted Social Services to mum's plight. Little did we know the Judas was a member of our own family.

Chapter 14

Social Services Child Welfare became involved. Mum struggled for many years to keep the family together with boundless love and affection. This did not meet the guidelines of Social Services. They advocated whatever was best for the children. They demanded stability, sustenance, a warm home and nourishing food on the table. Panacea differed to mum's.

A polite but quick tap at the door was an unrecognisable sound. A four-week countdown to eviction had begun by the Coal Board. Creditors soon learned of our imminent departure and circled like vultures, eager to get through the front door. Each creditor had their own distinctive call sign. Opening of the front door was dependent on their importance in our lives.

This door tap was unrecognised. A peep through the net curtains showed a woman and a man, both suited, carrying heavy briefcases, a clipboard held by each. They looked important, measured by their sallow look, official stance and deportment. We could discount a win on Littlewoods pools. You had to be in it to win it. They couldn't be from the Coal Board, they looked too intelligent. They couldn't be Jehovah's Witnesses, they were too sombre.

"Afternoon. I'm Mr. Anderson; this is Mrs. Walker." His deep, eloquent voice resonated importance and gravity, shrouded within a refined Edinburgh accent.

"We're from Social Services, Child Welfare........," he said in a refined Scottish accent.

Mum's heart sank. Stunned, as though a thunderbolt had struck. Her body petrified like the poor souls of Pompeii. Her brain became mortified by the prospect of losing us, split asunder by bureaucracy.

"Mrs. Walker? Can you begin, please?" Asked her boss.

"I'll come straight to the point, Mrs. Dalton. We understand your children are being looked after by your seventy-two-year-old mother. The youngest being only a baby."

"Another do-gooder sticking their noses into other people's business? I suppose it's that cow across the road, isn't it?"

"I can't divulge our sources, Mrs. Dalton. We must follow Departmental guidelines."

"I'll bloody kill her when you're gone."

"This is one of our concerns, Mrs. Dalton. We are aware there have been altercations at the hospital, the Coal Board, and with your neighbours," said Mr. Anderson.

"This is not an acceptable atmosphere for the children, dear," said Mrs. Walker, compassion not being her strongest point. "Our information is that you often leave your children in the care of your own frail mother," she continued.

"Only because my husband was in hospital, after that pit explosion? I needed to visit him in the evenings. How could I find a babysitter willing to look after four children?"

"Exactly. The supervision of your children is not adequate."

"Are you saying I'm not a dutiful mother?" Said mum, choked by anger and annoyance.

"We're not saying that at all. Our information is you had been absent for at least six hours, every day from four in the afternoon, until ten o'clock," said Mrs. Walker.

"I have to catch two buses to get to the hospital. That's how long it takes."

Social Services needed solutions. They were about to deliver the cruellest of conclusions.

"You cannot expect an elderly lady, in her seventies, to be minding the children," said Mr. Anderson with deep concern. "This is not acceptable for the children, your mother or our department," he continued with grave concern.

"For God's Sake. What else could I do?" Said mum, becoming rattled by interrogation.

"So you do admit you left your children with your elderly mother?" Said Mrs. Walker, her head bowed, tilted to one side.

"You know I did. Somebody ratted on me. I was only trying my best to keep us all together. You have the bloody evidence right in front of you. So why ask stupid questions?"

"We're trying to assess the allegations. We need to see if there are alternatives that we can explore, in the interests of the children," continued Mrs. Walker.

"I can tell you now, Mr. and Mrs. Fancy-Pants, you will not take my children away from me. THAT will not happen. I'll kill myself first," said mum. Her blood pressure boiled.

"Being like this is not helping your cause, is it, Mrs. Dalton?"

"My cause? Is looking after children a project?" Said mum.

"We're also concerned about accommodation arrangements. Four boys, your mother and you. Six people crammed into two bedrooms and a tiny box-room. How can we allow this?" Said Mr. Anderson. His deep and slow voice exuded authority. He glared at mum for a response.

"I would love to have in a bigger house. But a Coal Board pit house is what I've got. I don't have a bloody choice."

"Now, now, wee hen. No need for that kind of language," Mr. Anderson remarked with his naturally calming intonation.

She clutched her stomach, her face grimaced in agony. Sharp stabbing pains persisted as her stomach muscles seemed to collapse.

"Needing a larger house is not the problem. The fact is, an elderly person takes care of your children on a regular basis. The youngest two boys are of immediate concern to us. Someone has brought it to our attention they are malnourished and lack adequate clothing for the winter," said Mr. Anderson.

"My boys never go hungry; they have breakfast each morning, school dinners and a meal at five."

"As we have said, you're not at home between four o'clock and ten. We're getting into the realms of neglect, Mrs. Dalton. When this happens, the law requires us to step in and take control."

Child Welfare took notes as mum looked over their shoulders to glimpse at their scribblings. Enduring so many of life's traumas in such a brief space of time, she felt deflated. Crisis after crisis seemed like a pinball machine, catapulted from pillar to post. An unsung hero, she continued her battle to protect us from the tentacles of Social Services.

Mum seemed devoid of answers and solutions as the Child Welfare officers delved deeper into the quagmire of her life. They were like barristers with admissible evidence. The options diminished as each question bombarded her brain and speared like a javelin to the heart. She became irate, answers became more abrupt and colourful.

"I know what you're getting at. You don't have any right to take my children away from me," said mum, in tears.

"We can. We might not have any option in your present circumstances," said Mrs. Anderson in a curt tone.

"My children are staying with me. Would you let someone take your children away, Mrs. Walker? Do you even have children, Mrs. Walker?" Said mum with a bitter reply.

"The Coal Board Estates Department has informed us you've lost your tenancy here at Bishop Road," said Mr. Anderson, alert to the simmering atmosphere.

"I haven't lost the tenancy. My husband has abandoned us and left his job at the colliery. The Coal Board is taking the house from us. It's scandalous. You should all be ashamed of yourselves, throwing us on the streets."

"Only because you didn't pay the rent. How can anyone rent you a house if you don't pay your rent on time?"

"The government don't give me enough money. My husband doesn't give me ANY money. How can I pay the rent and feed four boys?"

"You do understand if the children don't have any satisfactory accommodation, we may need to step in and take them into care. Your children are our prime concern. We have a duty of care," said Mr. Anderson, emphasising his professional stance.

"Yes, I agree with you. But my children are MY prime concern," said mum with fury.

Mum burst into tears. Ultimately, she knew that Mr. Anderson had given a rational view in simplistic terms. Social Services had loaded the dice against her. Nothing she said would placate Social Services. They needed a way forward. They needed answers and solutions, 'poste-haste.'

"We can't afford to live. We can't afford to eat. Where can we go? Who can I turn to?" Said mum, despondent, crying into an abyss of darkness and uncertainty.

"Mrs. Dalton, Child Welfare have concerns about what you have said. Can I give you some helpful advice?" Said Mr. Anderson with empathy.

"Can I give YOU some advice? The last word ending in 'off," said mum as a sharp rebuke.

"I know you're hurting and feel let down with all this. I can see it's not in any way your fault what's happened. But the department tie our hands. We have to follow guidelines set by the government," said Mr. Anderson. His soft Edinburgh accent taking the sting away.

"Can we take a quick break here, Mrs. Dalton? Do you have a room where Mrs. Walker and myself can discuss some of the matters raised today? We will need some privacy."

"You can use the front room. It's the best room. I would offer you a cuppa tea, but we don't have any tea or milk? Sorry, I have nothing else to offer you."

Mum kept the best room in pristine condition. Though she allowed none of us in the room, it was 'Hoovered' and dusted every week. Mum polished the walnut furniture and radiogram without fail. The furniture being bought 'on tick' years ago when mum and dad got their first house. Mum always reserved the room for royalty, but they never visited.

Fifteen minutes later, Mr. Anderson emerged from the best room. He looked down to the floor, with deep lines creasing his forehead. Sadness clouded his face as he delivered tragic news. Mrs. Walker, likewise, had darkened eyes of gloom. Her face frowned and appeared as though neither of them enjoyed this part of their task. They both looked professional but held an air of melancholy.

"We hate to say this to you Mrs. Dalton, but we have no alternative solutions. We have considered many options for you, but we have to adhere to government guidelines."

Mum wiped her eyes as warm tears dribbled down her cheeks, her hands shook with anxiety.

"I can't believe you're doing this to me," said mum, tearful and whimpering. "After all these years of bringing my boys up, you walk in and destroy my family. Why does this happen?"

"We feel we will have to take your youngest two boys into care….." Mr. Anderson looked across for a reaction. He felt mum could descend further towards the edge of a breakdown.

"You're having tremendous difficulties coping with looking after your children," he continued. His voice plunged the room into stillness.

Mum didn't want to hear the rest of his comments. Her mind drifted to images of her own mother's stories of children being taken into care in the 1920's. Maybe never seen or heard from again. She was heartbroken that her life had come to this horrendous moment. Mum would never allow such a tragedy to happen, but our destiny was no longer in her hands. Her head was buzzing, her flooded eyes could no longer focus and stung each time she wiped away the tear. Within herself, she was prepared to fight to the end.

"I won't let you take any of my boys away. You can't do that."

"We can. You must understand this. Allow me to finish."

Mum grabbed my youngest brother, baby David, and smothered him with love and hugs. She grabbed Glenn and squeezed him tight. Then huddled me as we locked into a passionate embrace. Each one of us bawling without control. We were all like sacrificial lambs, huddled together knowing the axe was about to fall. Alex was at his girlfriend's house. Grandma Cooper had seen similar events in her own life, forty years earlier. She had a particular distrust of the Child Welfare department, distant memories that would never fade. She knew how her daughter felt. She could not intervene against Social Services. They were Demi-gods within the sphere of child welfare. She could only comfort mum and be by her side in the one sanctity closest to every mother's heart.

"I won't let you. Not even over my dead body, My boys stay with me," said mum, screaming whilst holding us tighter.

"Don't make matters any more difficult than they are already, Mrs. Dalton."

Mum wept as she had ever done before. Her fortitude, almost depleted, was now in danger of total collapse. She edged closer to a nervous breakdown. Her mind became overloaded with stress, her body overloaded with worry and her soul overloaded with grief. Social Services taking her boys would take her to the limit.

"Give me a chance! Please let me sort this mess out," said mum weeping, almost unable to mutter any words.

Mum looked at us with deep love. Deep emotion scorched her eyes, redder than her auburn locks that became matted with sweat. I felt her heart thumping within our embrace. She was drowning in her own grief but hurting more knowing of our fate. My youngest two brothers couldn't have realised the size of the miscarriage of moral justice. They were the victims of a travesty. Innocent bystanders caught up in an avalanche of epic proportions, recipients of Child Welfare's ultimate solution. Incarcerated in one of their homes of dubious notoriety.

The chances of pleading with Mr Anderson remained limited. Emotional blackmail didn't have any chance of succeeding with them. Her heart pounded with the fear of failure. She fought with tenacity, whilst ever a chance remained of keeping us under the same roof. She dropped to her knees, with eyes blisteringly hot, a headache blindingly oppressive. She clasped her hands, prayer-like, and screamed a spine chilling cry to the heavens, as loud as her lungs permitted.

"No-ooooooooo!" She yelled.

Mrs. Walker helped mum up from the tiled floor. She wrapped her arms around her like a mother would for her children. She caressed her and held her to her chest. Then smiled towards Mr. Anderson as a gesture to leave them alone for a few minutes.

"I'll be back in ten, Mrs. Walker. Just nipping out to get a wee bit of fresh air," said Mr. Anderson.

Mum recovered and composed herself after a few minutes with Mrs. Walker. Dejected and despondent, mum trudged upstairs to the bathroom. Her face burned with frustration and rage; she needed to wash in tepid water and cool down. Mum felt disconsolate and defeated against a gigantic wall of bureaucracy. She plodded back to be with grandma, who had been taking care of us. She needed her mother in these times of stress. She needed her support and unwavering love.

Mr Anderson returned minutes later, his clothes smelling of sweet Old Holborn pipe tobacco. He used the moment for deep contemplation of the actual issues, causes and workable solutions, but in line with policy and guidelines. He chatted at length with Mrs. Walker in the privacy of the best room. They toyed with potential alternatives, each having their own remit of duty of care.

"Right! That's it then," Mr. Anderson deliberated softly. His eyebrows raised as if he had captured a eureka moment.

The door snecked open as each of us huddled together. Mr. Anderson and Mrs. Walker returned with furrowed foreheads and grave faces; their eyes narrowed with determined intent. Mum's heart sank to another depth, her eyes stared at the frayed, decrepit carpet. She feared the worst; she expected doom and envisaged even worse. Her colossal nightmare of losing her devoted children was unfolding into unquestionable reality.

"Please listen carefully Mrs. Dalton. Time is of the essence. We understand you have to vacate the property in twenty-eight days. We need to organise papers within the next seven days."

"No… No…. You can't do this to me. Please….don't do this…Please. Please don't take my children away. I've done nothing wrong. The only thing I'm guilty of is giving them all the love a mother can give. Is that a crime?" Said mum.

She had hit the bottom of despair. She had no solutions to offer Social Services. Her mind filled with images of us being dragged away from her arms, crying into the distance.

"You need to listen to me. This is difficult.…," continued Mr. Anderson in a stern tone, demanding mum's careful attention. He was about to pronounce his professional judgement.

"I honestly can't take any more," said mum, her heart becoming heavier with angst. Her breathing was on the brink of an uncontrollable panic attack.

"Listen, please. We are both on a critical time scale. We have decided to postpone…."

Mum interjected with a sudden outburst of euphoria. Her eyes lit up with instant relief.

"Thank you, thank you, thank you," she said and wept at his knees like a disciple of Jesus.

"Please, Mrs. Dalton. Let me finish. There are stipulations attached that won't be easy for you to overcome. If at all. We have decided to postpone our decision until Friday this week. You have four days to organise where you will live. Your boys need stability. By then, we need solid, concrete arrangements in place. Not 'perhaps'….. or 'maybe.'…. Do you understand?"

"Thank you, Mr. Anderson, I won't let you down," I promise.

"You won't be letting US down, wee hen. We have a job to do. By Friday you need to find a solution; one way or another. I regret that this situation has occurred. We have little leeway with what is best for your children. We are bound by law to ensure their well-being is our priority. Their interests come before yours. You have four days to meet our requirements."

Our situation was precarious. Without a home, we had nowhere to live. Dad had abandoned us. We never saw him since the day he left hospital a few months before. He had never been at home at least a year before that. Our plight appeared to be in the hands of mum's side of the family. At best, they were lukewarm towards mum; they had their own family to support. Mum took the ultimate risk by leaving the boys with grandma once again. As it was Monday, she was still at our house.

Mum had virtually received a verbal warning, an ultimatum, from Social Services. A smidgen of hope existed; one last chance to save the family from being split up. Her options appeared limited. Grandma Cooper, her own mother, was out of the equation, as an ongoing solution. She was too old and weak for any more disruption to her life. Her health had deteriorated somewhat with grandad's passing and her age against her. The strains of helping to look after four boys, shopping, cleaning and cooking became obvious. Her face was gaunt. Her body frail and her bones ached every hour of the day. The trudge to Bradley's Corner Shop sapped her strength almost to the point of collapse, after all, she was seventy-two. Emotional and physical exhaustion drained her energy over the past few years, her efforts to support us were stoic.

Stepsister, aunty Ruth, with the help of uncle Jack, appeared to be mum's only hope of salvation. She had influence and respect within her own bloodline, a good organiser, a '*Winston Churchill*' in times of crisis. Mum wasn't a blood relative. Step-family connections were as thin as cotton thread; easily broken, but workable. In mum's mind, if Social Services broke the family up, it would be a better solution for us to stay within the broader family. Being dispersed by Social Services and put into a children's home, or an obscure local foster home, was always a worst-case scenario.

Mum dashed for the bus to visit stepsister aunty Ruth, four miles to the next village of Beighton. She couldn't lose any time. Family members may have needed time to contemplate the change in our circumstances. They needed time to consider the implications of their commitments. Taking care of someone else's children would always be a big ask, but there were no other options. Grandad used to say *'Don't ask, don't get.'*

Grandma stayed with us four boys. Although her strength had been greater a few years back, she seemed always exhausted. No matter what, her determination to help mum was immeasurable. Aunty Ruth called in a great favour from her blood-cousin Colin. He was a middle-aged single man and had a spare room where mum could stay. He could only offer accommodation; mum needed to prepare her own meals and sort her own washing. Mum needed to be self-sufficient. The situation was to be a simple self-catering understanding. The only commitment was for mum to contribute half towards gas and electric bills and pay for her own shopping needs. At last, mum had her own living arrangements in place. Grandma would return home to her own place at Woodhouse.

Brother Alex made plans to move in with his girlfriend, Gwen, at her parent's house. They were now inseparable and Alex seldom came home. Alex was now almost eighteen, safe from the auspices of Social Services. I was almost sixteen; maybe I could escape the clutches of a children's home. Mum had made arrangements for me to stay with aunty Ruth's son, Tony, and his wife. This would be a temporary setup for just a few months.

Accommodation and care for Glenn, now nine and David four, represented an immense headache for mum. Being so young meant it was impossible to find anyone prepared to look after them, even for a brief period. Their well-being had to be paramount. There were no options left, and only three days to go before Mr. Anderson's return.

If mum could not find care for David and Glenn, Social Services would assume control of their welfare. Glenn and David, the youngest of my brothers, faced uncertain futures within a children's home of questionable repute or standards. Uncle Jack drove mum back home. Darkness fell like a black cloak. Mr. Anderson's prophecy sounded ominously realistic. The following day dawned with typical uncertainty.

Chapter 15

A hefty rap at the door woke the house after a late night of mum sitting alone. The unrecognisable beat of the door caused concern on the Wednesday morning. We had not expected creditors.

"You've got a nerve, Eddie, showing your face here," shouted mum. "How dare you? What do you want? You're not welcome here," said mum. She scoffed in disbelief of his unwelcome presence, a knee-jerk reminder of the devastation he created.

"Just thought I could help."

Mum's annoyance flared, her body locked with rage that flashed through her veins like an electric shock. She trembled, fearing that an all-out slanging match was imminent. She was in no mood for recriminations on top of the anxiety that already existed within her life. She didn't want to shed any more tears; to him, a sign of weakness. Instead, she wanted to throw punches at him, to rid herself of pent up anger. She expected she would lose the fight. Her stomach winced with a stab of pain, irritated by stress.

"I have an idea. I reckon it would work." said dad.

Mum looked into his eyes with indifference. She had heard all his pipe-dreams before. She wanted him to go without upsetting us. He couldn't even take care of any one of us, not that we wanted to go with him. There was only his mother, grandma Greaves, in a position to help with accommodation, but she was eighty. Social Services had already rejected the idea of grandma Cooper taking care of us, even if we had suitable accommodation.

"I'm listening. Go on," said mum. Her croaky voice weakened.

"My mother and I had a serious chat," said dad. "She's got a three-bedroomed terrace. As you know, she lives on her own since my father died years ago......." said dad.

"There's no way I can live under her roof." Said Evelyn. "No way. She hates me, and she hates the boys. Always has, ever since we got married. She never wanted us to get married, remember?"

"Listen. My mother expected you would say that. There's no love lost between you both. I understand what you're saying. But she will help with David and Glenn," said dad.

It was ironic that dad's idea of help was to enlist someone else to do it; his own mother. He gave no physical input whatsoever, not even taking his boys out for the day.

"Your mother is eighty-years-old. Social Services won't agree to an elderly lady being a carer. We know that already. They point blank refuse to accept that idea," said mum.

"I suppose she wants to do some good. Be closer to God. She reads the Bible a lot," said dad.

Mum had become sceptical. Favours from grandma Greaves had been non-existent over the years. She was the epitome of the wicked witch. I guess she expected the best place for children was in a bubbling cauldron of green liquid. Mum had explored every possibility to save us. Sleepless nights followed by tearful days. She was at the end of her tether. Her options had dissipated.

"I know this idea will work. Make your mind up whether you want to try it. If you feel okay with the idea, you can and let Social Services know," said dad, at least trying to be helpful.

"So what's your suggestion?" Said mum, still unconvinced anything could work involving grandma Greaves.

"Glenn and David can sleep in one room. I can 'make out' in the second bedroom, my mother in the third. It will appear natural when Social Services pay a visit. Dad at 'home' looking after his boys. At least that's how it would appear."

"Can your mother cope, caring for a four and a ten-year-old?"

"It's only until you get a council house," said dad.

"Do you realise there's a four-year wait for a council house?"

"You'll be high on a priority list; a homeless mother with three boys under the age of sixteen and one under eighteen. It may only be for a few months," said dad.

"It's worth looking at, if your mother accepts with the idea."

"The boys will be at school, anyway. I can call round sometimes, to make sure they are alright," said dad.

Mum pondered over the shock suggestion. She had run out of options. Though grandma Greaves had been a heartless grandmother over the years, this fresh attitude, for whatever reason, appeared to be helpful. She never seemed at ease with children, but at least she could tolerate them.

"Have a think about it. Tell me soon," said dad.

"No need to think about it. I have no choice. Your mother has said some nasty words over the years. Me and her need to talk. There's a chance the arrangement is workable."

The walk to grandma Greaves' house on Digger's Hill gave mum time for thought. David and Glenn needed a place to live. None of us could ever envisage any love and affection from grandma Greaves. She had never shown her only grandchildren any compassion or tenderness. Arguments between mum and grandma became inevitable. Scores to settle could agitate dormant wounds. If mum spoke her mind, harsh consequences could follow. They had not spoken for the past five years, even though they lived in the same village and even crossed the road whenever they saw each other.

"I need reassurance everything will be alright. No arguments. No animosity. I need to feel happy where the boys will sleep, how they'll get to school. How will they eat…..?"

"My mother and I have discussed it. It will be alright," said dad.

"The boys have seldom seen grandma Greaves. How is that going to work?" Asked mum.

"I realise it will be very difficult for the boys and my mother."

Halfway up Diggers Hill, the long, steep gennel looked foreboding. A cavernous alleyway between two sets of terraced houses created an echo of spine chilling proportions. On the rare occasions dad took us to visit grandma Greaves, Alex and I played competed many times to see who create the best echo. We pretended we were in the Alps, yodeling are mimicking Tarzan in the jungle. At least until grandma came out with her broom to 'shoo' us away. It was brilliant fun, but grandma seemed to have puritanical views. Enjoying oneself in public was tantamount to playing with the devil. Whenever she spoke, the bible sanctioned her words, quoted by chapter and verse.

Mum tapped on grandma Greaves' door, apprehensive of the monster beyond.

"Oh…... It's you," gibed grandma Greaves.

"Nice to see you too, I'm sure," said mum with sarcasm.

"Eddie said you were coming round for a chat. You'd better come in," said grandma in her bitter, spiky voice.

"I needed to make sure you're okay with everything," said mum, trying to be conciliatory.

"I will take care of your YOUR boys. Alright?" Said grandma said in a frosty tone.

"Your grandchildren? Your son's children; remember?" Said mum with sarcasm.

"Not helping you, Evelyn. I'm helping my son," said grandma. Conversations between mum and grandma had remained sensitive. Tempers could flare-up at any moment. The atmosphere became more tense the longer it lasted.

"Thought it best to talk," said mum.

"That's understandable, I guess," said grandma Greaves with her smug attitude.

"Why do you care?" Said mum.

"The Bible says: 'Let the little children come unto me,'…. Matthew, Chapter 19," said grandma with unexpected verve. It seemed an angel of mercy had visited her conscience.

The first nasty feelings between mum and grandma Greaves had resurfaced. Grandma did not want a reconciliation. Pent-up feelings burned through her face as her intense, piercing eyes narrowed with bitterness and scorn. Grandma's lips tightened like a snake. Mum knew home truths were imminent.

"I've never liked you. I can't hide the fact," said grandma.

"You're a spiteful old woman. Whatever have I done wrong to hurt you?" Said mum.

"You mean you don't know?"

"I've never hurt you. I gave you four lovely grandchildren. You snubbed us all."

"You stole my only son, I can never forgive you for that."

"Eddie couldn't live with you forever. He was never a mummy's boy, was he?" Said mum.

"You were a teenager during the war. You wanted to go to dance halls," said grandma.

Mum frothed at the mouth by grandma Greaves' distorted view.

"Luckily Eddie didn't join the army. My son had a choice. Either become a soldier or work down the coal mine. Many times he got into fights when local village people gave him a 'White Feather,' for cowardice, for not fighting in the war."

"I still don't get it. Why are you bitter against me?" Said mum.

"You came along. Beautiful, flashing your skirt in the dance halls," said grandma.

"You got me wrong from the start. I only ever wanted Eddie. He was my first and only love."

"Why are you so cruel and vindictive? You can't paint everybody with the same brush."

"Trapped him, didn't you?" said grandma, her harsh voice carried little understanding.

"What?" shouted mum.

Grandma Greaves had hit a raw nerve. She spewed an untruth that needed answering. A sensitive issue, full of trauma and sorrow for mum, she had lost her first child. Even more heartbreaking, she lost a baby girl by miscarriage. The baby of her dreams.

"You trapped him by saying you were pregnant. Just to get a ring on your finger, wasn't it?"

"I WAS pregnant; and it was Eddie's," said mum louder.

"And the baby?"

"I had a miscarriage."

The heated discussion became hotter, the tone more caustic and a notch louder.

"I lost a baby girl. Your grand-daughter," said mum.

The room became silent. Mum's comment brought hostilities to an abrupt end, as though grandma subconsciously admitted to the truth. She was too proud to admit anything to mum, whether it was true or otherwise. Grandma's eyes glared with spite.

"I'll take care of your boys because you can't. What kind of mother gets into this mess?"

Mum stormed out with fury. The exchange had been sharp. She came with conciliation in mind, but she left agitated. Though she was angry, she regretted her bitter comments. David and Glenn still needed to live there. Mum was not welcome.

"Don't come back here again. Ever!" Said grandma Greaves, her parting 'goodbye.'

This was not an ideal scenario. It was now impossible for mum to visit Glenn and David in grandma's house. Mum had to meet outside the school gates at 3.30, sometimes taking them to the swing park. The saving grace being we were all close at hand, had a roof above our heads and a coal fire in every room would keep us warm. Food would be basic but adequate but it would meet social Services conditions as dad purported to be there.

Social Services arrived to find out the viability of any fresh arrangements that could be acceptable to them. This was the dreaded appointment with fear. All options seemed to be cul-de-sacs with nowhere to go. Mum opened the door to a waft of tobacco smoke. Mr. Anderson puffed on his briar pipe. It seemed to help him brood over a problem until he found a solution. A cloud of sweet Old Holborn drifted into the doorway. Mrs. Walker stood ahead, her designer tweed suit as pristine as the day she bought it. A matching tweed trilby complemented her slick, office image.

"Well, ma' dear. How are you today? Hope you and the boys are well." Mr. Anderson's soft Edinburgh accent flowed. His face sombre, bereft of any emotion.

"Better than I was earlier this week. Thank you."

"I expect you've had a few torrid days and sleepless nights, Mrs. Dalton."

"Quite a few. But we've got things sorted now," said mum with enthusiasm. "Their father will look after our two youngest boys. There are two spare rooms at his mother's house. She is more than happy for them to stay with their dad. He will look after them and make their meals. He can't work anymore, so he's at home all day. Their grandma welcomes the arrangements; she gets to see her son and grandchildren every day, rather than every week."

"That sounds promising. That's just what we need for them. Stability, decent meals and satisfactory accommodation. All held together by their own father," said Mr. Anderson.

"I can stay with a cousin," said mum, confirming everything was okay.

"It's only four miles away in Beighton, the next village. It seems it could work," said mum.

"I suppose families do rally round in troublesome times," said Mr. Anderson.

Mum was lying. Everything she had said to Social Services was the opposite of reality. Grandma Greaves would care for my youngest two brothers. A woman that had always shown total indifference to us. Love and kindness had vanished years before. Their father would still never see them. If Social Services knew the truth, could they imprison mum for perjury or deception? As mum said so often, she would do anything to keep her boys away from the dreaded children's homes or foster parents. With a degree of irony, godparents conveniently forgot about their vows in church:

'to fulfil their responsibilities to care for the children.'

With mum's crises, all godparents seemed conspicuous by their absence. A travesty of loyalty and integrity. They all ate the cake at the party, but never delivered on their promises. Deeds were more important than kind words. There were at least four godparents; none stepped forward with help.

"I can see and appreciate your passion for caring for your boys. I have noted that," said Mr. Anderson, his delicate intonation worthy of any Scottish orator.

"It wasn't easy," said mum, wiping the remnants of a tear.

"What we need to do now, Mrs. Dalton is to visit grandma Greaves and your husband just to make sure the accommodation for your boys is satisfactory. Visiting arrangements and financial support needs sorting out," said Mrs. Walker, marking her list.

"Aye. There's a lot for us to do now, ma' dear. We can't make any visits until Monday. But it seems we only need confirmation from Mrs. Greaves, now. We'll extend the deadline until we have met them. At least you've done your part. Well done, Mrs. Dalton," said Mr. Anderson.

"We didn't expect you to meet the conditions within the four days you had. But it appears you may have achieved it," said Mrs. Walker, scribbling notes into her report.

"We'll be in touch by next week. Fingers crossed eh?"

They left mum's Coal Board house for the last time and climbed into Mr. Anderson's gleaming MGA Roadster. He lit up his old briar pipe, puffed out a cloud of aromatic smoke, then a throaty blast from the exhaust sped them away.

"Well, Mrs. Walker. I feel a lot more confident about that poor lassie and her bairns now."

"Oh, my word! What a nightmare for her and her boys. All the family scattered around."

"I would have hated taking her boys away. I don't know about you, but wrenching bairns from mothers is my least favourite job, Mrs. Walker."

"I can agree with you there. It is a demanding job."

"Aye. It certainly is. Let's hope her fresh arrangements are as solid as she seems to think. I just feel that all the support has been on her mother's side, until now," said Mr. Anderson.

"There seems little input from the father's side. Now, at the eleventh hour, Mr. Dalton's mother comes to the rescue. It doesn't seem to ring true for me. We'll find out next week, when we meet everyone."

The probability of mum losing us had diminished to a possibility. Only grandma Greaves held the key to a positive outcome. As she was eighty, her stamina and willingness became vital for the arrangements to work. Grandma, looking after children, the youngest being four, was fraught with her own health risks. Mum had no options. For how much longer, God only knew.

Back in the city centre, Mr. Anderson's sports car came to a dramatic stop outside Sheffield Victoria Station. The day had been exhausting. He walked around the car to extricate Mrs. Walker from the low profile seat. He turned away as a discreet gesture, as a gentleman should. Her getting out of a sports car was undignified.

Chapter 16

Come the Monday, Mr. Anderson and Mrs. Walker met up with dad and grandma Greaves. They discussed all the arrangements about David and Glenn staying at her house. They duped social Services into believing our dad was to look after them, and all sleep at grandma Greaves' house. A ringing endorsement showed that we had met all the conditions. A few days later, mum received a letter of confirmation of their acceptance. Mum decided the time was right to let me David and Glenn know what was happening when we had to leave three weeks from now. Alex was at his girlfriend's house, almost on a permanent basis.

"David, Glenn, Jeff; Come and sit down. I need to talk to you and tell you some really important things that are happening right now. First of all, I want to tell you that all of you are the most precious thing to me in the entire world. I love you to the end of the earth. I always will. In three weeks, we have to leave here and live somewhere else for a few months until we can get a council house," said mum, holding back a tear.

"Are you staying with us, mum?" Asked Glenn.

"I can't love. There isn't enough room for us all to be together," said mum. Her eyes welling.

"Will we see you again, mum? Where are you sending us?" Asked Glenn. His face reddened as he became scared of being left in a strange place.

"Sweetheart; I'm not sending you anywhere. Your grandma has offered to put you and David up for a while at her house. It won't be for too long," said mum, feeling choked. "Jeff, will stay with your cousin Tony. I will stay near aunty Ruth in Beighton," continued mum.

"I don't want you to leave me, mum. I love you," said Glenn. Glenn and David's sobs turned into a deluge of outpouring and heartbreak. Mum had never spent one night away from them. She could not hide her anguish. She cuddled and squeezed them with her boundless love; her arms wrapped around them like a comfort blanket. They assumed she wouldn't be coming back into their lives. I gave mum an immense squeeze to reassure her at least I was alright. At sixteen, I could cope better with the devastating and wretched situation we had stumbled into. Mum's colossal anxiety was for my youngest two brothers. In three weeks from now, matters would get worse for them.

Mum continued to smother us all with her deep devotion. Her pain emanated from our hearts. There were no tablets for this kind of pain. Only mum's deep love could ease the suffering we all felt. David squeezed mum with another enormous hug. He put his arms around her neck, as though he would never let go. Mum put her arms around us all as we all continued our tearful grief. This was the moment mum dreaded.

"I love you so much mum. We all do. We will always be with you. No matter what happens," I said, unable to arrest any of my overwhelming emotions. Mum gave a generous smile, albeit difficult through her cascading tears.

"I love you too, sweetheart. Remember, I always will. This will last only for a few months, then we'll all get back to normal living together," said mum.

"Are we staying there forever, mum?" Asked Glenn.

"Not at all, love. Only until we get another house for us all. I'll meet you outside school every day. Then on the way home, we'll go to the park; maybe get some sweets," said mum.

"Can we get some sweets from the shop, mum?" Asked David, sniffling on to his shirtsleeve.

"I'm sure Mr. Bradshaw will be more than happy to see you."

David and Glenn settled after incessant crying. While ever mum was close-by, they felt safe. They knew grandma Greaves was not a loving person. With three weeks to go before the upheaval of moving house, they didn't want to go there. David and Glenn were being dealt a double blow. They had to cope with the trauma of mum moving away from them, and endure the awful situation of having to live with grandma Greaves, the wicked witch. Alex and I were the lucky ones, we were staying with people who we liked and knew them well.

Three weeks later, we moved out of our old home, the Coal Board house. Though mum was heartbroken, the embarrassment of moving out of the house in the full gaze of neighbours made matters worse. It appeared strange that nosey neighbours were eagle-eyed in times of personal crisis to see what possessions a person had, or to witness awful sad emotional moments. Mum's chat had taken the sting out of the traumatic move, but we all shed a few more tears that morning. Uncle Jack picked us up in his car and drove us all to grandma Greaves. She didn't come out to meet us or offer us a warm welcome. We weren't welcome; we were there, subject to tolerance and detachment. A cuddle and a handful of sweets would have helped to smooth their arrival. Instead, net curtains twitched with furtive glances.

Mum had achieved a major hurdle. Grandma had spared my two youngest brothers from the confines of a children's home, mum's paramount pledge. Uncle Jack drove us across the village to Diggers Hill, grandma's house. As we arrived, David and Glenn burst into tears. Mum gave them both an enormous hug, but they bawled even louder. Uncle Jack stayed clear of the emotional outburst and retrieved two bin-liners of their clothes. Mum and I held their hand as we climbed the steep narrow gennil leading up to her house. Primal screams became louder the nearer we stepped.

"Please, don't leave me mummy. I don't want to be here. Mummy, take me with you. I love you," squealed David.

Neighbours opened their doors to see what the commotion was.

"Mum, please take us with you. We are not welcome here. You know that," cried Glenn, pushing me away.

Mum could no longer hold back her tears. It broke her heart to see them both cry. Glenn sat on a step in the alley, refusing to budge. It would seem unfair if I picked him up. I knew he would kick and punch as best he could. David broke free of mum's hand and ran back down the slope. The steepness of the alley made him fall. He screamed as blood seeped from his knee. Grandma opened her door to see what had happened. The echo of her shoes in the gennil created a dramatic undertone. As the echo grew louder, so did David's screams.

"Mum, take me with you. Please, mum….. Please…..Don't leave me, mum, please….," cried David, his raw screams were as horrific as cruelty itself.

His shrill voice penetrated the walls of neighbourhood houses, causing net curtains to twitch with suspicion of a child's welfare. His fear of grandma paralysed his body to the point of paranoia. I could only guess he assumed our mum would never come back. His heart-rending screams embodied the devastation caused by mum about to walk away, abandonment of the first degree. He cried until there were no more tears left to escape. His throat became as parched and as coarse as desert sand. His voice subsided into a whimper. He was distraught and inconsolable. We sat for a short while on the cold concrete step by the side of grandma's house, out of sight. We huddled close to each other in a deep embrace, oblivious to the chill that scurried up the gennel.

I was out of my depth; mum out of her mind, coping, or controlling emotional outpourings. Mum and I still had to walk away. There was no painless way to achieve the delicate task of leaving David and Glenn alone. We edged closer to grandma's door and sat on the brick wall. Mum talked to us as a whole as she tried to pacify them. The heavy clomp of footsteps echoed up the gennil; uncle Jack appeared from around the corner with a welcome bag of chocolate bars and sherbet. Their eyes lit up instantly as they wiped their molten eyes on shirt sleeves.

"There we are, soldiers. Food for the troops, eh?" Said uncle Jack, handing out his goodies.

"Thanks, uncle Jack," we said almost in unison.

We gave him a thankful hug. At a stroke, he rescued the emotional situation. David and Glenn's tension subsided. Ten minutes went by. Mum took a tentative, brave step.

"Alright then. We've just got to get you into your new bedroom now and start hanging up your clothes for school on Monday. Are we all going to help?" Asked mum.

The situation became more tense. Not with my brother's stress, but with my grandma's. She had already said she didn't want mum anywhere near, let alone going into David and Glenn's room, to sort the clothes out and get the bed ready. The first complication of settling the boys succeeded with delicate nurturing and warmth from mum. The second hurdle could be a more formidable mountain to climb. Grandma greaves had kept her distance throughout the emotional ordeal. She stayed behind a closed door, maybe symbolic of her indifference. Mum now needed to face a potential slanging match with her. All this before my younger brothers had settled into their new surroundings. Mum knocked at the door, unsure how grandma Greaves would react.

"It's only me, Evelyn."

"Come on in," said grandma in her usual shrill, spiky voice.

Mum entered the lounge with trepidation, expecting a barrage of abuse. David, Glenn and I followed at close quarters. We stepped in as though we were treading on broken glass. Fear circulated through our veins. My heart thumped with the possibility of hearing a barbed comment, like '*Don't touch that,*' or '*watch where you're walking,*' rather than, 'it's good to see you all.'

"The boys are having the front room downstairs," said grandma in a curt tone but never looked directly at any of us.

"I'll go to the newspaper shop mum. I can get funny comics for David and Glenn; maybe a bar of chocolate. I've got enough money from my newspaper round. No problem," I said, happy to get out of the electric atmosphere.

Uncle Jack walked up the road with me as it was only a few minutes away, across from the comprehensive school I attended.

Back at the Stalag, mum took the opportunity and gave more hugs and cuddles. They had settled down from the anxiety issues of half an hour earlier. Uncle Jack went back to his car to listen to the radio outside grandma's house. As I knocked on her door, it became the signal for us to make our way to Beighton.

It was only four miles away, mum and I were to live there in separate houses, but close enough for me to see her when the opportunity allowed. Mum would visit David and Glenn every day outside school at Aughton; it was the only option mum had, to make sure they felt cared for and loved. Mum travelling on a daily basis wasn't great, travelling and waiting for two buses, rain, hail or shine. It was a task she had to fulfil for the well-being of my brothers. She still suffered chronic stomach problems and continued to collapse at random moments.

"Okay boys. I've got to be on my way now. I have to unpack my clothes at my cousin Tony's house. I'll be waiting outside school for you on Monday. Can you make me one of your special paintings?"

"I can do that mum. It will be my best ever. You'll see," said David with re-invented enthusiasm; his panic attack over.

The slanging match with grandma never materialised. She kept out of the way during mum's tough moments with David and Glenn. At least that was a blessing, that they had not caused upset again. Alex appeared oblivious to any of mum's difficulties. He came back from his girlfriend's house, once a week, to say hello. Other than that, we seldom saw him. My destination now was to stay at cousin Tony's house. Mum was on her way to stay with Colin, aunty Ruth's cousin. Grandma Cooper had finally earned some respite as she returned to her own place at Woodhouse. She no longer had any commitment to look after any of us, especially my youngest two brothers.

Moving from the Coal Board house created enormous upheaval for us all; except for dad. We were all heading to live at separate addresses. Mum, with no transport, could only take bin-liners full of clothes with her. Uncle Jack had collected several bags and delivered them to each of the separate houses. Mum left furniture and other belongings behind that wouldn't fit into uncle Jack's car. It was like abandoning a sinking ship.

The Coal Board workmen would become official looters, to grab anything of value as mum looked on, helpless and heartbroken. Fragments of her life would disappear into someone else's possession. At a stroke, it would sweep aside twelve years of our memories. Mum had ripped in half the hand-painted colour photograph of her wedding day portrait. Someone trashed broken frames with poignant photographs.

What little furniture mum owned, the walnut radiogram bought by grandad as a wedding present, would disappear into an unknown council workers' house. Mum now had nothing to her name. The Coal Board had taken her prized possession from her; her home. Only the love of us four boys existed. Mum cried as she carried bag after bag of what few things we had. Workmen from Coal Board Estates Department would trash everything else the following week.

Six months passed by; the temporary living arrangements worked well, most of the time. Grandma Greaves gave the occasional curt remark, but not too stressful. Everyone walked on eggshells and bit one's lips to keep the peace and a roof over our head. It devastated mum. She had fought tooth and nail to keep us all from a daunting life within children's homes and foster homes. We all suffered in silence, except that Glen nine, and David four, suffered the most. Randomly, they sometimes cried themselves to sleep, like being in a lonely dormitory.

Chapter 17

Mum eagerly awaited a letter from the Housing Department. She had been told there was a two-year waiting list for a council house, but mum was high on their priority list. On a rare occasion, Alex was visiting mum at her cousin's house. The letterbox clattered; an ominous brown envelope landed on the floor. Mum crept down the stairs with trepidation. She stared with fear and hope at the brown envelope, marked and franked across the top in red, '*Sheffield City Council, Housing Department.*' She closed her eyes, said a prayer, and crossed her fingers for double strength. She looked at the letter at close-quarters. Mum tried her best to read it by squinting a half-opened eye. She needed spectacles, but they were a luxury item; she could not afford them. Her fingers shook; the letter quivered like a shivering leaf.

"Woo-woo," screamed mum.

"Are we getting another house mum?" Asked Alex.

"We sure are. Let's walk around the corner and tell Jeff and my sister," said mum.

Mum was so excited. She couldn't wait to let everyone know, like winning the football pools. We caught the next number 10 bus to Aughton, to share the news with David and Glenn. As it was Saturday, they were not at school. Within the hour, we were all together with mum. It seemed like her own Christmas Day had arrived, keen to share her surprise. As soon as the boys dressed, got fed, and watered, there was another forty-five-minute bus journey to let her mother, grandma Cooper, know the exciting news. By midday, we arrived at grandma Cooper's house…….

A short while later, we all arrived at grandma's house

"Just come over to tell you some fantastic news mum. I've just got a council house," said mum, excited.

"That's good news, but more hard work to get it fettled," said grandma.

"It's in Richmond. Just the other side of the park."

"That's handy. Only a fifteen minutes walk away. I've just spent the last six months trying to get away from you. Now you come and live almost next door. What's that all about?"

"Hilarious mum; and I thought you liked me."

After a few giggles, mum told grandma about the council house and how she would decorate it.

"I have to see it first. Make sure it's okay for us," said mum.

"I've got the boys with me; Alex has gone to Gwen's place."

"Do I hear wedding bells not too far away?" Asked grandma. "I need to buy a floppy hat."

"Wedding bells are a long way off, mum. It's likely to be a christening before a wedding. Not like years ago. Young 'uns nowadays. What's happening to the world?" Said mum.

"Don't know what the world's coming to love," said grandma.

"Are you alright mum?"

"To be honest, I'm not feeling a hundred percent. Feel a bit 'off it' today."

"You don't look well at all. Best sit down in the lounge. I'll make you a nice cuppa, eh?"

"That'll be champion, love. I think I've been doing a bit too much housework, you know."

"Have you taken all your tablets this morning, mum?"

"Yes. As regular as clockwork," said grandma in a quiet voice, finding it difficult to breathe.

Mum stepped into the kitchen as grandma Cooper put her feet up in the lounge. Glenn and I chased about on the huge, secluded grass lawn at the back. Mr. Grumpy twitched his net curtains, as usual, in the flat upstairs as he kept watch over the grounds, like a guard on sentry duty. The only item missing was the searchlights, from Stalag 17 and Mr. Hardcastle was the Commandant.

Mum continued the small talk from the kitchen.

"Alex has still got a veritable crush for that girlfriend, Gwen, you know. They've been together six months now. Looks serious, I can wager," said my mum.

She continued chatting to grandma between kitchen and lounge. A lot had happened over the past couple of weeks in mum's life, grandma couldn't get a word in edgeways. Mum expected a few simple replies, like 'Really?' or 'That's nice.' but the lounge remained quiet. Perhaps grandma had fallen asleep. Mum made the cup of tea, then shouted…….

"Mum…...?" "Mum…...?" She shouted from the kitchen.

She paused and listened for a few seconds. Only the ticking clock broke a serene silence on the mantelpiece. Either grandma Cooper had fallen asleep or…….

"Mum?…. Are you alright in there?" Mum paused again, but there was still a stony silence.

She dropped a plate on the floor and ran into the lounge, screaming for her mother. The trickle of a tear traced down her cheeks. Then the floodgates of emotion changed her eyes to a cascade of heavy, burning tears as she burst into the lounge. Only blurred images around the room could be seen. Every sound had stopped in an instance. It seemed that the world knew grandma had passed. Mum knew her world had juddered to a halt.

Grandma sat in her easy chair. Her head strained backwards with eyes transfixed to the ceiling light as though she had talked with celestial angels moments before. My mum plunged to her knees, her head draped across her mother's lap. She clasped her mother's hands. A slight chill settled on her arms. She stared at her mother's whitened complexion. Life had drained from her mother's face. Mum's heartbeat raced, her body tensed into a panic attack. For seconds, mum could not breathe, her throat parched. Mum snapped out of her gaze with a knee jerk reality.

"Mum, noooooo...!. Please mum...... This can't be happening. Hey mum, talk to me, please .... I can't let you go. You can't leave me now. You can't go so soon. You can't leave me alone.

"There's no-one else to love me anymore. Please mum, say something to me."

Mum sobbed for an eternity. Her heartbroken apart. Just when great news had arrived from the Housing Department, grandma's passing came like a 'bolt out of the blue.' She screamed at the top of her voice in a frenzy of grief. She put her arms around grandma's shoulders and squeezed her.

"I can't let you go mum. Not now. I need you more than ever. Don't leave me alone."

Mum continued her outpourings for quite a while. Losing her sweet, adorable mother, friend and companion now burdened her head, a kaleidoscope of worry, ready to explode with more pressure. Grandma had gone.

'*Why me?.... Why now?*'.... Flashed through mum's mind as she looked to the heavens.

Mum sobbed rivers of grief, wiped by her fingers. Grandma's lap became a pillow for her tilted head. Fifteen minutes passed by as desolate sobbing subsided to whimpering like a vulnerable pet, crying for its' lost mother. A quietness descended upon the room as though celestial angels had arrived. This was too soon. Hopelessness and defeat shrouded mum's head. The serene quietness, only interrupted by the constant slow ticking of the Napoleon clock. The pleasant chimes of Big Ben played as the clock sounded at midday. We chased the ball as carefree as the wind. Mr. Hardcastle looking on from his window upstairs.

We played a few minutes more in the radiant sunshine at grandma Cooper's house. Oblivious of events only twenty metres away, we needed refreshments. Glenn and I came in from playing on the extensive lawn at the back of grandma's house. We were to discover the awful tragedy of the demise of our favourite grandma. A rattle at the letterbox broke the stony silence. Mum dreaded yet another confrontation, following her recent loud screams. She was in no fit state, mental or physical, to rebuff any slanging match with Mr. Hardcastle, the nasty neighbour.

"Ruth. Thank God it's you."

"Whatever is the matter?" Screeched aunty Ruth, seeing my mum with a blotched face.

"I thought it was horrible Mr. Hardcastle," said uncle Jack.

"Is he is mouthing at you again? I'll give that old bugger a piece of my mind."

Uncle Jack took off his sports jacket and flat cap, ready for a contretemps with Mr. Hardcastle.

"I'll have a real go at that miserable bugger. He can't upset people in this way," said uncle Jack in a belligerent mood.

"No. It's….. mum," said my mum, her head buried on her shoulder, crying.

"There, there, 'sis. What's the matter? What's happened?"

Uncle Jack never stood backwards when there was trouble. He had been mum's mentor as she grew up through her teenage years. He stood his ground without compromise.

"No Jack. Wait! It's not Mr. Hardcastle's fault. It's mum. She's collapsed in the lounge."

"Evelyn. Tell me what's wrong with mum!"

Mum couldn't answer, overcome by tears that blurred her vision, clutching a wodge of tissues in both hands. Her shoulders juddered with each sob. Her breathing became erratic; words became mumbled and incoherent. Mum stooped forward and grabbed the door-jamb to steady her stumble.

"It's mum…. She's....She's dead," whimpered mum.

"Oh God. I can't believe it. We only saw her two days ago."

"She sat down and said she wasn't too well. I made her a cup of tea. I was talking to her for a few minutes, and……."

"Did she fall?"

"No. I made sure she sat on her comfortable easy chair. I was talking to her as I stepped through to the kitchen. Two minutes later, she must have had a stroke. She never screamed, shouted, or said a word. She was sat in her chair, then slumped back."

"Come on, love, take a rest. Jack will ring for an ambulance."
Mum sat in the kitchen, out of sight of grandma. Aunty Ruth consoled her, waiting for uncle Jack to return and the ambulance to arrive. Mum dropped her half-drunk cup of tea onto the floor without warning, splinters of china cascaded everywhere. The tiled floor became stained by splashes of tea that resembled a splash of paint. Though distressed, Aunty Ruth didn't appear as distraught as mum. Evelyn was grandma's natural daughter, aunty Ruth was not. Twelve years older, aunty Ruth coped better, because of her older years or not of the same bloodline.

"What about my boys, their meal and the rest of the family?"
Mum collapsed into paranoia. Aunty Ruth tried to bring her back from her state of shock.

"Calm yourself, Evelyn. The boys are alright. They're just coming in now," said aunty Ruth.

"They'll need feeding. What about school?"

"The boys are alright. It's Saturday today. There's no school."

"Don't worry. We'll take care of the boys for a while."

"Who are you? Go away. You're not taking my boys. They're mine. You can't have them. I gotta do the ironing and the shopping…...."

"Evelyn, come on, love. You're in a bit of shock. Can you hear me? It's Ruth. Your sister..... remember?"

"I told you. Go away. I don't even like you."
Aunty Ruth and uncle Jack tapped mum's arm, gently at first, then a little firmer. They tried to shake her from her trance. Her mind had wandered into delirium and hysteria. There had been suggestions that mum wavered closer to a mental breakdown. The edge of the precipice became too close. Mr. Anderson from Social Services had mentioned it.

"It's my birthday tomorrow, are you coming to my party?" Said Ruth in childish garble.

Uncle Jack slapped mum across her face with the palm of his hand. Her eyes flashed wide open, and glared straight ahead, hypnotised. She shook her head, rubbed her cheek, and then her eyes came back into focus. A sharp rattle at the letterbox to broke her trance.

"What's happening?" Said mum, still smarting from her smack.

"Evelyn. You alright, sweetheart? You've just had a nasty turn. That's all, said aunty Ruth."

Mum broke down and wept like an abandoned child. Shock had numbed her senses like anaesthetic. A blurry dream had drifted by like a cloud.

"I just heard an ambulance. Was that someone at the front door?" Said Mum.

"Yes, love. It's the ambulance crew."

Mum blew a gasp of relief. The past ten minutes had been surreal, living in another person's mind. Dazed and confused, she looked around the kitchen. Her mum was out of sight, in the lounge where she had passed. Immune from the trauma, we still played outside on the lawn, shielded from the sight of grandma.

Mum finished her tea and recovered from her bout of paranoia, still upset. She was in a daze. She had been near to that point many times. The threat of losing us, and now losing her mother, pushed her to the brink of insanity.

"This way guys. Watch out for the grandchildren. They're running wild at the moment," said Jack, guiding the medics.

"How long ago did she fall?" Asked the medic.

"Half an hour, I guess. I hurried to the phone box and dialled 999 soon after we arrived."

The two ambulance crew stood on each side of grandma, one checked out the airways and the 'obs', the other asked history.

"Airways clear: No Respiration: No Pulse: No BP: Skin cold: No apparent bleeding out," said Medic One checking vitals.

"Did she fall, or stumble?" Said Medic Two.

"Sat calm one minute, then she collapsed. In an instance."

"Any medications?"

"She takes Amlodipine for blood pressure. Paracetamol when her bones ache."

"I'll call a locum doctor. He must examine Mrs. Cooper, to pronounce the causes, then complete the paperwork. It won't be long before he's here," said the ambulanceman.

"We'll move Mrs. Cooper into the bedroom for the doctor to make his examination. You can move around the house without sad reminders. The boys won't see her in there."

"Sorry we couldn't help in time," said the other medic.

The doctor arrived as requested. After his examination, he pronounced the cause of death as a stroke. He completed a medical report and stayed a few minutes to offer his sympathies.

"Very sad for everybody in the family."

"Thank you, doctor. Can my wife have any sedatives to calm her nerves?"

"Well. She's not my patient, but I can give her a placebo."

"Look, doctor. Placebos are for psychosomatic cases. She is ill, not mental," said uncle Jack firmly, indignant by the doctor's comment.

"She needs to contact her G.P. I can't help. I'd need to read her medical notes before I could even contemplate any medication," said the doctor. "There's no medication for sadness and grief. In my experience, mourning and grief are an important part of the healing process. Can anyone offer her a shoulder to cry on?"

"Thanks, doctor. You've been most helpful," said uncle Jack, loaded with sarcasm.

Aunty Ruth and uncle Jack helped to organise lunchtime snacks for us. We had played on, oblivious to the ordeal mum had seen. Even more agonising, our favourite grandma passed without us knowing. We came in for refreshments at one o'clock when we heard the ambulance sirens. Crisps, followed by a fizzy drink were our normal snack.

"Where's mum?" I asked.

"She's with your grandma in the bedroom. She'll only be a few minutes. Just rest a while. Your mum needs to talk to you. Hope you're not upsetting Mr. Hardcastle," said uncle Jack."

"Gotta try, uncle Jack," I said, in grandad's style of wit.

"Good. That's alright then," uncle Jack quipped.

Mum had crept into the bedroom. It devastated her to watch her mum in this way She needed solitude, some quiet moments alone with her mother. Grandma had kept her afloat through crisis after crisis, each one more immense and intense than the other. The room felt spirit-like and ghostly, even though grandma's body had expired a mere hour earlier. Blackout curtains had shielded bright mid-day sunlight and to prevent unsuspecting neighbours glimpsing through the window. Curtains were closed as a mark of respect and so we could not notice grandma lying in the bedroom.

Mum stepped towards her mother. Her body laid flat on her back, still and lifeless, her head peered at the ceiling. She reached out her left hand to clasp her mother's. Warmth contrasting with coldness, even in the early afternoon of a summer's day. Her right hand palmed her mother's forehead and cheeks, child-like, and felt the clammy coolness of her skin. Sat on the bed, she wrapped her arm around her in a warm embrace. Her mother's face positioned upwards, seemed younger as the wrinkles shrank with dehydration.

Her face was gaunt. She was now at peace.

In a flat, soft monotone voice, she spoke to grandma……

"With your hands held in mine, when I was a baby girl, what always made me so proud was being YOUR baby, and you were MY mum. Even though I grew up with stepsisters, your love radiated across everyone like sunbeams. You picked me up when I fell, when I grazed my knee, you kissed it to make it better. You always made me proud you were MY mum. I never meant you to share my burdens, but you were always there for me, unselfish, supporting me and guiding me. You were a rock in my life. I've made my mistakes over the years, but you never chastised me. You only gave me your love, your smile, your affection;

unconditional. You gave me part of you, the most important part, your heart. Now you must share your soul again with my dad, your husband. Without him, neither of us would have been here today. I'll remember you until my dying day. I can't find the right words to say, except these that I kept from an old book of poetry."

Mum paused to look through her old poetry book. As she read through poignant poems, a tear hesitated in her eye. She wanted to say a poem out loud, but her throat was dry and coarse. The hidden anguish of grief that few people ever saw. She read a poem of inner thoughts, then reached the ultimate line she needed to recite to her mother. Tearful eyes overflowed down mum's reddened face. Though she choked with a lump in her throat, mum summoned an inner strength to say a poignant message to her beloved mother. She wept as she spoke:

'Death leaves a heartache no one can heal, love leaves a memory no one can steal.'

Mum left the bedroom with puffy eyes and choked with heartache. She now needed to freshen up and compose herself ahead of the arduous task of talking to us about what had happened. She rounded us up to tell us the harrowing news of our grandma's passing. We nursed doleful eyes as mum reached out with a hug.

"Now we're all here, we can say a prayer for grandma together. Let's close our eyes and think of the happy memories she shared with us. We can thank her for all the enjoyable things she has done for us so many times. Even though grandma has passed, she has enriched all our lives and we should be so thankful she cared. We will all love her and miss her forever."

"Why do people have to die mum?" Asked Glenn.

"Do you remember your grandad used to say, dying is part of living? We pay our respects by saying prayers and we can reflect on our lives. We all grieve in our own ways. Your grandma and grandad were glad they were in your life because we were in theirs."

"We'll miss grandma," said Glenn. His face buried into her blanket to cover his anguish.

"I know, sweetheart. Let's say a special prayer for her. Your love will make her happy."

"Will we see grandma Cooper again, mum," asked David, my youngest brother. Mum gave him a huge cuddle and a kiss on his forehead.

"She's gone to be with grandad Cooper now, love. They've both gone to heaven. But they'll both be watching over us all now, to keep us all safe and happy."

As mum hugged David, my youngest brother, she wondered what it would have been like to huddle a daughter. Her first baby, a stillborn girl, would now be eighteen, a year older than Alex. Mum would have had the close emotional support she needed at this tragic moment. Though her four boys were by her side, we could never give the same support that a daughter could give. Grandad Cooper died in 1964, now in 1966, grandma was ascending to the heavens to be with him. I was content he would no longer be alone. Mum's heartaches had only just begun as each part of her life crumbled. An enormous part of mum's life had gone, vanished into a celestial world.

Chapter 18

A few days after grandma Cooper's funeral, mum could no longer persevere with her stomach pains. Every day she collapsed, clutching her stomach. For a few years, she hoped doses of Milk of Magnesia would subdue her stomach problems. Liquid chalk is how she described it. Violent pains came at random moments, and now more often. Now surfacing daily, another visit to the GP became an urgent necessity.

"Have you had these pains for some time, Mrs. Dalton?" Asked the doctor.

"A few years, I guess. I thought the pain would just go away."

"Pain and inflammation is the body's way of telling you there's something wrong."

"I don't have time to be ill. I just need a tablet."

"Perhaps you may need more than just a tablet, Mrs. Dalton."

"Why? What's wrong?"

"I think you may have an ulcer. Perhaps the problem is serious enough to need more than tablets."

"I don't understand about ulcers. I thought Magnesia took stomach cramps away."

"They're not stomach cramps, Mrs. Dalton; ulcers can be more serious than that, more-so if they're not treated. The medicine won't cure it. It just helps reduce the symptoms, keeps the flare-ups at bay. Paracetamol can reduce the pain."

"We need more blood tests, Mrs. Dalton," continued the doctor in his summation. "The results won't be back for two weeks."

Grandma had passed. A heavier burden now rested on mum's weary shoulders. Her only avenue of support had disappeared.

Mum's health became increasingly frail. Stomach convulsions brought her to her knees to the point of severe worry. Her screams of agony warranted serious investigation. For an accurate prognosis, the GP urgently required results from the hospital.

"If it is an ulcer, it may need surgery. They are always painful; as you've realised, it can flare up at random. All your symptoms lead me to believe there's a strong possibility that it could be a peptic ulcer AND a duodenal ulcer. Two ulcers in distinct parts of the stomach could be the reason you're in so much pain. The hospital will give you a thorough examination. I'll prescribe you some painkillers for the time being. Please continue taking the Milk of Magnesia, it will help to relieve the symptoms."

"So tablets and Magnesia might do the trick, eh?" Said mum.

"Can't say that at the moment. I'll arrange a hospital appointment for you. You will need a thorough examination, so we can identify if there are more serious issues. At least the prescription I'm giving you will ease the discomfort in the short-term. You need to put your feet up and rest more; your body is worn out, Mrs. Dalton. You're getting warning signs on a regular basis now. See me in two weeks. I will have your blood test results by then."

Mum glared as though he was on a different planet. Mum was too ill to rest. In an ideal world, she needed someone to help with all the household chores. In reality, she had little choice but to do housework for someone else. Ulcers still plagued mum's strength and sapped her energy. The journey to the junior school each day to see David and Glenn consumed much of her time. It was only a five-mile journey, but getting ready and waiting for buses seemed to be a major drain on mum. Especially when it was followed by a lengthy trek to and from school. Whatever her condition was, it was taking its' toll on her strength. Throughout the day, she was at a serious risk of convulsions. David and Glenn now lived with grandma Greaves, four miles away. The trek became a challenge in both directions. The sight of her two boys running towards the school gates became sufficient reward for her hour-long trek.

"My word! It's so good to see you. I missed you so much."

"Missed you too mum," said David, full of excitement.

"What have you been up to today?"

"I painted you a picture, mum."

David presented mum with a lovely picture of her with straight, straw hair, a red triangular-shaped blouse, a blue triangular shaped skirt; all complemented by orange pointed shoes. A masterpiece of modern art, worth a million pounds, needed to hang on the wall of our next home. She didn't show it, but a piercing dagger plunged deep into her heart. The straw hair that David had painted epitomised 'the other woman,' Roxy. Though it appeared to be an innocent painting, it raised other questions. The image opened a sore wound for mum. No matter where she went, reminders of Roxy seemed to appear everywhere.

Memories of places she had visited with dad came flooding back, but now she envisaged her by his side. Simply seeing a blonde woman, walking down the street, became a good enough reason to cross the road. At the hospital, mum had seen Roxy in smart clothes, with youthful looks and curves in the right places. This contrasted with mum's outdated, worn clothing, middle-aged looks, and curves that drooped in the wrong direction. David's painting also raised the question, 'Could he have seen blonde haired Roxy?' without mum knowing. Maybe a clandestine meeting with Roxy portrayed as an innocent bystander. Maybe worst of all, had he taken the boys out with Roxy on a day's outing somewhere? Either way, it seemed innocuous. An unintentional reminder of an unwanted image. A hint of paranoia surfaced for a fleeting moment.

A bolt from the blue left mum with another heart-rending dilemma. Since the eviction from the Coal Board house, I stayed with my much older cousin Tony. His house was only two streets away from where mum was staying in the village of Beighton. This allowed me to meet up with mum more often. During school terms, we met every day when she met David and Glenn from school. Afterwards, we took the same bus back to our cousin's houses.

"We're moving house soon," came the bombshell from cousin Tony. He had called in to visit his mother, aunty Ruth. During some of the day, mum spent time with her, rather than being isolated within the four walls of her cousin's house.

"Really?" Said mum, devastated by the implications.

"Yep, we're moving to Nottingham. The company has offered me the manager's job at their Midlands depot. It's a job I can't refuse. I get transferred in about a month."

"What about Jeff?"

"Well. We did only agree for Jeff to stay for a few weeks."

"There's nowhere he can go. We have exhausted all the options. To be honest, so am I."

Mum could only envisage one plan of action. She rang dad to come over for a chat.

"I'm at a total loss. There's nobody on my side of the family that can help. I knew that a month ago when we had to organise everybody's accommodation."

"Okay. I'll have a chat with my mother. There's still a spare bedroom there. As long as Social Services don't find out, we'll be alright."

"That's risky; your mother's in her eighties. I don't think she finds it too easy with David and Glenn as it is, let alone having to look after Jeff."

"No other option. We can only ask."

The following day, dad called in to see his mother, grandma Greaves.

"How's it going mum? Coping alright?"

"Just coping is a better way of putting it. Not as nimble now."

"Just wondered if you could do me a favour, mum?"

"I don't have any spare money if that's what you're asking."

"Not money; more difficult than that. Could you have Jeff just for a few weeks? Tony, his cousin, is moving house, so Jeff has nowhere else to go. Jeff is nearly 16; he can look after himself. More or less, he just needs a roof over his head. Besides, an extra pair of hands can help with David and Glenn. He'll be a help. Not a hindrance."

"A tough ask, isn't it? I can only JUST manage the other two boys, Jeff makes three. Let me think about it. I'll let you know tomorrow."

Grandma Greaves had a spare bedroom, so it was possible to provide me with a room. But could she cope with the extra effort, and more to the point, would she agree to it? A few days later, dad knocked on the door with trepidation.

"Hello Ma'. Are you alright?" Said dad to grandma Greaves.

"Strange isn't it? I don't see you for weeks on end, then when you want favours, you're like a bee around a honey pot," said grandma with annoyance.

"I'm busy ma'. I have to go to work. Any thoughts about taking care of the boys?"

"Look. I'll agree with it on two conditions. One; it's only for three months, and two; that mother of theirs doesn't show her face here."

"Thanks, ma'. You've just saved a whole load of problems. We can breathe much easier now."

"I'm not doing it for her or her boys. I'm doing it for you. Do you understand?"

I dreaded the prospect of living at grandma Greaves' house. None of us wanted to be there, but at least I would be with my brothers, and my secondary school was within walking distance. As I was the elder brother, I felt I had a degree of responsibility towards them, as a brother and on mum's behalf. The move would be fairly straightforward. I only needed to pack a few clothes; a few shirts for school, underwear, socks, and two pairs of trousers; the entirety of my wardrobe. Add half a dozen school books in a box and that was it. Done.

The atmosphere at grandma Greaves' house was as strained as expected. It felt as though we had been interned, like in a prison, with strict Victorian rules of governance. I was mature enough to be diplomatic, as and when required. That meant most of the time. David and Glenn, being much younger, suffered emotional upheaval. Mum met them each day at the school gates but was for a mere two hours at best. I joined them for an hour, as my school was further along the village. At the end of the week, I used to post mum a letter from us all, to keep her up to date with how we were. I had virtually become a diarist. I described how we all missed her and loved her so much. I said we all understood the situation about the Coal Board evicting us because dad had left his job at the coal mine. I mentioned how we were all okay, but the room we slept in was damp and noisy as it fronted the busy Rotherham road. This became our sleeping arrangement for six months, three in a bed. We didn't have a choice; beggars couldn't be choosers.

During one quiet evening as I lay on the bed and gazed upwards to the ceiling, thinking of what to say, I noticed an army of the tiniest red brick spiders I had ever seen. Strangely, they seemed cute, emanating from a crack in the ceiling, scurrying round in circles. I told mum about them, not as a complaint, just out of interest. I sealed the envelope and placed it in my sock drawer, ready to post. When I returned from school, grandma stood in the bedroom doorway, hands-on-hips. Her face was like thunder, her eyes narrowed with fury.

"And what is this?" She asked in a stern voice, waving the opened letter in my face.

My heart sank to new depths. Grandma was not pleased to find my letter. I listened to her rant about us being ungrateful, but at the age of sixteen, it seemed like character assassination.

"It's just a letter to my mum, grandma," I said, feeling I had let my brothers down about unintended revelations to my mum.

"You ungrateful child. Wait till I tell your dad about this."

She made me feel worthless. I had a feeling there could be trouble brewing because of my letter. She harboured grudges with a passion. The matter was not finished. In her eighties, she needed peace and quiet in her life, not mischievous boys under her feet, playing on the carpet or fighting as boys do. After three months of looking after us, the strain on grandma showed. She had become more irritable than before, more tetchy and her comments more caustic. I wondered if my unsent letter to mum was the final straw for our unwelcome stay there.

Evenings created the largest void as mum's absence deprived them of her love, hugs and cuddles. Often, they whimpered themselves to sleep; sometimes their cries were heartbreaking. Though mum stayed four miles away, the bus journey was of epic proportions, with a lengthy walk to the bus stop at either end. Mum persevered even though she became racked with pain, starved of money, and because of that, starved of food.

Three months later, whilst staying at her cousin Tony's house, a surprise envelope arrived. Franked with the caption 'Sheffield Corporation Housing Department,' it could only be marvellous news. Every scrap of awful news had already played itself out.

'Dear Mrs. Dalton. We are pleased to be able to offer you a three-bedroomed house in the Richmond District of Sheffield. The existing tenant has vacated the property. It will be available to view in seven days from today's date. Please attend the Housing Department offices with this letter and we will hand over a set of keys for you. The exact address of the vacated property will be given on your arrival. You can reject this offer.'

Mum dashed round to the next street to tell aunty Ruth the good news. She waved the letter as though she had won the pools.

"I honestly can't believe it 'sis. I got a house. After all this time. I got a bloody council house."

The news overwhelmed mum. It was the first morsel of good news in years. For once she cried tears of joy; the universe was a better place, after all. Her dreams had finally come true. After six hard months of drudgery and turmoil, tears and heartache, mum could bring us all together, under one roof again.

"That's fantastic love. What a lovely surprise. I'll get Jack to take you around in the car to let all the family know," said aunty Ruth, as excited as mum.

"It would certainly help. It's really difficult waiting for buses in the rain," said mum.

"Tell you what, love. We can nip up to the Primary School so you can see David and Glenn. I'll give them a run in the car. They'll love that," said uncle Jack.

"I do appreciate everything you've done for me Jack," said mum, her eyes watered.

Uncle Jack became a diamond again the following week. He drove mum and aunty Ruth to the Housing Department, picked up the keys, and then hastened to see mum's new council house. Council workmen had spent the week clearing rubbish and fumigating each room as part of their change-over policy. A skip full of trash blocked the front-drive. Brown goods, which used to be white goods, half-filled the skip. Old clothes and soggy mattresses filled the rest. With the help of aunty Ruth and uncle Jack, mum decided to take the council house.

The following day, mum was keen to tell Social Services her wonderful news. Having her own house meant we were no longer at risk of being taken into care. All that remained was for her to prove she could afford to live at the property and take care of us.

"Good Morning Mr. Anderson," said mum in a cheery mood.

"Looks as though the cat's got the cream," said Mr. Anderson in his soft Edinburgh accent. Mum jingled her set of keys before his eyes, as he glanced above his spectacles.

"I got something better than the cat's cream. I got its' whiskers. Look! I got the keys to my own house. Lucky number seven." Mum couldn't conceal her excitement, like winning the pools.

"Well, ma' dear. That's fantastic for you. It'll be wonderful to get the wee boys all together. I'm really pleased. Well done."

"I'll make arrangements with Mrs. Walker for us to visit the property. Make sure it meets the guidelines of the Child Welfare Department."

"It needs a bit doing to it, Mr. Anderson. A lick of paint and the gloss-work needs a coat. Me, the boys and the family will muck in to get it up to scratch."

"I'm sure you will. It's just a formality we have to do; to make sure the bairns will be alright, then sign off the papers."

Mum settled into her new home, number 7 Mason Avenue, quite well. Built-in the 1920's. It was larger than the Coal Board house and built of brick rather than concrete. There was no central heating, but a decent gas fire threw out enough heat. She still suffered from niggling abdominal pains, but painkillers and Magnesia helped. Blood tests proved inconclusive, but numbers showed there could be something wrong. With no other evidence, surgery became impractical. Milk of Magnesia became the norm to treat ulcers in the 1960's. Most diagnoses were virtually guesswork based on experience. They offered open surgery only when all other treatments had failed.

The euphoria of gaining a home soon became mooted and short-lived. Less than three months after moving into the council house, mum's life took another nose-dive when she became shaken to the core. Against the backdrop of destitution, chronic ill health, and personal tragedies, mum received a stunning shock. An official-looking letter arrived like a bombshell. The letter heading seemed ominous. The contents were blunt as mum opened it to read the exasperating news.

'Knox, Marwick and Jones, Solicitors.'

'Our client, Mr. Edward Dalton, has requested we commence divorce proceedings by way of an application for a Decree Nisi. Such proceedings are straightforward, providing all parties agree to the annulment of the marriage. Our client cites the reason as being the irretrievable breakdown of the marriage."

Chapter 19

Mum, completely taken aback and outraged by the letter, staggered to the armchair. She buried her head in her hands; her face registered disbelief as she stared into the orange glow of the gas fire. They had never discussed divorce. She always hoped one day, dad would come back home. It riled her even more as it did not bother him to tell her face-to-face. A cold-hearted solicitor's letter seemed as cowardly as anything he had stooped to before. She clutched her stomach in excruciating pain and edged towards the medicine cupboard. She looked long and hard at the painkillers in her hand. With pain so unbearable, she passed out and collapsed to the floor.

I arrived from school without the normal enormous hug and a fuss to greet me. Neither was Glenn and David at home; they would have been building something with Lego or playing with Action Man figures. This time, the living room seemed to have a bizarre quietness. The door was still locked, suggesting mum was still out of the house picking up my younger brothers from school. This was unusual as they should have arrived a half hour before me. I opened the door with my own key, the eerie quietness echoed my feet through the hallway. Though it seemed jarred, I managed to heave the lounge door open with the brute force of my shoulder.

Spread-eagled across the floor, mum obstructed the door. She lay motionless, but I noticed lethargic breathing. Her eyes were open but seemed transfixed with a drawn face. She clutched a bottle of paracetamol in her hand with an unscrewed top. Strewn across the floor where she lay were several of the tablets. I could only fear the worst.

"Mum. What's the matter? What have you done?" She didn't answer and stared into the hypnotic glow and warmth of the gas fire. Her eyes glazed in a trance without a blink, her face was passive and unresponsive.

"Mum. Wake up. What have you done? Speak to me."

"Aw, mum. Please tell me you haven't. Please."

With no response, mum seemed paralysed or comatose. Her frightening stare was as though she was in shock from a stab wound. I couldn't be sure whether she had taken an overdose. I read the letter she gripped and realised this could well be a step too far. She had already come close to a nervous and mental breakdown as her life spiralled out of control. Now, her body might spiral out of control, irretrievable from whatever she had done. The nearest telephone box was half a mile away. I couldn't leave in case mum needed me, realising someone was by her side. Mum breathed slowly, as I waited for my younger brothers to arrive from school. Glenn, aged ten, was old enough to walk home without mum, but David could be distraught, seeing mum laid on the floor.

"Mum wake up. Please mum. Don't go to sleep," I kept repeating.

Glenn, upset, burst through the door with David, who was crying.

"Mum, where are you? Why weren't you at the gates to pick us up from school? Shouted Glenn from the hallway. Aunty Ruth and uncle Jack walked in behind.

Unbeknown to me, the school had contacted aunty Ruth, concerned no-one had met David and Glenn at the school gates. After fifteen minutes of waiting, the Headmistress telephoned her. Uncle Jack and aunty Ruth dashed to pick them up from her office. No-one knew the reason for mum's delay. At least my brothers were safe.

"Mum, why weren't you there?" Screamed David from the hall.

"Glenn, hold David for a minute. Don't let him come through."

"Why, what's the matter? Where's mum?" Shouted Glenn.

"Just do it! Keep him back! I yelled again.

David wrestled to free himself from Glenn. He shed bitter tears as if there was no tomorrow. The more he struggled, the louder he squealed. He was still unaware, as we all were, how mum was. Aunty Ruth came into de-fuse the outpouring, while Uncle Jack drove to the phone box to call an ambulance as I comforted mum. My only thought was to wake her. I knew if she didn't respond, mum might slip away.

"Don't let your mum sleep! Keep talking to her! I'll be back in five minutes," said uncle Jack.

Mum's condition tormented me as she lay on the faded carpet, her face was pale and gaunt. I felt that something like this would happen one day. Logic would say it would be when there's no-one around to help her. With no telephone and living on the outskirts of Sheffield, mum's health was precarious. I hoped to God, for her and us, that she would pull through.

Almost sixteen, I now realised that should anything happen to mum, my youngest two brothers had no-one else to care for them. That thought must have crossed mum's mind as her health had diminished out of all proportions. I looked with fear at mum's face; battle-weary of life itself, she seemed helpless. She had endured every crisis under the sun. I could understand why she had taken those tablets. Her life was a miserable existence of the gravest order. No human should ever have to suffer as mum had done. Her life was full of injustice, just like the welfare system.

As mum lay in front of me, seemingly helpless, I stroked her forehead and palmed her hair back. A deluge of emotion overwhelmed me. Trickles of love escaped my eyes. Each droplet a prayer to God that he alone could prevent angels from taking mum from our lives.

"Don't leave us now, mum. You're too young to go. You're only forty-two. Angels can't take you from us now. We need you; more than ever. We love you, mum; always will. Come on, mum, talk to me. It's Jeff. Uncle Jack and aunty Ruth are here. There's an ambulance on the way." I continued, louder and louder, over and over again. I shook her shoulders and slapped the back of her hands; but still with no response. Uncle Jack returned; we both continued talking to mum until the ambulance arrived a short while later from Sheffield.

"Has your mum taken any of these tablets?" Asked medic one.

"Don't know. I came in from school about a half-hour ago and found mum on the floor like this. A bottle of tablets was in her hand with the top open."

"Has she taken any other medicines or tablets?"

"Sorry. I don't know."

"Her numbers seem to be almost normal. Her blood pressure is low; so we'll take her to A&E for a check-up," said Medic 2.

David and Glenn, initially distraught and panic-stricken, calmed from their trauma, as aunty Ruth cuddled them. Aunty Ruth set about cooking beans on toast for us as we had only just arrived from school.

"Look, Jeff. We're going to see how your mum is. You're almost sixteen now, so you'll need to take care of your brothers for an hour or two until we get back. Okay? Make sure you don't go out until we get back, okay? Hold the fort, yeah? We'll get back as soon as we can; we will stay at your house tonight. Then we'll know more about your mum," said aunty Ruth.

The following day, uncle Jack and aunty Ruth took David and Glenn to school, then went on to the hospital. By the time uncle Jack and aunty Ruth arrived at the hospital, staff had transferred mum to a recovery ward. Sat upright, she had just finished a slice of toast and sipped a cup of strong tea. She seemed to be well on the mend, rather than recovering from an overdose.

"So what's this all about then, sis?" Said aunty Ruth, her forehead frowned and anxious.

"Nothing really. I know I had a headache, went to get some painkillers, next thing I knew, I was in hospital."

"You are anaemic and you're not eating well," said aunty Ruth.

"Are the boys alright? I've been worried about them."

"Everybody's fine. We stayed over last night and made sure they were all fed and sorted. We dropped them at school before we came today." said aunty Ruth.

"So what on earth's happened?" Said uncle Jack.

"I'm fine. No need to panic. Did you read the letter, Ruth?"

"What letter?"

"It must have fallen on the floor at home; From that bas**rd's solicitor. He wants a divorce."

A nurse popped her head through the door.

"Mrs. Dalton. You're alright to leave if you wish. All your numbers are alright apart from the iron. You're anaemic. You need to take more iron tablets," said the nurse.

"How come you took an overdose? Because of the letter?"

"I didn't overdose. In fact, I didn't take any tablets. I must have gone into some kind of shock, then fainted after I read the letter. Next thing, I was in hospital. Obviously, they found nothing wrong. I didn't have time to take painkilling tablets for my ulcer. I managed to get to the tablets, then I was out."

"The nurse says you're okay to be discharged, Evelyn. We'll give you a lift home as we're already here. We'll stay until the kids come out of school. I'll pick them up," said uncle Jack.

Just after lunch, mum, aunty Ruth, and uncle Jack arrived back at our house. Aunty Ruth stayed with mum, to make sure she was well enough to take care of us again. Uncle Jack collected David and Glenn from school, then aunty Ruth prepared a meal for us all. Mum's episode turned out to be a brief scare, but that only served notice of what could happen with mum's health.

"Great to see you mum. Love you millions," said Glenn as part of a huge squeeze.

"Love you mum. I thought you were leaving us," wept David.

"Hey. How could I leave my adorable sons, eh? Come on, give me a special hug. Show me how much you love me. I just had a funny turn, that's all. Nothing for you to worry about."

Over the next few months, we got back to what we could call a normal life. A normal life for mum was of purgatory, destitution, and ill health. For me, her stomach problems were not going away anytime soon. Her GP still awaited results from the hospital following a thorough examination. Only then, could I feel at ease with mum's well-being. Her serious health issues could have a devastating impact on us all. She vowed we would never go into a children's home.

The solicitor's letter prompted mum to tell us all about it. She had ignored subsequent letters from that date until she received a letter marked: '*Urgent*' and required mum's signature as proof of delivery. As she opened it, it was a repeat of earlier letters they had sent, but with stronger wording. Mum decided now was the time to give her view of the situation with dad. Mum waited for a quiet moment when David and Glenn were happily building a Lego construction in their bedroom.

"I need to have a chat with you, Jeff. It's best if I only tell you and Alex about the letter. I need to know how you feel about your dad."

Alex wasn't around, so mum confided in me alone.

"Sometimes mums and dads drift apart for different reasons. Sometimes they can talk about problems and maybe get them sorted out. You know, for a few years, you haven't seen your dad because he lives at another house. He met somebody else and he says he's happy. But he just didn't want to come back and live with us again."

"Does he still love us?" I said.

"Of course he does. It's just that he's become busy and can't see us very much. Sometimes, it becomes a bit more serious and they get a divorce. That's like living apart but making it legal in a court. Dad's solicitor has sent me a letter saying he wants a divorce. How do you all feel about that?" Said mum.

"Divorce him mum. As simple as that. It might hurt you for me to say, but I'm being honest with you," I said, without any diplomacy.

Perhaps I should have been more compassionate. As much as we hated dad for leaving us abandoned, mum was devoted to him.

Mum sighed with disappointment. She gave me the impression she was trying to convince me her attitude and feelings towards dad was worthy of my support. I saw the situation in black and white, but mum was more forgiving. Her view was through rose-tinted spectacles, clouded by misplaced love and devotion.

"I love your dad very much, I don't want us to finish. We've been married for a lot of years, he might decide to come back."

The more that mum spoke, the less logical her reasoning seemed. I couldn't empathise with my own father. His solicitor's letters showed no remorse. He betrayed and abandoned us. Begging mum's forgiveness would have sounded better than demanding a divorce.

"It's not for me to say, but for your sake mum, let him go. You need to divorce him. He doesn't want to see us anymore," I said, without hesitation. "I know for a fact, Alex feels the same," I continued.

"I thought that's how you felt, but I can't help the way I feel. I need him in my life."

"If he wanted us, at least he would have come to see us. I don't understand how you can feel this way, after the way he has treated you. But we still love you mum; we all love you, with all our hearts."

Mum ignored the letter for the time being. As far as she was concerned, divorce wasn't part of her long-term aims and interests. The solicitor's letter showed that dad was determined to get a divorce sooner than later. It was another complication she could do without. She felt her strength had suffered from the horrendous traumas and the untimely bereavement of both her parents.

Chapter 20

A letter arrived the following day from Sheffield Hospital Gastro-Enterology Department, offering mum an appointment for the following month. Thunderstruck, they diagnosed her with gallstones that needed removal. Human biology was never my strongest subject at school, but it sounded dreadful; no wonder she was in so much pain. Mum knew from her constant convulsions, there was something serious. Mum had put off hospital appointments for far too long. With four boys in tow, she needed to be much healthier and certainly needed to be free from pain. There needed to be twenty-five hours in mum's day; she devoted no time for her own well-being; only ours. As mum said, she didn't have the time to be ill. She dreaded the worst-case scenarios with hospitalisation. She knew that whatever happened, it could have devastating consequences in her battle to keep us from being taken into care by Social Services. She feared more for our welfare, rather than her own. In her logical, but strange way, mum contemplated whether to attend the appointment. With grandma and grandad no longer at hand to offer support or guidance or support, aunty Ruth took on that mantle.

The day of the operation arrived with trepidation. We were all at school, apart from baby David who would take him with her to hospital. The knock at the door heralded uncle Jack's arrival. Aunty Ruth, the perennial organiser, helped mum pack some bare essentials. That's all mum had.

"Have you got the appointment card for the hospital, Evelyn?"

"Not sure whether I can do this," said mum, being faint-hearted.

"You need to do this, Evelyn; for you, and the boys."

"Should I take this bottle of Milk of Magnesia with me?"

"It's not helped too much for the past few years, has it? The hospital will give you any medications you need. Let's not delay any more; grab your bag. Jack's in the car waiting."

Within the hour, they arrived at the foreboding Northern General Hospital. The smell of clinical antiseptic wafted through the swing doors as if to fumigate everyone who arrived. The distinct aroma permeated the corridors and clung to clothing as cigarette smoke did in waiting rooms. Mum appeared more pale than ever. Her forehead wrinkled a frown. Her warm smile had vanished to become an expression of hope rather than confidence. People scuttled about, a mix of hospital staff and visitors. Patients hobbled about on wooden crutches with bandaged ailments. As each step edged nearer to Ward 20, it raised mum's palpitations and heart rate, multiplied as the reception desk came into view.

"Here we are," said aunty Ruth, concerned about mum's fears.

"I'm scared, Ruth. I can't help but think about what they're going to do. They're going to cut me open. It's so frightening."

"Listen. There's no need to worry. A nurse will give you a sedative to calm your nerves, help you relax. Don't worry about your boys. Jack and I are staying with them this week. You'll be fine. Doctors do this operation every day. It's a routine procedure for them."

Uncle Jack walked on to the Ward after parking his car. Mum had completed admin forms at reception, donned her gown, and sat in bed, waiting with apprehension for sedatives to work.

"Do you know what the diagnosis is yet?" Asked aunty Ruth.

"A lot of it is exploratory, but gallstone removal seems to be the most logical," said mum. "They won't know until the operation takes place. It seems all the time, doctors had been missing the actual cause of all the pain," continued mum.

"That will be Eddie, then?" Said Jack, with flippant humour.

"Hilarious," said aunty Ruth, mum couldn't help but smile.

Uncle Jack tried to make light of it all and laughed to himself.

"Jack, go for a walk if you can't be serious. My sister's in pain. More-so with you sat there."

Jack went for a walkabout. He never liked hospitals.

"The doctor reckons I've got gallstones," said mum, irritated it had taken so long to diagnose.

"That's quite simple nowadays. It is open surgery though," said aunty Ruth.

"Apparently, you only have to stay in the hospital for five days, then they transfer you to Fulwood Hospital, for two weeks convalescing."

"Quite nice out there at Fulwood Hospital. It's like a stately home with acres of grounds" said aunty Ruth with a wry smile.

"I've been told they've got the nicest doctors over there, you know," said mum.

"I've heard they have a lovely bedside manner. Know what I mean?" Said aunty Ruth with a wink and a broad grin.

They both giggled and teased each other about junior doctors and their own wishful thinking. Aunty Ruth tried to take mum's mind off the operation with light-hearted girly talk.

"You can't say that Ruth. Somebody might hear you."

"Swap places sis.' Doctors can feel my pulse any time."

"You're wicked, Ruth. What about Jack?"

"I don't think Jack would be too happy, would he? Especially if a doctor took his pulse," continued Ruth with innuendo.

"You are so common. Those doctors here are very polite."

"You mean they warm their hands when they check boobs."

They both laughed and changed the subject as Jack came through the swing doors.

"What's so funny then?" Said uncle Jack.

"She was just wondering which doctor she would have," said aunty Ruth.

They both smirked as the bell rang out to end visiting time. Chairs scuttled and screeched back.

"We'll come by tomorrow. Just to make sure you're okay."

"The operation is at about two-thirty today. I suppose I will sleep most of the rest of today."

"Let me know which doctor you had, I might book myself in, if he's good," Aunty Ruth winked, and turned to the door.

The operation to remove gallstones went ahead as planned with conventional open surgery. Mum was back on the ward an hour later. She felt groggy from the anaesthetic and drifted in and out of sleep a few times. Eldest brother Alex and I arrived for the evening visiting time.

"How you feeling mum?" I said.

"Tired. I'm not in pain at the moment. I'm filled up with drugs to keep me comfortable."

Idle chit-chat continued to the end of visiting time. Mum was drowsy; her speech slurred in between dropping off to sleep. She had been through a horrendous time. Even in 1969, gallstone removal required open surgery. A straightforward procedure at the time, but recovery tended to take several weeks with complete rest. The doctor's morning rounds began.

"Good morning, Mrs. Dalton. How are you feeling today? A little better, we hope," said the doctor on his morning rounds.

"Comfortable thank you. How did the operation go?"

"We carried out the procedure and found several gallstones. I'm happy to say we have removed them all satisfactorily. All being well, you should be able to have a speedy recovery. We're going to transfer you to Fulwood Hospital in a few days."

For the next three weeks, uncle Jack concentrated his efforts on collecting my brothers from school, then journeying to and from the hospital at visiting times. Aunty Ruth took on the role grandma Cooper used to do, taking care of us at home, then feed us and complete household choirs. Uncle Jack took David and Glenn to school and picked them up later in his gleaming Ford Capri. Dad no longer visited us, probably unable to cope with meeting mum's side of the family or unable to get away from his 'bit on the side.' To us, he became a lost cause, ostracised, and an outcast of the family circle. Now, it appeared the door had been closed by dad's antics of abandonment and desertion, especially with the impasse caused by his expectation and request for a divorce.

Mum continued her recovery following the removal of several gallstones. By day five, she became strong enough to be transferred, with care, to Fulwood Hospital, in the leafy suburbs of south Sheffield. A specialist convalescent unit, it resembled a modern-day private clinic with state-of-the-art facilities in each of the individual private rooms. Set in acres of ancestral grounds, it oozed peace and tranquillity. Looking through magnificent Edwardian windows resembled looking at a painting by John Constable. A week's recovery at Fulwood enabled a speedier recovery than normal; both physical and mental. Two weeks of top-quality hospitality went by way too fast.

"Ready love? Your carriage awaits," said the jovial driver.

"Yes thank you," said mum, pampered to high heaven for the first time in her life.

"Which residence would you prefer to visit today ma'am? Sandringham m'lady?"

"The Co-op will do. I need some fags," mum continued the banter. Fifteen minutes later, leafy Fulwood merged into Millhouses Park, then on towards home, Richmond.

"Here we are, love. Home sweet home," said the driver. David and Glenn raced up the garden path to hug mum.

"Hold on, sweetheart. I can't lift you up," said mum, fending off a high rugby tackle.

"Love you mum. Great to have you back," said David, eager for hugs and cuddles.

"Please don't squeeze me though love. My tummy's sensitive."

"It's fab' to have you back mum," said Glenn heartbroken.

"It's good to be back, love."

"Cuppa tea sis'?" Shouted aunty Ruth, standing in the doorway.

"Sounds good to me sis'."

Home became really busy for a few weeks. Cousins and aunties popped in out, the vicar called in for a cup of tea and Dundee cake.

A few neighbours brought mum up to speed with the latest tit-bit of juicy gossip. Aunty Ruth and uncle Jack became a rock. Mum, weak from the operation, and devoid of the comfort of her own mother, relied heavily on her vaguely reluctant, step-sister.

A few weeks after her convalescence at Fulwood Hospital, her recovery, mum got back to household chores. The vacuum cleaner buzzed around as mum tidied the house. She hadn't *'bottomed it, from top to bottom,'* but good enough to stop neighbours gossiping. Within an instance, mum collapsed to the floor convulsed with excruciating pain.

The vacuum cleaner buzzed away as mum, racked and tortured with agony, convulsed into a fetal position. Her stomach felt as though somebody's fist had reached into her intestines and strangulated them into a ball of paper. She was alone, weeping and in agony. The pain, so horrendous and more violent than ever before, she could barely speak. The nearest telephone box stood half a mile away.

"Hello?...Mrs. Dalton?… Anyone at home?" A woman's voice yelled through the letterbox.

The District Nurse, Carla Benson, had arrived for her weekly visit to change mum's dressings. This ensured the scar tissue was healing well and feeling okay. She could hear the vacuum cleaner, but it didn't make any tell-tale noises of back and forth sweeping. The nurse had tapped the letterbox, but the cleaner had drowned out all other sounds. Nurse Benson walked round the back of the house to peer through a window. She tried the door handle; it was unlocked. She took a step into the kitchen via the unlocked back door. The vacuum cleaner still buzzed without a pause.

"Oh no! Oh my God!" Screamed the nurse, shocked to find mum on the floor.

She saw mum flat to the floor, curled up like a baby, trying to scream for help, with muted shouts. Nurse Benson scurried through the door, medical bag in hand.

"Mrs. Dalton. I'm Nurse Benson. Can you hear me?" Mum gave a vague nod and a whimpered noise of reply.

"Stay as calm as you can. Just stay still where you are. Don't move. I'll ask a neighbour to call an ambulance. They'll be here soon," said the nurse.

The nurse checked mum's airways and made sure there were no signs of bleeding. She grabbed a cushion and raised her head onto it. Nurse Benson continued to talk to mum and reassured her everything would be alright.

"Can you speak at all, Mrs. Dalton? What happened?"

Within minutes, the ambulance arrived. Mum couldn't speak as the agony intensified; she felt as though a fish-hook had gutted her. Her stomach felt cramped and screwed up tight like a paper ball. Two-tone sirens echoed the ambulance's arrival. The crew asked Nurse Benson for an update.

"So what's happened here Nurse Benson?" The medic squinted to read her name badge.

"This is Mrs. Dalton. Gallstones were removed six weeks ago. Anaemic. She appeared to be making a steady recovery; then today, I found her as she is now, clutching her stomach in obvious pain. I called on my rounds, carrying out a routine visit. I needed to change her dressing, but I didn't get to that point."

"Thank you, nurse," said Medic One. Let's check vitals now.

After a few minutes of checking mum's vital health numbers, the medic appeared concerned.

"Mrs. Dalton's skin feels tepid and clammy. I'm gonna give her oxygen to help her breathe easier. She is struggling, though," said Medic One.

"Have you administered anything, nurse? Do you know if she's taking anything?"

"No. I've not given her any medication all. I think she only takes paracetamol and Magnesia,"

"Glad about that. It would have taken her blood pressure even lower," said Medic Two.

"Scar tissue from the operation seems intact on the outside. Numbers are up and down. Maybe an infection, but we'll find out more at the hospital. She's had gallstones removed so that shouldn't be the problem," said Medic One.

"A & E will run important checks," said Medic Two, as he gathered his bag over his shoulder.

Paramedics reassured mum she was in expert hands and said not to worry. The ambulance scurried off to Northern General Hospital. Nurse Benson contacted aunty Ruth as the point of contact as David and Glenn needed collecting from school. Mum arrived at A & E within twenty minutes. Nurses gave her powerful pain relief as she was in so much pain. Doctors diagnosed her with inflammation of the gallbladder. Removal of any suspected gallstones would be of critical importance. The reopening of the original incisions, though essential, was fraught with danger. Scar tissue would not have healed. With immediate effect, they rushed mum to the Intensive Care Unit.

"Mr. McKenzie to ICU, ..." Announced the intercom.

Chapter 21

The ICU team clicked into rapid response mode adjacent to the Operating Theatre. Once stabilised, auxiliaries transferred mum to the Theatre Team. They monitored vital obs and conducted their normal preps and pre-op procedures. Mr. Giles administered anaesthetic and waited one minute for drugs to kick in deeper. Minutes later Mr. McKenzie arrived and double checked medical equipment was in place for the procedure.

"Mr. Giles?... Ready when you are," said Mr. McKenzie.

"Vital obs are acceptable. Deep anaesthetic effective. We're good to go." said Mr. Giles.

The Theatre Team team scurried about performing each of their critical roles. Mr. McKenzie read through mum's patient notes and conferred with his number two, Dr. Hammond. They had both treated mum a mere six weeks before. It appeared the over-riding issue was that of remedial work. A second attempt to investigate inflammation of the gallbladder. Mr. McKenzie addressed his team.

"Listen up, everyone. The procedure today is to investigate problems in the gallbladder and remove gallstones. There may be unknown complications, but we won't know until the procedure begins. Just to remind everyone, we all need to work with the utmost efficiency. Everyone has a job to do. Do it well. The Golden Hour is ticking."

Theatre became more tense as the critical time factor ticked by. Time wasn't on their side. Blood pressure remained low. Consultant, Mr. McKenzie looked once more to his anaesthetist Mr. Giles, who gave another nod of the head to proceed.

"Scalpel. Incision made. Swabs please," said Mr. McKenzie.

After twenty minutes of open surgery, they had removed several gallstones once more.

"Blood pressure falling. We need to hurry Mr. McKenzie," said Mr. Giles, anxious of the narrow window of opportunity. Mr. McKenzie removed more, but was irritated by his anaesthetist.

"We are okay, MR GILES," said Mr. McKenzie, sharply.

He continued the procedure for another ten minutes, tidying the gallbladder area and examined for bleed out.

"Blood pressure continues to fall. Pulse racing. We need more urgency, Mr. McKenzie."

"Slow bleed out. More packing please, Clips, quick but be careful. Swabs."

"Blood pressure critical. Still falling. Breathing erratic. STOP! Stop Mr. McKenzie! Stop!" Said Mr. Giles. "Time out, please! We need to address critical blood pressure levels."

As protocol demanded, the procedure paused because of the critical low blood pressure. Erratic breathing and a racing pulse all required stabilisation to prevent cardiac arrest. The anaesthetist's dilemma was that to allow the BP to track lower would help reduce bleeding. To increase BP would improve the vitals, but creates a serious problem with stemming blood loss.

"We are fine MR GILES. Please calm yourself!"

"Mr. McKenzie. We need to stabilise the patient; now. Whether you like it; or not."

"I hold you responsible for unnecessary delays."

"To keep the patient alive is my remit. Time is of the essence. I can't hold her stable for very much longer," said Mr. Giles.

"A successful operation is MY remit, Mr. Giles."

The atmosphere became almost intolerable. The Theatre Team and mum, fighting for survival, were in the centre of a war of wills. Eyebrows were raised in disbelief as the theatre team stared at each other and glared at Mr. McKenzie.

"I will submit a damning report, Mr. McKenzie. Consultant or not. Be warned!"

"Are you threatening me, Mr. Giles?" Asked Mr. McKenzie.

"There are eight witnesses, Mr. McKenzie' Swallow your pride before it's too late."

"I'll take that with the contempt you intended," said Mr. McKenzie as a sharp rebuke.

The two-minute pause allowed vital obs to stabilise. Mr. Giles glared at Mr. McKenzie. The surgical team stood back and paused. Mr. McKenzie stretched his back and closed his eyes to re-focus. He stared at his Theatre Team like a Regimental Sergeant Major.

"All organs seem to be functioning. She is anaemic. We may have serious bleed out issues," said Mr. McKenzie.

"We need to work hard to stem any haemorrhaging. Time is of critical importance, MR McKENZIE," said Mr. Giles, raising his concerns and his voice a decibel.

"Just do your job, Mr. Giles. I'll do mine. RIGHT?"

Conversations degenerated to emphatic stares and evil glances. The atmosphere became electric; tensions were at fever pitch.

"Patient vitals stabilised. Blood pressure low but manageable," said Mr. Giles, giving a cursory nod to Mr. McKenzie.

"Okay Dr. Hammond. Remove packing and clips. Complete the sutures," said Mr. McKenzie.

"Clean up the scarring, please. Apply wound dressings, but without pressure, nurse."

"Patient vital obs acceptable. Transfer to Recovery Room please," said the anaesthetist.

Following housekeeping and scrub down, Mr. McKenzie, Dr. Hammond, and Mr. Giles began a heated discussion of the procedure before writing their reports.

"Prognosis Mr. McKenzie?" Asked Dr. Hammond, his protege.

"A tough one. Inflammation of the gallbladder is evident. Gallstones found and removed."

"Blood pressure and pulse, remains low, Mr. McKenzie. There has been a significant amount of blood transfusion during the operation. Mrs. Dalton has lost a substantial amount of blood. I just hope that you have stemmed the bleed, Mr. McKenzie," said Mr. Giles.

"Follow up treatment?" Asked Dr. Hammond.

"There is heavy bleed out. I believe that was a major reason for a blood pressure drop. There has been a successful removal of several gallstones," said Mr. McKenzie.

"I'll make sure we monitor her hourly and prescribe sufficient sedation," said Mr. Giles.

"Overall. She is ill and getting weaker. If blood pressure deteriorates over the next few days; it's a problem, sh*t hits the fan. One thing is certain, opening her up again is not an option. Her body can't take it. Her numbers will be through the floor," said Mr. McKenzie, concerned but optimistic.

"Thank you, gentlemen."

As they walked away from the theatre, Mr. McKenzie chatted with his number two, Dr. Hammond. Mr. McKenzie and Mr. Giles brushed past each other without saying a word.

"Phew. That was tricky for a while," said Mr. McKenzie. "You did a superb job, Dr. Hammond. I'm glad you're in my team."

"Conclusion?" Asked Dr. Hammond.

"I'm concerned that her blood pressure continues to creep lower. I can't understand it. I checked everything; bleed out from the gallbladder wasn't present. We must keep a close watch on that. Write up the patient notes, Dr. Hammond. Make sure we give Mrs. Dalton sufficient morphine. We need her sedated for at least another twenty-four hours. See you tomorrow morning."

"I'll ensure the Blood Bank is on standby," said Dr. Hammond.

The next twenty-four hours were at a critical phase for mum's well-being. In relative terms, the operation had been a success. Mr. McKenzie removed gallstones and was adamant there was no blood seepage in that area. The overwhelming priority was to stem the apparent blood loss. Logic emanating from the vital obs meant that there was indeed haemorrhaging. No clues were apparent within the body. There were no scanners able to identify and locate the problem.

Without a precise location, the consultant had said mum was not strong enough for a third attempt, even if they could trace the errant blood loss. Mum's only hope was if they could stem the seepage to stabilise her blood pressure.

Relatives drifted in and out of ICU during the day. The hospital allowed this as it was an ICU unit. Alex and I arrived after work and chatted in the waiting room until a cousin ended their visit.

"What the heck is happening, bruv?" It's been twenty-four hours since the operation and still no improvement" Said Alex with anger. Patience had never been one of his virtues.

"Just relax. These surgeons are professional guys. They know what they're doing," I said.

"Do they? This McKenzie guy has had two attempts at a simple operation. Was it a trainee doctor the first time and it went wrong?" Shouted Alex, showing his aggravation.

There were no improvements to report. Time seemed to stand still. Everyone waited for snippets of news and signs of recovery.

"Mr. Dalton. Can I have a word?" Said the Sister.

We both stood and walked towards her. I hoped Alex wouldn't blow his top. We had waited in a disinfected waiting area without news. Each time the doors clattered open, it raised then dashed our hopes of any semblance of improvement.

"Is mum okay? Has she come round from the anaesthetic yet?"

"Your mum is very weak. The consultant has decided to keep her sedated for another twenty-four hours. You're welcome to see her, but she won't be coherent until tomorrow."

"Okay, we'll both go in just to say hello."

"Perhaps you would care to see him tomorrow afternoon after his rounds," said the Sister.

Though Alex was in a foul mood, his temper cooled somewhat when we saw mum. She looked pale, but at peace as sedatives kept her sleeping.

We stayed for a while and talked about mum's surgery. We both spoke to each other with affection, but we knew she couldn't hear. I tried to hold her hand, but that was difficult because of the cannula inserted in the back of her wrist. Any other embrace became prohibitive because of the wires and tubes attached to mum. An eerie, irritating noise bleeped, buzzed and pinged as monitors checked the numbers. Connected to mum's face was a scary-looking breathing mask. The rubber bladder expanded and contracted to deliver oxygen at a controlled rate. I watched mum sleep, motionless. Her struggle to breathe and survive seemed to epitomise her battle in the outside world. An everlasting image cut deep into my heart. I held her hand so as not to interfere with the cables and tubes, then kissed her pale cheek before we left. Before we left, she looked weak and vulnerable; we hoped the operation cured her problems.

In ICU, the following morning, the staff kept a close check of life support monitors. There had been no improvement in her vital numbers since the surgery. In fact, it was now worse, her breathing now became erratic. Throughout the day, blood pressure remained low. The visit to mum seemed to have become a vigil of hope and prayers. An irony set against the vigil of miner's wives, who's loved ones fought to survive a colliery disaster.

Twenty-four hours afterwards, a major development surfaced. Body temperature increased at the same time as blood pressure dropped further. Mr. McKenzie arrived to complete his post-op rounds for the second time. He must have harboured his own fears. He knew the only reason for the continuous slow drop of blood pressure was internal seepage. The paradox was that he was adamant the gentle oozing emanated from the gallbladder area. The mystifying conundrum was not knowing why, but not knowing where. No equipment was available that could identify the problem. The fear of the unknown became insoluble.

Alex and I suspected there had been a misdiagnosis harbouring on malpractice. The scanning technology was in its infancy and undeveloped. A few short years later, scanners would be a boon for medical science. This was of no consequence for mum. She was now within the jurisdiction of prayers and hope. Neither of which entered the annals of a medical handbook.

"Medical notes Sister?" Said Mr. McKenzie arrogantly snapping his fingers.

"Blood pressure remains low, breathing is erratic," said Sister.

"We thought haemorrhaging was a possibility because of low BP; that seems to be the case. Iron levels are pitiful; low because of anaemia. Mrs. Dalton has very jaundiced skin now. We'll keep her on a high dosage of morphine. We need constant monitoring until further notice."

"What about visitors?" Asked the Sister.

"We must limit visitors, Sister. We must keep her under heavy sedation with plenty of rest. Page me if needed."

Blood pressure continued to drop. Vital numbers remained below par. Her heart fading, her lungs became weaker. It appeared to be a dreadful dream. A nightmare of falling from the sky in slow motion into a bottomless pit, hoping never to enter oblivion.

"Sister. Is it okay to see mum? I'm Alex Dalton."

"A quick word, please."

"Medication has sedated your mother."

"Something wrong?"

"We have removed gallstones but your mum is anaemic."

"Gallstones again? How can that happen? Why weren't they all removed last time?" Said Alex, his voice raised enough for other patients to notice.

"Is there a problem, Sister?" Asked a passing duty doctor.

"This is Alex Dalton….. Mrs. Dalton's son."

"Look, Mr. Dalton, your mother is extremely ill. She is only twenty-four hours into recovery."

"No! You look, Doctor Hammond? There's something wrong here. I need to know the truth; now," Alex's temper raised another notch to anger; registering nine on the Richter scale.

"Calm down, Mr. Dalton……."

Alex pushed him back two steps. Doctor Hammond grabbed a screen to catch his fall. It ricocheted into the wall with a clatter, curtain rings whined like a zip wire.

"Don't tell me to bloody calm down……." yelled Alex.

"Get Security Sister."

"I can assure you, your mother is in excellent hands, Mr. Dalton," said Doctor Hammond as he wrestled to his feet.

"Assurances? I want bloody answers, not assurances. I want to speak to the consultant. Now."

Two Security Officers arrived and tried to restrain Alex. He shoved one of them to the floor, the other jumped on his back, forearm around his neck. Two orderlies grabbed Alex's arms. Four of them bustled him into a side-room. His legs lambasted out like a trapped tiger, to land where pain hurts the most. Plastic chairs jettisoned into the wall and bounced back.

"What's happening here?" Said Mr. McKenzie, the consultant.

"Mrs. Dalton's son. He's just arrived. He's not happy about progress," said Dr. Hammond.

"Security. Wait outside, please," said Mr. McKenzie. Mr. Dalton, calm down or Security WILL escort you from the hospital. Understand?"

"Who the heck are you?" Said Alex, his blood boiling.

"Mr. McKenzie, senior consultant. I performed the operation."

Alex glared at him and said nothing. He didn't know whether to lash a fist at his jaw or listen. His chest heaved with anger and frustration. Deep breaths snorted through his nose.

"McKenzie?" Shouted Alex with derision. His eyes narrowed with anger.

"Mr. McKenzie, if you don't mind."

"McKenzie. Get those notes. Tell me what's gone wrong?"

"I don't need to see notes. The operation went well."

"Doesn't look like it to me," said Alex, his heartbeat racing.

"She……?" Mr. McKenzie stalled and corrected himself.

"Mrs. Dalton had complications. We discovered gallstones, a blocked bile duct, and pervasive inflammation of the gallbladder. We suspected a knock-on effect to the pancreas and the liver. An understatement, your mother is very ill."

"You removed gallstones six weeks ago."

"Successfully, I may add."

"And then there's more?"

"It happens sometimes," said Mr. McKenzie.

"You didn't do the job right in the first place. Did you?"

"We found other complications."

"Caused by not taking all the gallstones out the first time?"

Alex jolted his chair back and stooped forward with aggression, then feigned a head butt. The two security guys dashed into the room. Mr. McKenzie expected another physical attack and raised both arms in defence. Security restrained Alex in a painful arm lock, almost to breaking point.

"Security. Get Mr. Dalton off the premises. I don't need this."

"You've not heard the end of this McKenzie. Be warned!"

"Hmmm. Neither have you."

An hour later, Alex had arrived home, his blood still simmering. He reached for a glass of water, then smashed it against the wall.

"So. How's your mum?" Said aunty Ruth, back at home looking after Glenn and David.

"There's something wrong aunty Ruth. I can feel it," said Alex.

"Meaning?"

"They seem defensive, evasive. They just spiel jargon out. Mum is in deep sedation. Asleep."

"Jeff's going in tonight. Isn't he?"

"Sure. On his own. Straight from work."

"She might be awake by tonight, love."

"She didn't look good. Stayed asleep all the time I was there. She was unconscious."

"Early days yet. She might be up and about soon."

I arrived at the hospital for the evening visit. Her room quiet and dimly lit, only the monitors made a sound to prove mum was alive. I looked at the patient notes, but numbers remained virtually the same as the day before. A graph of blood pressure showed a gradual downward slope.

"Mum. It's me, Jeff. Come to see you. Can you squeeze my hand? Can you nod your head?"

There was no response. The constant ping of the heart rate monitor irritated the silence as it traced up and down. It was a clinical piece of equipment that seemed vital to mum's care.

"Mum. Can you hear me? Flick your eyelids if you can hear."

Again no response, no eye movements. She seemed drained of life, of spirit, of hope. Her face looked serene and content, like a child. She looked at peace with herself and the world beyond, wherever that was. Outside the window, people walked in the rain, reflections of headlights hit the wet road. Everyone was oblivious to the anxiety that existed a few floors above them.

"I'm going now, mum. Aunty Ruth and uncle Jack will be here tomorrow afternoon. I love you lots, mum. Just want to hear your soft voice again, soon. To feel you squeeze my hand and to touch my face. To see those lovely green cat's eyes you gave to me. To see your loving smile, radiate sunshine and warmth. Ineed you mum. We all do."

I brushed a tear away before I spoke with the Sister. She could only give me solace, but no answers.

"I wish we could do more. It's a waiting game at the moment. Let's hope for better news tomorrow," said the Sister, despondent. She must have said those words many times over the years. She was doing her professional job with empathy. Everything seemed frustrating. Whilst mum was still alive, I hoped they could do more.

Chapter 22

Three days after the operation, mum's health continued its' downward spiral. With stubbornness and frustration, not only did blood pressure stay low, but in a fresh development, actual blood levels were dropping to a dangerous level. The agonising truth pointed towards an unchecked blood seepage, oozing from an unknown source. Mr. McKenzie was adamant that a puncture of nearby organs had not taken place. Within the area of the gallbladder, he insisted there was no blood seepage. There was no equipment available in the 1960's, that could isolate any bleed-out from within the body. Without determining the precise location, intervention operations could never be a practical option. Harder than finding a needle in a haystack, or 'pinning the tail on the donkey' in total darkness. Blood clotting agents and medication had not worked. Mr. McKenzie and Dr. Hammond convened a meeting to assess every option.

"We seem to have reached a brick wall," said Mr. McKenzie.

"Blood pressure cannot continue to drop, unless……."

"Haemostasis," said Mr. McKenzie.

"Bleed out? Blood seeping out from somewhere in the body?" Said Dr. Hammond.

"Correct. Internal haemorrhage. But not anywhere near the gallbladder. The operation went well. There was no internal bleeding from there," said Mr. McKenzie.

"What next? We're short of options," said Doctor Hammond, disturbed by mum's numbers gliding downwards.

"A wing and a prayer aren't in the Medical Dictionary. But that's all we have to go on."

"The only option is a Life-Support machine. If we could stem blood seepage, BP would stabilise and medication would lift her numbers. Then life-support would keep her alive until the blood clotted," said Dr. Hammond.

"Plausible. But haemostasis is impossible. She's losing more blood than we can put into her. At this rate of loss, she's only got twenty-four hours before her organs begin to shut down. Inadequate blood supply. Organ failure. More blood transfusion would be futile. From that point onwards, kept alive only by the LSM and morphine to make her pain free. She would be brain dead. A vegetable," said Mr. McKenzie.

"There's something we've overlooked. I'm sure. But I don't know what," said Dr. Hammond.

"We'll wait until mid-day. Blood could still crystalise at source," said Mr. McKenzie. "Then we must put her onto a life-support machine," he continued.

"Mid-day? WHY bloody wait another three hours?"

"I'm head consultant, Doctor Hammond. Don't cross me. Think about your career."

"She needs help NOW. Three hours later is three hours lost. For God's Sake."

"I have noted your comments, Dr. Hammond. In red ink."

Mum was connected to life-support at mid-day as directed. Her blood pressure continued to drop towards the danger zone, but breathing stabilised. Aunty Ruth and uncle Jack came and went without mum responding. Alex arrived for the evening visit, in no mood for weak excuses. His own blood pressure was sky high as he drove to the hospital. Anger management was not his forte.

"What the heck is going on with my mum?" Alex said loudly.

"It's a life-support machine," said the Sister, pressing the alert to Security with prudent concern.

"What?"

Alex walked into mum's room. Nurses had connected mum to the monitors, machines, and tubes like a spider's web. She seemed trapped in a harness waiting for her release.

"The blood pressure dropped again today."

"So that machine says she is fighting for her life?"

"It's not that, Mr. Dalton. It also helps her breathe better."

"Oxygen masks?"

"I demand to see McKenzie. NOW!" Shouted Alex in a rage.

The two Security Officers arrived.

"We have called the police, Sister," said the first officer.

"Calm down sir. No need to get agitated. Not in the hospital, please," said the second officer.

"McKenzie……..NOW!"

"Come through to his office. He's on his way," said the Sister.

Alex, two Security Officers, the Sister, and Mr. McKenzie walked into his office.

"Got your bodyguards, have you?" Said Alex, braced for any reaction.

"Listen, Mr. Dalton. Let me explain. We have……..."

Without warning, Alex dived across the desk, fists clenched, his nose scrunched up with temper. He'd had enough of weak excuses. The two Security Officers had expected a violent confrontation and wrestled his hands behind his back ready for the police to arrive.

"Calm down Mr. Dalton. One more move like that and you'll spend the night in a police cell."

"Why is that bloody contraption in my mother's room? I said something was wrong."

"There has been a slow bleed for days. She's anaemic."

"Meaning?"

"It's difficult for her blood to coagulate."

"Talk in bloody English, will you?"

"It's been impossible to stop her from losing blood. She is losing more blood than we can get into her body. When she loses blood, her blood pressure drops. She's lost so much blood now, even with blood transfusions, she is getting weaker."

Alex breathed heavily with frustration. He struggled to contain his anger against a rising tide of possible negligence and ineptitude by Mr. McKenzie. He struggled to avoid a physical fight, being his normal release if anyone riled him. Many times in the past he lashed out, then walked.

"You mean she might......."

"We have put her on a life-support machine, a respirator, to make it easier for her to breathe. Her blood flow is being regulated by a blood transfusion."

"If the worst comes to the worst, there'll be hell to pay. I can tell you that much," said Alex.

"We have done everything humanly possible. We can only hope the internal bleed stops in time. If it does......."

"If it does. You're in the clear. Is that it?"

"The care she is receiving will get her on her feet again."

"Last month, she came in to have gallstones removed. This week, my mother came in for the same operation. Now she's fighting for her life. Am I missing something here?"

"This time, there were complications," said Mr. McKenzie.

"The only complication my mother has had is you, McKenzie."

The room went quiet. Alex and Mr. McKenzie glared at each other. One with incitement, the other with indictment written on his face.

"I'll make my own way out. Wouldn't like to fall down some steps. Would I?" Said Alex.

Uncle Jack and aunty Ruth arrived later, with Glenn and David, and took them to the children's playroom. I arrived from work and went straight to mum's bedside. Wires and tubes criss-crossed around her body from the monitors and life-support machine. Mum looked frail and weak. Her face drawn and sallow showed her fragile existence. Her face and arms yellowed with deep jaundice and void of any other colour. Her lips, always rouged, were now dry, bloodless and wrinkled. Her skin had shrunk like an ageing pensioner, an irony considering her age of forty-three.

"Hi mum. It's Jeff. I've come to see you. Can you hear me?"
She struggled to breathe even though the LSM was in operation. Deep-throated gasps of air seemed inadequate to sustain her body. She seemed to have lost the fight against the inevitable; drifting away from me, minute by minute, hour by hour.

"Can you move your eyes or your head? Squeeze my hand mum." There was no response, not even a twitch of recognition of my voice or even my presence. The atmosphere seemed to be one of melancholy and gloom. A shiver ran through my body as spirits seemed to gather in the lonely room. Distant angelic voices sang incoherent chants through my mind. My heart saddened as a coldness descended, like a mist across a valley with a bright light beyond. I kissed her cold cheek and put my arm around her. She was in another world, but still, the machine helped her breathe. I held her hand for what seemed to be a lifetime, then said.....

"Time for me to go mum. Alex is on his way. David and Glenn
are here for you as well."
Alex stepped into mum's room and chatted for ten minutes and gave her hugs and kisses. It was the first time I had seen him cry, even when he had been on the losing side in a street fight. He seemed hurt in a physical and an emotional sense. He WAS hurt; deeply hurt. A side of him no-one ever saw. His emotional outpouring fuelled his pent up anger. Mum was hanging on to life by a thread. Alex wanted vengeance and retribution. As he saw it, Mr. McKenzie had bungled a simple gallstone removal operation.

"You can't beat up hospital staff, Alex. You'll go to prison."
"Can't get McKenzie out of my mind," said Alex.
"Alex. Let's meet Mr. McKenzie. Just you, me and the doctor,"
said uncle Jack, trying to defuse a volatile situation.
"If somebody upsets me. I fight."
"What about that girl Gwen?"
"What about her?" Said Alex, in a defensive mood.

"Would she be happy to visit you in Wakefield Prison every other Sunday?"

"Suppose you're right."

"Just gotta see sense. Not see red," said uncle Jack.

"Point taken."

"Hey. Mr. McKenzie?" Uncle Jack shouted down the corridor.

"A word please?" Continued uncle Jack.

He looked apprehensive, unsure whether to call Security. He just gave an uneasy nod.

"Apologies for Alex. He's had a lot of stress," said uncle Jack.

"I understand that," said Mr. McKenzie.

"A quiet word?" Asked uncle Jack.

"Any arguments and he's out."

"Agreed," said uncle Jack.

"Mrs. Dalton has had serious unforeseen complications. I agree, gallstone removal last month was a success. She made a full recovery. This week we diagnosed more gallstones and inflammation of the gallbladder and the liver. Blockages within the intestines and suspected problems with other organs made matters worse. My staff have worked with tireless spirit, day and night, to stem the haemorrhaging, but it's been difficult. We've put Mrs. Dalton on a life-support machine to help with lung and heart problems. She's extremely weak, but fighting.

"Sorry Mr. McKenzie," said Alex.

"Forget it."

Day after day seemed to be the same, haemorrhaging and blood pressure dropping. Mum's heart and lungs became weaker. The life-support machine continued. Everyone hoped and prayed a spark of life would ignite. Embers were fading by the hour. It all seemed to be a dreadful dream. Images of happier times plagued my mind, past conversations appeared real. Unexpectedly, Mr. McKenzie summoned Alex from our constant vigil.

"Mr. Dalton, you spoke out quite a few times this week."

"As I said, I'm sorry about that."

"Now, let me speak mine," said Mr. McKenzie. "You're a strong young man. You now have to be strong for others."

"I try to be."

"We have tried everything within our powers, to get your mum back in good health. We performed complicated operations, then gave her the best care available. As she became weaker, we began using the LSM. We have tried our very best."

"Why are you telling me all this?" Asked Alex, expecting some kind of an apology.

Mr. McKenzie took a brief pause before he could deliver the inevitable bombshell. He looked into Alex's eyes and without twitching an eye muscle; he spoke with a subdued voice.

"Alex, we can't save your mum. She's fading away. We can't hold back the tide. There's no other way to say this. We need your permission to turn off the machine."

The room quietened. The stillness stunned Alex. His eyes filled with burning tears that jarred everything out of sync that mattered. Images of mum blurred into soft focus. Life itself would no longer be meaningful. Mum's radiant warm smile shone above the cruel adversity that purveyed her life. In halcyon days, her smile had been like the evening sun, a warm glow that cast auburn shadows. The same deep richness as her own hair. Life's indifference had cheated Alex. Mum was in the throes of being cheated of her own life. He wished he could exchange her life for his. She deserved more from life than the raw deal bestowed upon her. Shell-shocked, Alex's mind was blown asunder. Fragments cascaded into a kaleidoscope of random thoughts of life's betrayal and a loved one's imminent departure.

For a decade, Alex nurtured a heart of stone, battled with fearless courage, and was as resilient as a diamond. His heart was now n meltdown. The street-fighter in him became as meek as a lamb with as much growl as a kitten. Less than a week ago, mum had been generous with her hugs and love to us all. Today, the silence was deafening. He stared ahead in shock. A droplet escaped the corner of each eye. The bitter sting dribbled into the corner of his lips. He hadn't expected to adjudicate to end mum's life. The unwelcome burden on his shoulders was a horrendous task no son should ever have to make.

Mr. McKenzie's summation had stopped Alex in his tracks. The dilemma had hit him square between the eyes. A tremor shivered through his body, like the after-shock of an earthquake. It was something he had never experienced. The ambience of the room seemed surreal, as though he was in a transient dream. Alex's heartbeat quickened like a panting dog. His eyes, normally scornful and with cold menace, filled with deep pain, burning with sorrow and reality. His brain became jaded with random thoughts, weighed down by responsibility, and drowned in an immense wave of self-doubt. He alone controlled mum's destiny. Recriminations of guilt bombarded his mind.

Mr. McKenzie stared at a pathetic soul. He made critical decisions every day and controlled people's lives. Now that painful duty fell into the unexpected lap of Alex. Like a Roman Emperor witnessing a fight for life and death within an arena, Alex held the mantle to sanction the infamous 'thumbs up or thumbs down' in one mighty swoop. He agonised for minutes, seemingly hours, contemplating her demise. His dilemma didn't sit well with his own conscience.

"Alex. There is no blame attached to you," said Mr. McKenzie with an empathetic tone.

"How could I walk back into mum's room and face her, knowing what you ask of me?"

"Your mum's peace and tranquillity are more important," said Mr. McKenzie.

"How could I face my family with a clear conscience?"

Alex continued to stare at the floor, paralysed by grief and gripped by the dilmma. He retreated into his own mind. Under normal circumstances, he would lash out in panic situations, then ask questions later. Now, subdued by the moment, he contemplated the action he must take.

"How could I live with myself? How could I tell my own brothers or look anyone in the eye for what I've done? What could I say to mum's grandchildren in the years to come?"

"You owe this kindness to your mother, Alex. You owe it to your brothers and yourself."

"I'm not a Judas," said Alex. "My mother's blood will be on my hands, it will make me feel like a murderer," he continued.

"Alex, it's not for me to persuade you. I can just tell you the purest of truths; your mother has already passed. It's only the machine that keeps her heart beating. She is unable to live without it. If you wish, we can wait until visiting is over. Your family will have said their goodbyes. It will give loved-one's quality time at your mother's bedside. She is comfortable now and unaware of what is happening. We can switch off the life-support at midnight, then a short while later, she will pass away in tranquillity. A dignified departure, you by her side."

Alex again sat motionless in deep thought. His hands covered his face, wondering about the right thing to do. His breathing became heavy. The inevitable truth filled his glazed, watery eyes.

"You're right," said Alex as he summoned inner strength to cope with his own ordeal.

"You can be at her side all night, her dignity preserved in the privacy of her own room," said Mr. McKenzie in a soft voice.

"Isn't that euthanasia?"

"No. Your mother cannot survive."

"But I would be assisting her death. Illegal? Ten years inside Wakefield prison?"

"We could keep your mum alive 'ad infinitum.' A vegetable on a ventilator. Do you want that? That's not a life, it's an existence. This happens every day, all over the world. Patients appear to pass naturally," said Mr. McKenzie.

"Assisted suicide?" Asked Alex, harbouring on reality.

Mr. McKenzie gave no reply and looked at Alex with a benign smile. From Mr. McKenzie's viewpoint, there was nothing more he could do.

"Midnight, you say?" Asked Alex, despondent, his heart heavy with guilt and pangs of being Judas.

The conversation stopped. Alex racked his brain, contemplating his dilemma. A few minutes more of silence slipped by. Remorse reverberated through his brain and echoed a biblical statement:

'…. *forgive them, for they do not know what they do.*…

Chapter 23

Mum's destiny became inescapable. The next few hours became darker for Alex. His mood dominated by circumstances he could control, but declined as common sense prevailed. He trudged back to mum's bedside, as though he carried a heavy wooden cross. Impending recriminations racked his brain; to be moral and keep mum in pain, or guilty, and turn off the machine. Peace or pain became his moral dilemma. His chest heaved a heavy sigh of despondency as he plodded down the corridor to mum's room. A choice that he alone had made, a secret buried in time.

Members of the family congregated on both sides of mum's bed, waiting for Alex to return from his meeting with Mr. McKenzie. They hoped for better news. Maybe they had considered other treatments or even a transfer to a specialist hospital. They pondered how long she could survive. Mum remained gaunt and lifeless, oblivious of anything or anybody in the room. Questions surfaced of how this could have happened and why attempts to revive her had been futile. Alex had been away for an hour. Maybe Security had ejected him for violent behaviour. His mood pointed in that direction. He had a motive. He had suspicions about Mr. McKenzie. The door opened to interrupt the morose atmosphere. All eyes focused towards Alex.

"There's no news. Mr. McKenzie has no more solutions," said Alex, looking subdued.

"Is that it?" You've been talking for an hour," I said with impatience. "You can't come back after an hour and say there are no more solutions," I continued.

"Only life support is keeping mum alive," said Alex.

"I can't believe it. Gallstones? Then she's gone. How can that be possible?"

"They found complications," said Alex.

"This is an ICU. They deal with this every day."

"They've run out of options. Nothing left, bro."

"How long has she got?" I said, leading the inquisition.

"Can't tell…...Tomorrow…...The day after maybe."

"She'll not survive. Will she?" I said, but nobody commented.

We all listened to the conversation, expecting a glimmer of hope. Alex looked dejected. I was distraught. Alex hid his tragic secret of guilt. He deflected the inevitable point-blank questions as we wrestled outcomes. Heads shook in disbelief. Only Alex knew the ultimate solution. Only Alex knew the darkest hour edged closer. It would not be his finest.

Alex stormed out of the room, his face emblazoned red with shame and fury, tightened by acrimony, irritated by questions. I chased after him to calm his angst before he could smash a window, wreck a chair or disable a coffee machine. I grabbed his shoulder and stopped him halfway along the corridor. It was late. A handful of us had stayed as a vigil. Many of us bleary-eyed by lack of sleep, some of us blurry eyed by hot tears.

"I need fresh air," said Alex, in a loud whisper, the hospital eerily quiet and deserted.

"You're hiding something," I said.

"Get out of my way!" Alex shoved me against a wall; my head whiplashed against a door. I grabbed him again and shook his shoulders to awaken him from complacency. I hoped a fight wouldn't break out. This was not the place for animosities.

"Surely in 1970, we have the technology to remove gallstones without it being fatal?" I said, with a puzzled, deep look of consternation and demanding of the truth.

"It is what it is. RIGHT?" Alex snapped back. His temper boiled as he clenched his fist.

"Only saying," I said, taken aback by his venomous snipe.

Alex took a deep breath and let out a slow sigh.

"Sorry, Jeff. It's getting to me. I just can't handle it," said Alex, shaking with guilt.

"Don't lose it Alex. It's hard for all of us."

"I've never been on the losing side. Now I am, and it hurts, deep within me," said Alex.

"It's mum who is on the losing side; her life; her will to live; everything."

His bleak eyes, cold and piercing, shifted away from mine.

"Alex, you always looked me dead straight in the eyes without flinching I see a mask hiding something. What is it? Tell me!"

Alex glared with frustration and anger. He gave me a look of knowing. I could sense he harboured much more than he would tell. His eyes, misted with a tear, frowned and shied away from mine. He couldn't look straight at me and evaded contact.

"What do YOU know that I don't?" I said in a sharp tone.

There was black horror in his eyes. He wore a mask of fear, having seen the apocalypse. Ominous clouds loomed like a praying mantis as he wrangled his clammy hands with nervous effect. Alex raised his eyes, seemingly about to speak. He cleared his throat with a vague cough, then ran his tongue around inside his mouth and took a deep breath.

"Can I give you a lift home, Jeff?" Shouted uncle Jack down the echoey corridor.

The moment had gone. Uncle Jack had rescued Alex. He had missed his chance. I had missed the last bus home. It was ten o'clock, nurses had dimmed hospital lights, some turned off.

"That's good of you uncle Jack. Thanks." I said.

"I'll hang on a while longer with Gwen," said Alex, staring.

As had happened many times before, we both went our separate ways. This time, me with uncle Jack, Alex to mum's bedside with girlfriend Gwen, to continue the lonely vigil. All the while, mum drew deeper, erratic breaths. The occasional breath missed a beat, as though each one seemed to be the last. The heart rate monitor peaked and troughed. Flashing, oversized numbers became hypnotic as mum wallowed closer to the precipice.

"A matter of waiting, isn't it?" Said Alex as Gwen hugged him.

"You SHOULD be here," said Gwen as she squeezed his hand with warm affection.

"You know, I can't help but think……., her favourite record," said Alex, tearful.

"She's not alone. You're by her side. She knows that."

"Stranger on the Shore."

The clock ticked closer to midnight, seeming to get louder, yet the hospital became quieter as night shift nurses settled to their duties. A nurse popped in to check the monitors.

"Mr. Dalton, the Sister would like a quick word with you both," said the nurse.

They both stood up and sauntered to the Sister's desk.

"Would you both like a coffee? Not from the coffee machine though," said the Sister,

"I could do with it. That might keep us both awake," said Alex.

"It's been an arduous day," said Gwen, clutching Alex's hand.

"Nights shifts seem longer for me," said the Sister.

The nurse returned, the door closed behind her. She gave a polite smile and a meaningful glance towards Alex but said nothing. Alex had agreed with the Sister, that at midnight, she should switch off the monitors and life-support. He and Gwen would grab a coffee from the vending machine as a distraction. The nurse, with tact, switched off the hypnotic monitors in his absence. Staff knew the symbolic sight of switching off life-support could be traumatic. Alex realised the coffee break ploy and with trepidation trudged back to mum's room with Gwen, knowing what the nurse had done

As Alex opened the door, an eerie lethargy pervaded mum's room. A disconcerting sensation overwhelmed him and hit him head-on. The gravity of Alex's decision to sanction the equipment being turned off was like an airplane in the sky, and the engines had stalled mid-flight. There would be a gradual descent until the inevitable impact, but like the Marie Celeste, no-one on board. As mum still hung on, Alex burst into heart-wrenching sobs. Gwen pulled his head into her chest, in part to smother screams of anguish, and in part to reassure him of her own love.

They both sobbed together, clutching each other. Tears streamed with relentless abandon until their throats became as parched as desert sand. His shoulders juddered with each cry. Mum was still alive, but only just. Each breath could now be her last. The nurse had administered morphine before she had left, so mum remained calm. No-one was about. No doctors. No nurses. No-one. She deactivated alarms in the room. The final descent had begun. At least mum was pain-free and comfortable, hanging on to our world, soon to be in hers.

After a short while, the duty nurse entered mum's room, as a matter of protocol. She knew mum's passing was imminent. The clock seemed to echo louder as each minute ticked by. Mum's breathing became erratic with frightening gasps. Minutes later, mum took her last breathe, passing away in peace. The nurse was present but then walked out of the room to afford Alex and Gwen quality time with mum. The nurse closed the door, then walked ten paces before a thunderous scream hailed from mum's room.

"No! ….Noooooo!.. Mum don't leave."Please mum, I love you; I need you, more than ever.

Mum had gone. She sighed her last breath of air. Alex and Gwen blubbered without control. They hugged each other and looked towards mum, lost in the wilderness of time and ether. Alex screamed blue murder; his cries resonated down the corridor. The duty doctor arrived within ten minutes to pronounce mum's death, then issued a Certificate.

"You stayed with your mum to the end. That's what she would have wanted. A loved one to hold her hand, to say '*I love you.*' said Gwen, holding Alex with a firm hug.

"That's all she ever craved from dad. All she ever wanted from him," said Alex in tears.

The duty Sister arrived and assisted the doctor with medical notes. She heard his cries down the corridor but gave them space to unleash pent up emotion, like releasing a coiled spring. Alex and Gwen stayed at mum's bedside, talking to mum with soft voices. He comforted mum with kind words and reminiscences of happier times. He eulogised about how she fought all of life's battles, but ultimately lost the war. He spoke of fond memories at Great Yarmouth and many of his escapades that worried mum at the time. He reflected on funny moments of my misfortune, such as when I put Mr. Hardcastle's window through with grandad's walking stick.

"Remember when dad was a Gunner in the Territorial Army, you always said he was 'Gunna do this' or 'Gunna do that', but never did. All of your battles were never over until today, mum. But you won in the end. You've gone to another place, a better place. As usual, you didn't have a choice. Taken by angels to be with your mum, your dad and your baby girl Dorothy, who never survived, with sadness, never recorded. The sister we never had and never knew about for years."

Alex took a few minutes out and wiped his eyes and his dribbling nose. He needed to compose himself after the torment of mum's last moments. Tears flowed as mum's family photograph evoked cherished memories.

"You never lived to see any grand-kids, maybe one of them could have been the baby girl you never had. One day you will see them as you look down from heaven."

"I love you mum. I miss you so much."

A few minutes of quiet reflection and a last glance towards mum as she lay at rest, ended the night on a low. The air was still and quiet. Nothing moved, there was no sign of life. Machines became silent, all the alarms muted. A serene silence filled the room. No more battles to fight. A sheet covered her body and all the blinds remained closed. At two o'clock in the morning, even the echoes of feet in the corridor had stopped. The clatter of trams outside had retired to the depot. Traffic had vanished, only an electric milk float whirred along the road with effortless nonchalance. Alex and Gwen got to their feet and swept their tears aside.

"Ready?" Said Gwen, looking into Alex's bloodshot sore eyes. Alex attempted a sardonic smile of acquiescence as they walked out of the hospital. Every image blurred by tears, oversized '*EXIT*' signs were unintelligible. Outside it was frosty, the sharp, crisp air jolted the body and the brain into reality. Vapour drifted from the mouth with each breath, with each word spoken. Gwen drove back to her mum's house with Alex. He was incapable of driving, concentration levels shot. They grabbed a few hours' sleep before contacting the wider family about our tragic loss.

At ten o'clock, a phone call came through in the office where I worked. I could not make or receive private phone calls. We had no telephone, so receiving an outside call was odd.

"Jeff? It's Gwen."
Gwen deliberately paused the call. It wasn't easy to deliver tragic news over the telephone. There was no other way to deliver the awful news than straight to the point.

"It's about your mum, Jeff. She passed away this morning."
I dropped the phone. It clattered onto the wooden desk and echoed across the room. I sat in stunned silence, gazing straight ahead. My eyes filled as blurred images of unrecognisable colleagues plied back and forth before me. As they looked, I saw their mouths move, but with muted comments. I saw their frowns of empathy and concern. My entire body went into shock. I was sixteen, the youngest member of the team.

A lady colleague, Angela, empathetic by default, realised the phone call had been devastating news. She put her motherly arms around me like my mum used to do. Perhaps it was my mum, sent by an angel incarnate, who sat beside me. This act of compassion and kindness triggered a torrent of tears, a floodgate of emotion. My minutes of silent shock exploded into a scream, tears like molten lava flowed down my face. Colleagues I barely knew huddled around me and hugged my shoulders in a warm embrace. Office activity stopped other than to console me and to offer tissues. Fifteen minutes later, I had recovered enough to speak to the team leader.

"My mum…….She's…..She's just passed away."
The office became a library of silence. She couldn't conjure any words in reply but looked with agony towards me, her stern face melted with compassion. The warmth of feeling generated within the office was spontaneous. The pain and grief I felt prevented me from saying anything more. I was numb, devoid of any ability to think or speak.

"Call a taxi, someone!" Yelled the team leader. "I'll send Jeff home. Angela, can you go with him? Stay with him for an hour. Maybe get a taxi back. He might want to go to the hospital so I'll leave the arrangements in your hands."

I could hear garbled voices that became incoherent. Random actions around me made little sense to me. I could only imagine I was in a state of delayed shock. Once home, I grabbed a few casual clothes. Angela made a coffee for us both. My mind couldn't focus on anything I should be doing. I wandered about, moving things from one place to another. I tidied my bedroom, hearing mum's voice in my head. My eyes became glazed. I couldn't see anything in focus. Tears streamed without control. Embarrassed to shed tears in front of a female colleague, she could see I was struggling, even to co-ordinate myself. As she walked towards me, I wasn't able to speak. She held me in a motherly embrace. I could sense she knew that all I wanted at that moment was an enormous hug. A brief time passed by before I could conjure anything coherent.

"Thank you for being here with me, Angela. It means a lot."
"Hey. I can't have you making me a drink. I've tasted your coffee at work," she said.
She timed her jovial comment to perfection. We both agreed and sniggered. It snapped me back into focus. I freshened up and got ready for the bigger task of seeing mum at the hospital. Angela called

another taxi from the phone box, for me to go to the hospital and her to go back to work.

Under the circumstances, the hospital staff allowed unrestricted visiting times to bereaved families. I ambled down the long corridor, still dazed by mum's demise. I couldn't imagine the pain she suffered over the years, emotional, then ultimately physical. They say people can't see pain, but I could see mum's. It showed in her face, most of it showed in her heart. She worshipped dad. She never tired of trying to win his heart back. Mum suffered years of agony and torment, but she still believed he would return. With travesty, his long-awaited return could be at mum's funeral.

Mum's room appeared in front of me with blinds down and the door closed. The Sister looked up from her desk and smiled with empathy. She nodded without saying a word. I couldn't cope with any form of conversation from anyone. I wanted to be alone. I wanted to share the last day with mum before she disappeared to the mortuary. A potential autopsy was far from my mind. I wanted to see the old mum, the more familiar mum that I knew and remembered with such great affection, without machines and tubes. I sat for a few minutes in meditation before my mind clicked into the words I needed to say. Hours of vigil had transferred much of my thoughts. Now, mum was at peace. As we were alone, I spent the precious moment speaking softly to her as tears escaped.

"It wasn't meant to be like this, mum. Grandma told you to fight for the things you want in life, the things important to you. You struggled to keep us all together, to keep us under one roof, and somehow to put food on the table. You fought and won. You fought to bring up four young boys on pennies and to keep us rom going into a children's home. You fought for the man you have loved all of your life, dad. I know, if angels above had not taken your life so early, things might have been different. I know that one day, dad will live to regret the hurt and the pain he gave to you and us. One day, he will ask for your forgiveness. Ghosts of his past will haunt him to his own grave. On that day, you will have won. How cruel can life be, mum? As we all got together, demons stole your life."

I took a drink of water; my mouth acrid with tears, my throat parched and thick. Outside, rain hit the window that tracked down in the same way as teardrops tracked down my face. It seemed surreal that this day had arrived. Grandad told me to be brave.

"Grandad Cooper never allowed me not to drown in self-pity. He often said, '*One thing in life is certain, death itself.*' He taught me to get on with life, the way it was. '*Adapt to the world, the world won't adapt to you.*' He said many times, '*Only the good die young.*' Never a truer word spoken mum, forty-three years young. In the whole of your life, you did nothing wrong to anybody. But you suffered the most. I will love you forever, mum. Thank you for loving me. When I think of you, I will always smile. Do you remember what you put on grandma Cooper's headstone?" I said.

'*Don't cry because it's over. Smile because it happened.*'

I didn't have the mental strength to turn back the sheet that covered mum's face. I was alone, very alone. I felt vulnerable. I felt mum's soul had left the room as I was leaving. My spine shivered, goosebumps covered my arms. Tears burned to the point of sting. "Goodbye, for now, mum. Sleep well."

Chapter 24

Ten days later, the heart-rending funeral of mum took place. Neighbours gathered at the roadside and at the end of garden paths. I couldn't help but think it was like witnessing a major accident on the motorway. People slowed and stopped to witness someone else's grief, rather than grieving themselves. Perhaps I was cynical; perhaps they did pay their last respects.

"Tragic. The family has only been in the house six months," said a neighbour as they watched four of us climb into the black limousine.

The first car carried mum's coffin, adorned with red carnations and wreaths, annotated with '*MUM*' and '*SISTER*'. Gwen, Alex, Glenn, David and myself, stooped into the second car. I sat opposite Alex, both of us tearful; glazed eyes stared at each other in disbelief that this painful day had arrived. Words were not forthcoming. Every memory that I cherished of mum consumed my mind, like a subconscious eulogy. Glenn, who was now ten, cried a constant stream of tears. Gwen put her arm around him and held him tight. David, now four, couldn't understand what was happening. He was the only one of us who said anything:

"Mummy. I want my mummy," screamed David; his cries quivered in a shrill, penetrating voice.

He needed the love of his mother. We all did. All that we had was a memory of someone we once knew. We needed mum at this exact moment. She was about to make her last journey. She wasn't coming back, only in our dreams.

As we all shuffled into the car, dad attempted to climb in with us.

"Don't even think about being in this car with us. You're not wanted. Why are you even here?" Said Alex. He pushed dad backwards and closed the door. Dad didn't deserve to show his face at mum's funeral.

"Four boys with no mother," said a neighbour, from their gate.

"Doesn't seem right, does it?" Said a neighbour.

Dad, embarrassed by rejection, stepped into the third car with his two brothers and his mother. Any feelings we had towards dad had dissipated when he closed the door on us and abandoned us a few years back. Dad's presence seemed to rekindle unpleasant feelings. He wasn't welcome. The sight of dad's mother, grandma Greaves, evoked images of the bad atmosphere spent living under her roof. Alex, already in a foul mood, and volatile by nature, his temper simmered and could erupt.

The funeral journeyed the two miles from Richmond, and on to the traditional stone-built church of St James in Woodhouse. My eyes welled as we drove with decorum along the streets I walked with grandad Cooper only five years back. Life had turned full circle, as I remembered when grandad and I stopped to pay our respects to a passing cortege.

Now, it was his own daughter, my mother, who travelled the same journey in the shiny black car. Neighbours bowed their heads and removed their caps as the cortege set off. Along the way, people who walked to the shops or the park likewise stopped to pay their respects. A poignant moment arose passing Richmond Park; a pensioner had stopped with his grandson to pay their respects, just like grandad and I had done years before. For a fleeting moment, it seemed to be me and my hero.

Fifteen minutes later, we arrived at the church. A crowd of mourners had gathered and threw single flowers over the passing cars. The immediate family stood at the church entrance, each side of the path. As we extricated ourselves from the limousine, we stood by the entrance door of the church, to await mum's coffin adorned with red carnations. Alex, me, Glenn, and David, stood mournfully. Gwen stood by Alex and clasped his hand. Many others lined the path from the church gates. Four pallbearers retrieved the coffin and began their slow walk of respect and dignity. Wailing and sobbing, from mourners, permeated the church grounds and grew louder as the cortege halted alongside us. Each of us held a single red carnation and in sequence placed them on mum's coffin.

Uncle Jack needed to lift David and Glenn for them to offer their respect. Mum's stepsisters sobbed and touched the coffin as it proceeded into the church. Pallbearers slow-walked down the aisle, resting at the altar where mum had married only twenty years earlier. A bouquet of red carnations seemed appropriate resting on her heart, with four individual stems from us. The vicar delivered eulogies and prayers. Popular hymns reverberated through the old nave and echoed high into the vaulted roof. It became impossible to focus on anything or anybody as my three brothers and I had blurry eyes and wet faces. I couldn't sing or say prayers, my dry throat refused. The hymn, 'All things bright and beautiful,' finished me with pangs of deep emotion.

Aunty Ruth gave me and my brothers' enormous hugs. The vicar said a few more prayers before the pallbearers returned. They lifted the coffin and walked along the aisle, to her ultimate resting place, the family grave alongside grandma and grandad Cooper. Mourners gave condolences and handshakes, then drifted away. With tragic irony, mum had no blood relatives alive, only us, her four sons, since grandma died. Stood on the periphery were dad and his side of the family. They tried to avoid any close contact, especially with uncle Jack visible close-by. Words needed saying.

"Mum got her wish," I said, with sarcasm, in earshot of dad.

Alex frowned at what I meant.

"What?" Said dad, surprised and fearful of any arguments on this, of all days.

"Mum said you would come back one day." I said, "Ironic, her words came true."

"Just paying my respects," said dad with a frown.

"You don't have any respect. Least of all for mum."

"Come on, Eddie. Leave it!" Said his brother.

"Just coming to make sure you got what you wanted, eh?" I raised my voice in anger.

"I don't want any trouble," said dad, subdued by the funeral.

"You don't need a divorce now. Do you? Mum's gone, we told her years ago to divorce you."

"Mum was always too good for you dad," Alex said, joining in the heated argument with his blunt statement.

"God knows why she ever loved you. We hate you," I said, "In the same way you hate us."

"We hate you for what you've done to us. I hate what you've done to mum. Look around you. YOU have done this to us. Why? What did mum ever do that was wrong? What did WE ever do that was wrong?" Continued Alex in a bitter tirade.

"Mum loved you, with all her heart. We loved you, but look what good that did for us. In the end, you only ever loved yourself," I said.

Uncle Jack came over to calm the tension as the heated conversation became noticeable by others.

"Come on, lads. Let's cool it a bit. Eh? Don't spoil it for your mum," said uncle Jack. His eyes penetrated dad's as they squared up.

It seemed a suitable cue to walk away and pay our last respects at the graveside. Dad and his family walked off in the opposite direction. The thorny issue of childcare for Glenn and David still needed resolving. Contempt and bitterness still simmered beneath the surface with grandma Greaves. She was a reluctant and indifferent part of the dilemma. This became an underlying theme over the next few months, not the most conducive atmosphere for us to live under the same roof.

The situation remained as an uneasy quagmire. Nasty blood existed between mum and dad's side of the family. Mum's untimely passing created a whole new raft of tension. Spontaneous outbursts of tears erupted from each of us at different times, confined to the privacy of the bedroom. Counselling wasn't forthcoming for bereavement. It was hard to believe that there wasn't any. At least, the local authority departments had never offered it over the past five years of crisis and chaos in our young lives. My mind and my life had become a rudderless raft. There was no meaning to life. Two weeks later, bereavement was still painful. Missing mum was still a bitter taste. Tears erupted at random moments, whether alone or with company. I was sixteen when mum passed. My heart still yearned for her to be alive. I wanted to say sorry for all those silly things that upset her. The trivial arguments with my brother, the mardiness of being young and knowing everything in life. My spontaneous outpourings left passers-by wondering why.

For my youngest brother David, at the tender age of four, it must have seemed his world had collapsed around him. Mum had disappeared overnight. He was an abandoned child, orphaned by a cruel twist of fate. Glenn, at the tender age of ten, had his life decimated by the loss of his mum. Her deep love, stolen from our hearts in an instant, theft of the highest order, stolen as we lay asleep in the darkest of nights. They constantly woke screaming, with awful dreams and bed-wetting every night. Nothing could ever substitute mum's love and tenderness. Overnight, an old woman offering indifference from her own bitter heart and her own icy feelings had substituted mum's deep love for us all.

The move to grandma Greaves' house, four miles away, went ahead under the same arrangements as a year before. The exception being, mum wasn't around to visit as she had done every day. This created a horrendous void on the emotional side of care. We had no genuine loving relationship with anyone, any more. Grandma Greaves was cold, heartless, and mean. She seemed unable or unwilling to have any compassion towards any of us. In essence, staying with grandma Greaves became a purely clinical arrangement to help dad with his non-existent childcare. It seemed dad didn't actually care where we lived, or how we lived, or even if we lived. We seemed to be an inconvenience. His life and love were pre-occupied elsewhere. Our lives had changed. Love had left our lives.

Even orphans had some kind of love. We had no-one to love us. Only distant memories remained.

Homeless, motherless, fatherless and unloved, we were all split up once more. Fate seemed to be against us, ever since Alex and I broke mum's large mirror in 1962. Alex was now a permanent fixture at Gwen's parents' house. Since mum's passing, he awaited the letter from Social Services with eagerness. Alex and Gwen had requested to be foster parents to David and Glenn. Two weeks after mum's funeral, the dreaded brown envelope arrived. It wasn't the letter they expected.

The hammer blow read:

'We have received a letter of complaint from a member of your family, expressing their concern about the role of fostering David and Glenn. We have taken into account the difficulties of such an arrangement and have concluded that the welfare of the children must come first. Because of your age and financial circumstances, we have no alternative but to deny your request to foster them.'

"I don't believe it," said Alex. "Fostering David and Glenn would have been the perfect solution for their care. To be with someone who loved and cared for them, day and night. It can't be right. I need to speak with aunty Ruth and uncle Jack. I need to find out what they think. I'm the nearest flesh and blood they have got," Alex continued.

Alex and Gwen dashed to aunty Ruth's house as quickly as they could. Alex was seething. He envisaged that somewhere along the line, if we stayed with grandma Greaves, aged eighty, she wouldn't be able to take care of us for very much longer. She would struggle to cope with the extra burden. The frosty atmosphere was as unwelcoming as it had been ever since we were born.

They arrived at the village of Beighton, ten minutes later. Speed limit signs were a blur as he raced through the village. Only the railway crossings could have stopped him. In a rage, following the letter, his temper was effervescent. He was in a belligerent mood, like a coiled spring, ready to explode, capable of striking without reason.

"What do you make of this letter, Aunty Ruth?" Said Alex, unable to hide his frustration.

She read it out loud to uncle Jack, who sat in the corner reading. *'The Sheffield Star'* newspaper.

"It says what it says. Doesn't it?" Said aunty Ruth, sounding like a barbed comment.

Her immediate response came as a surprise, flippant and abrupt. Her indifference seemed to speak volumes as though she already knew. She appeared unconcerned that anyone could do this.

"What about the letter of complaint? Who do you think might have sent that?" Said Alex.

Aunty Ruth hesitated with her answer. The silence pointed to her uninvited involvement.

"We did it for the best, Alex," said aunty Ruth, unable to stare him in the eye as she spoke.

"For the best? How do you mean?" Said Alex, his face reddened with fury and temper.

"Your grandma Greaves proved last year she could care for your brothers. So what's changed now?" Said aunty Ruth.

"Can't you see what will happen next? Grandma Greaves is eighty. Her bones probably ache."

"Life is becoming harder for her. We're not talking about a few months of care here. We're talking about at least twelve years. Would you take care of grandchildren you hated, up to the age of ninety-two, maybe longer?" Said Alex. "Do you not realise what you've done?"

"How do you mean?" Said aunty Ruth.

"Soon she'll be asking Social Services to care for her, let alone her looking after three boys. I can't believe you've done this. Mum struggled for years to save us from going into a children's home. You spent ten pence on a postage stamp and destroyed her efforts by the stroke of your pen. You've just condemned my brothers to a lifetime of misery in a children's home. What on earth could you have been thinking?" Said Alex, his voice became louder.

"That's enough," said uncle Jack, agitated. "Perhaps you'd best be on your way, lad. Don't want no trouble."

"I appreciate you looking after my brothers over the past few months," said Alex. "But mum would hate you for what you've done. You had bent over backwards to help us. Now you've gone out of your way and destroyed us," said Alex. "It proves blood is thicker than water, doesn't it? Here's ten pence for the stamp. Thanks for nothing," he continued.

Alex shook his head in disbelief and slammed the door on his way out. Gwen had sat quietly in the corner of the room. Alex's temper was at boiling point, but it hadn't spilled over into an all-out argument. Aunty Ruth had surprised him beyond reason. How could do such an act? It seemed she had misinterpreted how matters would pan out. Only time would tell how long grandma Greaves could cope looking after young children again. We tried to keep ourselves away from grandma as much as we could. But kids fresh out from school want to play, eighty-year-old pensioners don't. I took my brothers to the park as often as I could, to play on the slides and the swings. When it rained, there was nowhere to go. Three of us shared one bed in a tiny room, nine square metres. Being cramped was an understatement. In years gone by, grandma used the room to store well-read copies of the daily newspaper and magazines. They had turned brown with age and dampness and smelled as fusty as unwashed football socks. Grandma had never cleaned or fumigated it before we arrived; however, it was ONLY for us. Even the dog slept in the lounge in front of the fire. She was a hoarder. I never understood her obsession.

The heavy clunk of a car door closing made me peer out of the front bedroom window. David, Glenn, and I spent many hours building Lego houses and monumental four brick towers in that claustrophobic nine-metre square room. Out of the car stepped Mr.

Anderson and Mrs. Walker from Social Services Child Welfare. I recognised them from a few months before. They looked up to the window as I looked down. I assumed they were conducting a routine visit to see how we were all were coping under one roof. I could hear their voices in the next room, soft but incoherent. Mr. Anderson's refined Edinburgh accent carried well. After a short while, a screeching voice emanated from next door.

"David, Glenn, come here," shouted grandma, in a sharp tone.
I waited in the bedroom, but not yet summoned. The atmosphere seemed secretive. We were all penned in like segregated sheep, partitioned in two separate rooms. It seemed strange that Mr. Anderson didn't ask for my feedback. David and Glenn looked at me with a frown and deep hurt in their eyes. They seemed to ask me for answers, but I didn't know what was going on either.

"I'm coming," They both shouted to grandma, as though they had done something wrong again.

"This is Mr. Anderson. He needs to chat with you"

"My word. You two are growing up fast, aren't you?"

"They most certainly are," said Mr. Anderson, expanding on professional empathy.

Minutes went by before the lounge plunged into silence. I heard the outside door open by its noisy sneck. Old hinges creaked as it opened. Seconds later......

"Jeff!" Shouted Glenn, as loud as he could.

David began crying as loud as I had ever heard before.

"I want my mum," yelled David. His screams developed into squeals of terror and fear, getting more piercing by the second.

"Mum!...... Please don't let them take me away...... Mum!" David continued his cry for help.

He screamed and cried as though he was being abducted. The heart-breaking cry of a four-year-old, begging for help, stays in the mind.

"Jeff. Please... Help me... Please," screamed Glenn, both of them now sobbing out loud.

Memories of shrill, heart-wrenching cries of helpless brothers could never go away.

Chapter 25

I burst through the door, clouting it back against the wall with a heavy thud. David was just being led through the outside door by Mrs. Walker. They tugged against each other furiously, David trying to extricate himself from her tight clutches. He squealed as they forced him outside towards the minibus. Tears streamed down his face, wiped by his coat sleeve. Grandma Greaves left the room, devoid of any emotion. She didn't want to get involved. We weren't her children. Her indifference showed by inaction and ineptitude.

"What the hell is going on?" I yelled out at Mr. Anderson as he dragged Glenn, squealing as though he was being kidnapped. Glenn, being ten years old, put up more of a struggle. He kicked out with both feet, punching his fists randomly like a street-fighter, before being lifted from the ground by the burly Mr. Anderson.

"Now, now. Calm down, laddie. Everything's alright. We're going for a lovely ride up to Wakefield," said Mr. Anderson in a firm tone, gripping Glenn with disproportionate firmness. "Bring my brothers back," I shouted. Put them down. They're not going anywhere." I continued, my temper simmering to boiling point. This was one time I needed Alex's physical strength and aggression. He wouldn't allow this to happen. He would fight, then maybe ask questions later, if the perpetrator was still conscious.

"Jeff. Please help me," screamed David. His voice became distant as they carried him away down the long gennel to the minibus. His voice dissipated as they bundled him into the car. I felt frustrated and powerless at this act of attrition. Mrs. Walker, with Glenn, had disappeared into the car. Any attempt to thwart Mr. Anderson, a giant, twice my size and weight, seemed futile and more than formidable. He appeared more than capable of palming me off like a rugby player, without batting an eyelid.

"You can't take me. I'm not going. Tell him, Jeff. Please tell him," said Glenn.

"Put him down, Mr. Anderson," I shouted. Glenn now gripped by a panic attack and screamed as though he was being kidnapped by a stranger.

"Back off, laddie. Don't make me come back with a Restraining Order," said Mr. Anderson.

As we passed through the kitchen to the back door, my mind focused on the kitchen knives hanging on the wall. The set of sharp carving knives glistened, caught by a shaft of sunlight. It was as though a demon took control of my mind, willing me to grab them and use them against Mr. Anderson. My blood boiled with anger. Irrational thoughts clouded my judgement. In the heat of the moment, common sense didn't exist. I clutched the largest of the knives. We glared at each other as my heart pounded with fury. I gripped the handle so tightly, my arm shook with rage. We stood a mere two metres apart. Mr. Anderson stopped in his tracks but held Glenn with a vice-like grip. His face paled as he froze with fear. The shiny blade captured his attention. A Mexican stand-off ensued. He knew what could happen when he turned his back to leave; I didn't. Fury took control of common sense.

"Come on, laddie. Let's not do anything silly. Eh?"

"What's happening, Mr. Anderson? Why haven't we been told anything about this?"

"Put the knife down, laddie. Let's not make matters worse. We don't need the police, do we?"

We glared at each other. My heartbeat raced like a panting wolf, baying for blood. My biceps locked with tension, my hands and fingers shook with adrenaline flow. I couldn't think logically, my mind was consumed with protecting David and Glenn. They were helpless and sinking into the clutches of a Social Services Children's Home. Mum vowed this would never happen whilst she was alive. A travesty of how cruel life could be showed within weeks of mum passing.

I had become their Guardian Angel, their protector, at the age of sixteen. Mr. Anderson, as mild mannered and as eloquent as he seemed, was brutal in his conviction. He was a heavyweight in comparison to my bantam-weight as his opposition. The knife in my hand seemed to redress the balance of power. As my grandad suggested so many times…

'I feared no evil'

"Let's calm it down laddie," said Mr. Anderson in a soft tone.

My whole body was tense in the heat of the moment. I had nothing to live for. My two youngest brothers were my entire family. They were about to be abducted by a Highland Warrior into a dubious Edwardian house for under-privileged children and orphans. Tears and pain had clouded my judgement. I never said a word. I could only stare into Mr. Anderson's steel eyes. The silence seemed an eternity, but slowly, he began to elaborate on the circumstances surrounding the situation. I listened without conceding my thoughts. My right hand gripped the serrated knife as I shook with rage looking for vengeance and retribution for the unwarranted act.

He spelled out, with professional calmness, the decision Social Services had reached, then deliberated on the train of events that transpired. As Mr. Anderson spoke gently, the agonising, painful truth of the situation became apparent. I couldn't believe I had grabbed the knife to prevent my brothers from being taken. I placed it back on the wall as we sat in the room. Mr. Anderson's calming voice was well suited to situations of family crises and traumas.

"That's better. Let's all calm down shall we?" Said Mr. Anderson, visibly shaken but in total control. Annoyingly, he still kept hold of Glenn, preventing his escape. Glenn continued to cry and looked towards me for help and writhed to escape. Mr. Anderson went on to explain.

"A few weeks ago, when your mum passed away with deep sadness, Social Services were presented with an enormous problem. Glenn and David needed care. Your grandma Greaves stepped in and agreed to look after you three boys."

"My brother Alex and his girlfriend wanted to foster us,….. job sorted," I said.

"We considered that as a potential way forward, but that idea failed on affordability. Also, the fact Alex and Gwen were only eighteen years old, unmarried, and living with Gwen and her parents. What if Gwen's parents changed their minds? Where would everyone be after that? None of it seemed practical," said Mr. Anderson.

"So what's the problem now?" I asked with frustration.

"At eighty years old. She can't cope any more. Your dad contacted us to let us know. We came over last week to see your dad and grandma. Talked about a few things. It became obvious your grandma could no longer take care of David and Glenn. She no longer had the strength or stamina to care for two growing boys."

Social Services involvement became inevitable as dad walked away from his responsibilities; namely us. Mr. Anderson continued explaining the role of Social Services, unpalatable as it was. It showed how callous and heartless dad was towards us.

"Your dad said he could not take care of David and Glenn. We agreed the only option was for Social Services to take control of their well-being. As we came under the jurisdiction of West Riding County Council, Sandall Hall in Wakefield was the only children's care home that could take two young boys. He signed the papers last week. Here we are now."

"But Wakefield is forty miles away. That's unfair. Visits will be difficult," I said.

"It's the nearest place we can get, a lovely place. Large play areas. An excellent atmosphere."

"So this proves how much my dad cared. He doesn't want us. Grandma doesn't want us. What about me?"

"You're sixteen now. Beyond our remit. Grandma has agreed to
look after you for a while. Roll of the dice, laddie."
Mr. Anderson stood up and shook my hand out of respect. I knew he
was carrying out his professional duties. He saw a tear in my eye as
he turned to the door.

"Don't worry, Glenn. You'll be okay at Sandall Hall. I'll visit as
often as I can." I said.

"I'll walk down the gennil with you," I said, needing to see their
faces as they disappeared.

Glenn climbed into the minibus and thrust himself into the seat. Mr.
Anderson put two suitcases of clothes into the boot, that grandma,
without doubt, had prepared hours before. Tears trickled down my
face as I looked at David. He began crying again, still shouting for
his mum. Glenn had settled but looked disconsolate. He seemed
forlorn as though their journey to Sandall Hall was a Puritan
punishment. I continued to weep as the minibus pulled away and
sobbed just as much as I had done at mum's funeral. The only saving
grace being that mum never saw them being driven away to a
children's home, forty miles away. It hurt deeply. As the car
disappeared over Diggers Hill, heading towards Wakefield, I turned
to walk back up the gennil to face another trauma; grandma Greaves.
The curtains twitched, with grandma secreted behind them. With the
expectation of a full-on row, she caught me off-guard when she asked
me to sit and chat for a while. Again, it felt as though she sat me on
the naughty chair.

"I know it was painful, Jeff, but I'm too old to look after young
children anymore."

"You needed to tell me what was happening," I said softly.

"But you wouldn't have reacted any different."

"Leaving through the back door without telling me was so
deceitful."

"Your dad thought it best that way. I'm many things, but I'm not
spiteful."

"You never liked us or mum."

"It's not what you might think, your mum had secrets herself."

"Heartless. How could you have done this to them?"

"That was your dad's decision. I just listened."

"It condemns them to countless years of misery, with uncertain futures, at the mercy of dubious childcare professionals."

"Ask yourself. Where was your dad today?"

We learnt the hard way what mum knew years ago. Dad didn't want us or mum in his life. He signed the papers to put David and Glenn in a home. It was dad who sent mum to an early grave. I was lucky. I only had to endure a few more months of a cold atmosphere of indifference.

Like a prison sentence, Glenn was to spend spent six years at Sandall Hall. A ten-year-old boy when he arrived, a sixteen-year-old man when he left. David was to spend twelve years at Sandall Hall, a four-year-old child when he arrived, a sixteen-year-old when he was 'released.' In the absence of parents, Glenn became his saviour at the children's home. He protected him like an older brother would and helped him through his stay at the home. Within their minds were suspicions and doubts as to why they were incarcerated. They probably felt it was a kind of punishment.

On the occasional visit, talking about family became a taboo subject as painful memories still cut deep into hearts and memories. I found it difficult to hold back my emotions. Discussing the future seemed as remote as walking on the moon. Social Services now controlled their destiny. My face burned hot, my eyes streamed bitter tears. We talked a little about dad, but they knew even less about him. Over these years we had grown apart.

We had become distant cousins rather than close brothers. Tea and scones on the occasional Sunday afternoon seemed to be as much as we all could manage. So many avenues of conversation were closed. Mum was gone from our lives. Dad chose to be absent. Both David and Glenn benefited from a decent children's home, and a decent education at the local schools. My fears of misery, with uncertain futures and at the mercy of dubious childcare, proved to be unfounded. On the positive side, their earlier years of destitution and chaos was substituted for a life in a comfortable home with stability. Funding seemed bottomless, in sharp contrast to mum's struggle to live on a pittance.

By surprise, the following week, Alex phoned me at work. Since mum passed away, we barely contacted each other. We all had separate lives in unfamiliar places. We were all drifting further apart, like icebergs in the ocean of time.

"Hiya Jeff. Can we meet up somewhere tomorrow?" Said Alex.

"Tomorrow's Sunday. How about Rothervale Country Park?"

"Okay, for Gwen to come as well?"

"More the merrier," I said.

We met at the old cafe inside the converted stone barn. It overlooked the vast expanse of the mile-long lake, bordered on all sides by the gently rolling hills. Wayfarer dinghies plied up back and forth across the lake, honing their skills, tacking and gibing for fun. We bought coffees and sat outside in the late summer sun.

"Not like you to contact me at work," I said. "Not like you to contact me at all, to be honest."

"Thought it might be time we got together. Remember, it's been a year since mum passed."

"Do you ever go to mum's grave?" Asked Alex.

"I can't Alex. I get too emotional……." I lost tears just saying those words and broke down weeping like a lost child.

Gwen put her arms around me to help me pull together. Just the mention of mum brought a tear to my eye. One year on, her absence was still a deep wound, her presence sorely missed.

"How can it be like this? I'm a grown man," I said.

"I'm the same Jeff. Memories are still painful and bitter."

"Jeff you're only seventeen. It's normal to cry, even years after losing your mum," said Gwen.

It pleased me that Gwen was with us. She gave some needed emotional support. Since mum had passed, all family connections disintegrated. People got on with their own lives. Aunty Ruth's letter to Social Services destroyed the last strands of contact with her. She probably meant well, but it backfired to the detriment of us all, David and Glenn in particular.

"It's impossible to catch a bus back when your eyes are streaming and your face is red. I think of mum every minute of the day," I said, choking up. "I think of every sweet smile she gave. It still hurts you know. I got upset last week when I went to see David and Glenn at Sandall Hall. They've been there a year. It chokes me up inside, just thinking about their pain. It's like visiting somebody in prison. It tears my heart up when I have to leave," I said.

"Mum tried so hard to keep them out of a children's home."

We sat for a few minutes in quiet reflection, staring into our coffees, then composed ourselves. The agony mum must have gone through, helpless and alone, consumed our thoughts. We talked for ages about our happy memories with mum. We spoke of the love she gave unconditionally, as she smiled through her own pain and grief, hidden from our innocent minds. I still wondered what Alex knew about mum's operation. It seemed the authorities covered up the truth. It was inconceivable that Alex could agree to whatever happened that night.

"Did anything ever come out of mum's autopsy?" I asked.

"Certificates stated she suffered 'Thrombosis and Sustained Internal Haemorrhaging' following Gallstones Removal. It sounded technical, but in basic terms, it was a sustained and slow loss of blood," said Alex.

"We knew that was happening, but the genuine question was why? Was there incompetence, negligence, malpractice?" I said.

"The autopsy found that the bleed-out was from a ruptured duodenal ulcer. Probably caused by overwork and a poor diet. The peptic ulcer didn't help the situation. They had treated her for ulcers for a long time. They knew mum had gallstones removed six weeks earlier, but they found more."

"Her GP suspected a duodenal ulcer. He sent for blood tests the week before mum collapsed."

"That's right. The major problem was getting the letter back to the GP. Vital information that crossed in the post always meant results became delayed. By strange irony, mum's results came through a week after she passed away. A cruel twist of fate. The hospital doctors knew nothing about the duodenal ulcer. Had they known, mum might have survived with surgical treatment."

"When mum collapsed in agony, that would have been the duodenal ulcer being ruptured. She got rushed into the hospital with suspected gallstones. They overlooked the ulcer. From that, slow blood poisoning and bleeding remained undetected."

There was no equipment that could detect internal haemorrhaging. Postal communication caused critical delays. Medication and blood clotting agents didn't cure the problem. Blood tests could have picked up the blood poisoning, but there were no suspicions of duodenal problems. Excessive bleed out contributed to mum's gradual organ failure.

"The Coroner's Report could find no evidence of neglect or incompetence. After all said and done, they followed correct proceduress. She passed away peacefully, as they say."

Our thoughts drifted back to how tragically mum had slipped away from us. I couldn't help but think Alex still harboured secrets as to what genuinely happened in those last hours of mum's life. For him to contact me randomly and spend a few hours socialising at Rothervale Country Park didn't ring true. I expected him to reveal some dark truths, some knowledge that only he was aware of.

Chapter 26

White sails glided with serenity back and forth like majestic swans, rippling the still water in their wake. We walked around the lakeside for an hour, then arrived back for another coffee and cake. Our meeting seemed surreal over recent years, we had never been close enough to socialise together. We spent an hour reminiscing with smiles, laughter, and a random escape of a tear.

As we sat, we continued to look back at events that shaped our lives. This was probably one of the few times that Alex and I were not at loggerheads with each other. His girlfriend Gwen calmed his temper from belligerence to rationality.

"Do you believe in superstition, Alex?" I said.

"Sometimes. Sometimes things are just a coincidence."

"Think back to 1962. I was only eleven, you were thirteen. That was the biggest fight we ever had between us."

"I reckon I can still feel the bruises," said Alex sarcastically.

"It was a massive ding-dong of a fight in the best front room, mum's little palace where no-one could enter, only the Queen."

"That massive wall mirror was her pride and joy. Grandad Cooper bought it as a wedding present," said Alex. "It was such a fight, we knocked the mirror clean off the wall. Shattered into a thousand pieces. Mum panicked and shouted for ages. It was a hammer blow for her. To break a mirror was expected to bring seven years of bad luck."

Mum was extremely superstitious. Devastated, she seemed to cry more about the consequences of breaking a mirror, '*Seven Years of Bad Luck*', than by damaging the mirror itself. From 1962 -1970, seven years of bad luck descended upon our family. Superstition or not, it happened that way. To mum, this was a cardinal sin. Sacrilege beyond comprehension.

"You know, from here, you can see our old house on the White City estate," said Alex.

"When you think how things turned out, all of mum's prophecies came true. We did have seven years of awful luck," said Alex.

"Can you see Holbrooke Colliery where dad worked. He was involved in that horrible accident. He nearly died there," I said.

"Nearly?" Said Alex, with a frown that begged a comment. His chat coming to an abrupt end.

A moment's pause followed. Alex looked at me straight in the eyes. That moment had arrived; Alex must have judged the time was right to let me know what was on his mind.

"I thought you were hiding something. You would never arrange for us to meet socially."

I knew something was amiss.

"There's something I have to tell you, Jeff. Just found out for myself. Sit down before you fall down," said Alex, completely altering the tone of our chat. "We need a strong coffee."

Gwen volunteered to buy another round of strong coffee. We all sat at a picnic table outside in the warm afternoon sunshine. A quiet spot that overlooked the gentle lapping water seemed ideal to gain privacy. Swans glided past in slow motion. Baby ducks babbled in the distance to keep up with their mum. I looked at Alex's poker face. He never flinched a muscle. We had talked about old times and childhood memories for over an hour. Then our eyes met. His eyes glazed somewhat, without a tear escaping. We stared for a few minutes, neither of us saying a word. I tried to second guess a hidden meaning. The conversation stopped.

"Dad's dead," Alex said abruptly.

The world seemed to stop, statuesque; a sudden clatter of thunder. Voices in the distance appeared further away. I felt my heart beating through my shirt, goosebumps stood on end along my arms. There seemed to be no words to be said, even though a hundred questions needed to be answered. I couldn't speak as my throat clammed with dryness. I tried to comprehend what Alex had said. Another significant silence followed. The impact was a bolt from nowhere. Mum had died a year ago, aged forty-three. Dad was only forty-four. Gwen put her arms around me.

Though dad had grown away from us over the last five years, the news still came as a sudden shock. Only Gwen was strong enough to elaborate.

"Two police officers knocked on our door yesterday to notify Alex. We invited them in to explain what their problem was."

A lengthy silence followed as my eyes glazed with disbelief. Gwen clutched my hands that shivered with shock. The impact created a hundred questions, beginning with how, why, where and when. Each burning question created random images in my mind of potential gruesome scenarios. Each question begged a gruesome answer. For the first time in years, Alex seemed close to me, forged together by common mutual grief; death. We had grown apart from dad; he divorced us all, not legally, but physically. Mum could never agree to a legal divorce. Not out of spite, but she knew one day he would come back to us. We never expected it would be as tragic as this.

"The police officer said it was 'apparent suicide.' They needed to do forensics to confirm."

"Took his own life?" I asked.

"Yesterday morning. Carbon monoxide poisoning. Two coal miners found him in his car. The engine still running. A garden hose led from the exhaust pipe through the back window. He had sealed the narrow gap with towels. They found him slumped over the steering wheel just after four in the morning,
 on their way to start the morning shift."

"That must have been a shock, first thing in the morning."

"They called an ambulance from the Pit Deputy's office. By five o'clock, they pronounced him dead at the scene. He would have just fallen asleep and died," I said.

"What a waste of a life. He must have been desperate. He was somewhere in a black place. Experts reckon it's a cry for help."

"I didn't expect any of this. Why now?" I asked.

"I reckon dad could never get over mum passing away. It was a year ago. His conscience became haunted by ghosts of guilt," said Alex.

"Mum always said he would live to regret what he had done to us all."

"I guess there must have been lots of arguments over the past eighteen months between him and Roxy. Mum begged him to come back. Roxy must have had arguments of jealousy."

"She had a son, didn't she? That must have created some issues. Dad having four boys with mum. I never knew whether her son was dad's. It must have caused some jealousy issues; arguments about his priorities," said Alex.

"Mum's passing last year must have caused a tremendous impact on dad. He turned up at the funeral with Roxy. She sat outside the cemetery and waited in his car, seething at being dragged along to witness dad's own pain and suffering, and mingling with mum's family."

"That might have been the final straw. Seeing scores of mum's relatives chatting," said Alex.

"I heard that when mum passed away, he suggested we all live at Roxy's house." I said. "That wouldn't sit well. Roxy looking after mum's boys. Red rag to a bull, I should guess with some certainty. There was no way that would ever happen."

"He must have felt guilty that he signed over the documents to put David and Glenn into a children's home Social Services took him away for twelve years. It was like imposing a prison sentence; every inmate a stranger. What kind of punishment is that when you've just lost your mum? Dad left when he was not quite two. David never knew him."

"Glenn lived in the children's home for six years. Another prison sentence for an innocent child, committing no crime. They must have despised dad every single day," said Alex.

"Dad lost the love and respect of us. But it was self-inflicted."

"On the anniversary of mum's death, his mood must have plummeted like a stone," said Alex.

"His head must have been ready to explode. Arguments with Roxy, guilt about making mum's life purgatory, shame about abandoning four young boys. To add insult to injury, he signed the papers to condemn David and Glenn to a Children's Home for years," I said.

"I reckon that all these arguments and guilt came to a head. Roxy must have kicked him out for good. His conscience riddled with guilt. He could only think of one solution. Down that country lane, where they found him," said Alex.

"The police said carbon monoxide filled the car. They found him slumped over the steering wheel with an empty bottle of whiskey in his hand," said Gwen.

"I assume the whisky was his only friend that he nurtured in his last moments alive," I said.

"He must have really agonised about all the wrongs he had done and all the grief he caused us and mum. The whisky would have plunged him deeper into depression," said Alex.

"Dad must have driven away that night, with tears in his eyes, almost unable to see the road in front," I said.

"He knew where he was going. He drove six miles to get to that old access lane between the railway track and the colliery. He must have set the engine running, downed the last of the whiskey, then fell asleep. He had no-one left. All of his hope and respect had gone," said Alex.

"He left a note in the car. Police gave it to us this morning."

She sat down, calm and composed, and looked Alex and me in the eyes. I appreciated she had agreed to read the note. Her soft Yorkshire voice possessed a calming northern tone. She cleared her throat, hoping she wouldn't get choked by an emotional outburst. She took a deep breath, then looked at us both again. We gave her a nod of readiness as she took a sip of the strong coffee and began reciting dad's handwritten message, slowly, with great empathy:

'To whom it may concern, being of sound mind and body...

I have written this letter to say I am sorry for all the hurt and pain I have caused to my dear beloved wife Evelyn and our lovely boys. With sadness, I followed a path in a different direction. I believed I had chosen what was right for me and followed my own heart. I have lost everything I had in my life, my wife, my boys, my family, my job, my home. There was nothing else left, I had lost the respect of others around me. My dear Evelyn, you never wanted us to part. In a cruel twist of fate, you passed away. To honour your wishes, I have decided to be with you. At least I have done something right for once. Many would say I sent you to the grave. I hold myself responsible for giving you a hard life. One year after you passed away, I find I have no reason to live. You were right when you said I would regret what I had done and that it would haunt my conscience for the rest of my days. Dear Evelyn, with all my heart, I agree with you. I hope you all understand.

All my love. Dad.

The End

A Postscript is added on the next page.

Postscript

As mentioned in the Preface of this book, perspectives do change over time. Medical advances and innovations have improved our health and well-being. Such things could have saved mum's life; scanners can now detect accurately the source of internal haemorrhaging. Modern medications can stem internal bleeding more effectively. Misdiagnosis of mum's symptoms was the main factor that became cataclysmic. Evidence gleaned fifty years later shows that mum had a stomach rupture caused by caesarean sections years earlier. Gallstones created excruciating pains, but even worse I now know she suffered from pancreatitis, creating even worse pains than gallstone problems. Current medical practice solves gallstone problems by removing the gallbladder. The Death Certificate states mum passed away as a result of Thrombosis. This could not have been the case as consultants were unable to clot her blood as she was anaemic. It appeared, mum slowly bled to death. This is not true, it was not known fifty years ago, but Sepsis claimed mum's life. Sepsis was unheard of, all those years ago. Mum was given "Kurari," to aid her recovery. She never recovered. She suffered from misdiagnosed and undiagnosed symptoms. Continuous loss of blood, combined with the devastating consequences of Sepsis was how mum lost her life. It was officially recorded as Thrombosis – untrue. The saving grace in mum's demise, is that she has gone to be with Angels. She is at peace, she no longer suffers. As for me and my three brothers, we all survived. But the pain of mum's loss is still with us every day. Between us, we had 12 children. They would have been mum's grandchildren. Sadly, she never saw any of them. We miss you mum. Always x.

Though this was a tragic, but true story.

I sincerely hope you enjoyed the read.

For me, Jeff, it has been a "closure."

Please be kind enough to leave a review.

Acknowledgement

Extra special thanks goes to my partner Joy who supported me whole heartedly throughout the writing of this book. She has been pivotal in the structure of the story and edited the book painstakingly from inception to conclusion. Joy deserves much more than I could say. Without her support/patience, this story could not have been told. Sincere thanks go to Gwen for much background information. Special thanks goes to Julie who provided a wealth of research.

Website: www.authorjayaston.com
Facebook www.facebook.com/authorjay.aston.3
Twitter: Jay Aston @ JayAston12
IG: www.instagram.com/authorjayaston
email: jayaston01@gmail.com

Sincere appreciation

to Sheffield History, Picture Sheffield, Sheffield Libraries
"We Love Sheffield," Francis Frith Collection
Very special appreciation goes to the kind people of my home town of Sheffield. In particular, the surrounding districts of Rotherham, Aughton, Swallownest, Aston, Ulley, Beighton,, and the place of my birth, Woodhouse, Sheffield, UK
Appreciation to all readers and Facebook, Twitter & Instagram

Please be kind enough to leave a Review.

Notes on the use of British & USA Grammar. The book has been written and published in the UK using British grammar. For International and USA readers, there will be some basic differences with spelling certain words. The most common difference will be words such as "summarise" (UK) as opposed to "summarize" (USA). Bear this in mind as the book is read.

9 781838 537227